ELECTRONICALLY HEARING:
COMPUTER SPEECH RECOGNITION

John P. Cater is employed as Manager of the Intelligent Systems Development Engineering Section at Southwest Research Institute, San Antonio, Texas, where his responsibilities include the generation and successful conduct of electronics research and development.

Mr. Cater has a BS in Electrical Engineering from Texas Tech University, and an MBA from Trinity University, Texas. He is a member of the American Association of Artificial Intelligence (AAAI) and a registered member of the IEEE Technical Committee on Personal Computing. He holds a patent on digital data transmission techniques. In addition to writing books on computer applications, John has presented papers at the 1980 and 1981 Computer Faires. He is the author of *Electronically Speaking: Computer Speech Generation*, another SAMS book.

ELECTRONICALLY HEARING: COMPUTER SPEECH RECOGNITION

by

John P. Cater

Howard W. Sams & Co., Inc.

4300 WEST 62ND ST. INDIANAPOLIS, INDIANA 46268 USA

FIRST EDITION
FIRST PRINTING—1984

International Standard Book Number: 0-672-22173-X
Library of Congress Catalog Card Number: 84-50051

Edited by: *Richard Krajewski*
Illustrated by: *Donald B. Clemons*

Printed in the United States of America.

Preface

Consider, if you will, the possibility of a not-so-futuristic scenario. A computer scientist approaches a stainless steel door in the brightly lit hallway of a computer research facility. As he nears the door, which is unmistakably conspicuous by the lack of a door knob, he speaks into the nearby wall-mounted intercom, "Entry requested." A soft, somewhat monotonic voice from the wall unit asserts, "Please speak your last name and the word 'cyclone'." The scientist responds "Smith— cyclone," which immediately produces a raspy buzz from the door. The soft voice from the wall announces, "Please enter Dr. Smith." As Smith enters the windowless room, he utters, "Computer?" The same soft door-voice answers from a nearby console, "Ready." Then, in response to Smith's query of "Computer, status," the soft computer voice answers, "Awaiting your command." Following this initial precursory verbal interchange, the scientist requests that the activities from the previous day's research be read by commanding, "Computer, please read yesterday's project record." After a rather lengthy computer reading of the previous day's research efforts, Smith again verbally activates the computer with, "Computer, transcribe yesterday's record, begin verbal input of today's record." The computer's line printer starts with a quiet churning; the computer voice answers, "Awaiting verbal project entry for 1 April 1996."

The conjectured verbal interchange between Scientist Smith and the computer represents the evolution of the computer as we know it today. The technology for computer-generated speech, while still relatively young, is well understood and is progressing as a mature scientific discipline. My previous book, *Electronically Speaking: Computer Speech*

Generation (Cat. No. 21947) encompassed the technology of speech synthesis from its beginning to the present time. This book continues the study of verbal interaction with computers by providing you with the fundamentals of speech recognition technology from a hardware and software approach. In light of some intrinsic technological differences between speech generation and speech recognition (primarily involving intelligent language understanding), this book must delve rather deeply into the realm of artificial intelligence. Of course, adequate consideration is also given to the electronic and acoustic qualities of speech and the electronic and mathematical requirements for speech processing and analysis.

The subject of computer speech recognition covers eleven chapters in this book. Chapter 1 contains an introduction to voice processing, which discusses the direction of current trends in "hearing" computers. The predominant concepts of computer speech recognition are presented and immediately contrasted with some of the obstacles encountered when trying to create computers that listen to us.

The intent of Chapter 2 is to provide you with a technical background in speech acoustics adequate for the understanding of the remainder of the book. Since the initial path of speech into the computer is from your mouth to a microphone, interactive acoustics must be considered. These are reviewed in Chapter 2. Chapter 3 ingresses into the field of syntax and semantic understanding of language. In this chapter, we have our first glimpse at computer-implemented artificial intelligence, in order to create an accurate understanding of our language and its meanings by machine. Synthetic languages such as *Loglan* and *Unifon* are examined and analyzed as possible solutions to the voice-entry dilemma. Also covered are the problems encountered when attempting to electronically resolve the nuances of different dialects and accents in combination with syntactical ambiguities.

Chapter 4 begins the analysis of speech in electronic terms by covering the most prevalent means of digital acquisition of speech signals. Specifically, direct waveform acquisition (or digitization of audio signals) and spectral signal acquisition are described. Both analog and digital filtering systems are proposed for spectral analysis techniques.

The fifth chapter contains an in-depth look at some of the most efficient methods of speech signal analysis. Included are the DFT (Discrete Fourier Transform), FFT (Fast Fourier Transform), and Cepstrum Analysis of Formants. These methods describe the means by which the various features of speech are isolated for further analysis by methods described in Chapter 6. The sixth chapter covers the processes for speech feature extraction and speech pattern recognition. The information within this chapter is considered to be some of the most vital and technical information for the creation of the voice recognizer. Contained in this chapter are descriptions of feature extractors for parameters such as speech pitch and phoneme identification, in combination with envelope contour measurements. The pattern recognition techniques described include template searching and chain code matching for correct identification of words and utterances. Then, Chapter 7 describes the functions of speech recognition that must occur once the words and utterances have been identified as the target language. This chapter eagerly scrutinizes the topic of artificial intelligence because at this point the computer is really beginning to understand the illogical meanings and ambiguities of our spoken language. The information given here refers primarily to connected speech recognition, but it also applies to isolated word recognizers.

The last four chapters of this book deal with the hardware of speech recognition and their applications. Chapter 8 contains a survey of the applications for voice recognition equipment. Present uses are identified and discussed in terms of system cost and complexities while future systems are proposed for your own exploration. The information in Chapter 9 provides the reader with a review of currently available voice recognition systems. These pioneering recognizers are on the market today and may (for a price) be purchased for your own use. The voice recognition systems reviewed in this chapter span the range of technology from complete stand-alone voice recognizers down to voice recognition chip sets. Each manufacturer's product is listed with a complete description and a short theory of operation. Also listed is the cost of each unit as this book goes to press.

Chapter 10 provides those of you who like to tinker with hardware and software with a design description for a *working voice recognizer.* Although this system may not be as elegant as those that are commercially available, the concepts and theories of voice recognition and its circuitry are certainly exemplified by this chapter's contents. Finally, in Chapter 11, the evolutionary trends that may be expected to continue in the extremely dynamic field of voice recognition systems are described. Following the last chapter, there are several appendices which contain a glossary of terms and some suggested advanced reading material for those masochistic readers who like to immerse themselves in equations and pages of technical formulas. As you complete this book, you will have seen the intricacies of voice recognition from a number of major disciplines which exist outside the realm of computer science. The knowledge of these seemingly superfluous sciences is crucial to a working understanding of the voice recognition systems of tomorrow.

Now that the stage is in order, sit back and relax as the house lights dim. The musicians raise their instruments as the conductor taps his baton on the podium. The symphony starts . . .

JOHN P. CATER

Acknowledgements

I would like to thank the following for their assistance in the completion of this book: Bob Manville for being a fantastic editor and accepting this chronologically late, although possibly technically premature, manuscript; Dr. Jackie Hipp for his assistance in my understanding of signal processing; Bob Robison for furnishing some of the graphs in Chapter 10; and Diana Drenner for being my manuscript stenographer.

Dedication

To my loving parents, Elva and Paul,
who have always believed in me,
and to my dear wife, Jaye,
who patiently slept through another book.

Contents

CHAPTER 1

Introduction to Voice Processing

In the opening paragraphs of the preface, a thought provoking futuristic scenario was proposed and explored. It was presented there to illustrate some examples of speech input to computers. For example, our fictitious computer scientist gained entrance to his laboratory through a voice lock system—this was an example of speech input used for *speaker identification*. As he entered the laboratory, he exercised, through conversational speech, vocal control over the computer when he requested the computer status and the previous day's project record. This procedure was an example of *voice command*. Finally, Dr. Smith's dictation of the project entry for the current day was an example of *voice data entry*. Each of the above activities may be considered to be an independent application of voice input to a computer. They may also be used in conjunction with each other to provide computers with complete voice entry capabilities similar to HAL, the computer in Arthur C. Clark's *2001: A Space Odyssey*. In this chapter, the techniques for speech input to computers will be introduced and examined in detail with full consideration given to the problems involved in their implementation.

It has been said that the technology for creating accurate and reliable speech control of the computer is easily 100 times more complex than that of speech generation from a computer. The reasoning therein lies in the fact that a voice input computer must not only hear the spoken utterances, it must also understand and interpret them. This dilemma brings about some rather startling conclusions:

1. The computer's apparent intelligence must exist at a level approaching that of human understanding. (This takes us quickly into the field of artificial intelligence.)

2. The computer must respond to vocal input in near real time, thus indicating an extremely fast and powerful voice processing system.
3. For the voice input system to be a viable peripheral, it should respond with equal accuracy and speed to any randomly selected human voice (speaking the same language, of course). Now, taking into consideration the variety of accents and dialects in existence for a given language, this computer must employ extremely flexible and adaptive input and recognition techniques.

The scope of these conclusions extends through many disciplines of science from acoustics through mathematics and spectral analysis to the eventual thinking computer. Each must eventually be utilized in harmony to orchestrate what some computer scientists and philosophers declare will be a new species on earth: machines that reason.

Why Should Computers Listen to Us?

The first question which should at least be resolved, if not answered, is: *Why in the world are we as a human race trying to create machines that can eavesdrop on our every spoken word?* Now, before acute computerphobia begins to attack your reasoning power, let's examine the possible answers to that question for some justification in our logical madness.

First of all, I would like you to ponder man's struggle to expand his capabilities over the ages. First came the wheel, then the lever. In fact, up until about 50 years ago, man's major obsession was in increasing his physical powers through the use of some form of strength amplification. And, as you walk through the construction site of an 80-story high-rise building and see a crane operator hoist a 30-ton concrete slab to the top, you might concede that we have succeeded in this effort. However, the struggle for capability expansion continues. The invention and implementation of the first computing machine gave man one of his first tools for true knowledge amplification. After this discovery, a single man with a computer could solve problems by himself that normally would have taken a team of expert mathematicians much longer. The only fly in the ointment here that has irritated computer researchers since their efforts began is the means of data entry and output from computers.

The most significant problem seems to be the operator's distraction during data entry or retrieval. Since the normal means of these interactions has been through keyboards and printers or visual displays, the computer operator must momentarily remove his attention from the task at hand and focus it on the computer to interact with the computer.

This procedure produces a considerable efficiency loss in the man-machine interface. And inevitably, man has begun to search for a more efficient means of creating the man-machine interface through voice control of computers. This will obviously provide the computer operator with a means of interacting with a task at hand while more or less subconsciously controlling a computer through voice commands. The only other means of computer input that might be more efficient would be that of direct mental waveform input through electroencephalograms (and don't think that this isn't being researched in some cybernetic research facilities).

As you might expect, the major drive behind the flurry of activity in voice entry is commercialism. Experts in the field have said that the first company to the market with a fully functional voice-activated typewriter will be financially secure for an eternity. This elusive goal would certainly be of benefit to book authors if not to all of mankind. But this is only one application for computers that hear. There will surely be others.

Another reason for our frantic rush to perfect voice input for computers might be that of personal recognition and fame. The person or team of workers who eventually succeeds in creating accurate and reliable speech input for computers will certainly go down in the scientific hall of fame with great men like Alexander Graham Bell and Thomas Edison. Those researchers, if questioned as to their obsession with their work, would most likely answer that they are simply trying to solve an unsolved problem. In the eyes of researchers, this is definitely an acceptable and honorable justification for the continuation of their work. In the eyes of the rest of mankind, the way that this research will help our society is the real justification.

Having taken the previous arguments into consideration, it begins to appear that the answer to the question "Why should computers listen to us?" is that it will advance our own species by making life easier for us. (The real reason is probably that most computer scientists hate to type.)

Now that we know why computers should hear, let's look at the kinds of information they will have to listen to. They are: data entry, commands, and speaker identification.

Voice Data Entry

This class of voice input system is often referred to as a voice data entry (VDE) terminal. The environments in which these systems might be found include data processing offices, factories, banks, and any other place where a large amount of numeric or alphanumeric data entry is required. These systems have several characteristics that may be exploited for the sake of system simplicity. For instance, in most data entry operating scenarios, the people operating the system have been hired for that function and will normally be consistent users of the VDE terminals. This means that the voice entry systems chosen may be *speaker dependent* type systems. In other words, they can be trained to recognize a specific user, and thus do not have to respond equally well to randomly chosen speakers. This constraint, which does not really affect the voice data entry capability, lowers the cost and complexity of the system considerably.

Another characteristic of voice data entry which may be utilized to simplify a system is that of *isolated word recognition*. For instance, in entering a column of numbers for tabulation, the data entry operator may speak numbers separated by pauses: one . . . two . . . nine . . . decimal . . . three . . . four. An entry transaction such as that would input the number 129.34 into the computer without the use of a 10-key pad.

The advantages of such a system are obvious since the operator needs no typing skills at all. However, the speed of such a system is probably going to be much less than that of a 10-key typist working at full speed. As the technology for speech recognition improves, the isolated word restriction will be lifted, allowing the operator connected word numeric entry (without the pauses between numbers). Such systems should become as efficient as the 10-key operator over prolonged periods of time. Do not, however, expect this switch in technology to occur in the next few years. The efficiency of manual key entry will remain (at least for a while) much higher than that of speech input for applications involving computer data entry.

Other considerations must be given to restrictions that might be placed on the operator during the process of data entry. For instance, if the operator has his or her hands occupied during the data entry transaction, then the 10-key input approach would be less efficient than that of speech. This situation might be found in banks where bank tellers must manually process deposit slips and checks while simultaneously entering the transaction amounts into the bank computers.

In the opening paragraphs of the preface, Dr. Smith utilized a form of voice data entry into the computer when he began to dictate the current day's project record. Of course, this form of data entry would require continuous speech recognition with an extremely large vocabulary for its implementation. For this visionary system to become a successful reality, it would also have to be speaker independent. The problems associated with the creation of such a machine will be described in later chapters.

In general, vocal data entry when viewed as a possible alternative to manual data entry through keyboards is still a rather inefficient and costly method. As the barriers of speaking inconsistencies slowly fall because of technological innovation in computer hearing, voice data entry will become a more viable procedure. Meanwhile, there are other uses for speech input technology, uses that provide definite advantages.

In some cases, voice input can perform tasks that could not otherwise be done. Take, for example, the need for voice control over computers and computer-controlled machinery.

Voice Command

As Dr. Smith entered the computer research facility during the preface opening, he ordered the computer through *voice command* to respond with its status, followed by a vocal request for the previous day's research records. Applications for voice-command computers are prevalent throughout industry and society. An example of such a system available to the consumer today is the television set with the voice recognition system for changing channels and controlling the television set's operation. In this particular piece of equipment, the capability for voice control (of which absolute necessity may be questionable) allows the tv viewer to remain in his easy chair while ordering his television set to go to Channel 13.

A more exotic form of voice command is being developed by the United States Air Force for use in highly maneuverable aircraft where the operator's physical response time might be too slow for emergency situations. The vocal command given by a pilot can be issued and recognized in a shorter time than would be required for him to move his arm to an emergency control. In view of the fact that the pilot might have crucial tasks for his hands at the same time, the voice control would be of paramount importance in this situation.

Another situation in which voice command over computers might prove to have life-saving consequences is in the control of industrial robots. In remembering the Japanese factory worker who was reportedly killed several years ago by an industrial robot gone berserk, one must wonder if his life might not have been saved if the robot had been able to understand the word "Stop" (or the Japanese equivalent). A red emergency stop button ten feet away is useless if a rotating 200-pound robot arm is hurtling at you at a rate of five feet per second. As I mentioned earlier, this is an application for voice command that no manual entry can replicate.

There are also more mundane uses for voice command over computers. As computers shrink so that they might be planted in commonly used items, then we might use voice control in house lighting, automobiles, and, eventually, other domestic instruments too numerous to mention. A rather trivial example of such an application is that of a listening light switch. Although there are several sound-activated light switches on the market today, they only turn on the associated lights for a preset period of time upon sound activation. Imagine in the future the light switch that responds to the spoken words "off" and "on." These devices will probably be introduced first because of their novelty; however, as costs plummet through improvements in technology and production efficiencies, there might be a future for such a trivial device.

The applications for voice command over computing systems is limited only by the designer's imagination. While researchers are finding that, in some instances, people do not want voice control for specific applications, there are instances where the availability of voice command would be very advantageous. Problems associated with interpretations and execution of vocal commands are thoroughly discussed in later chapters of this book.

Speaker Identification

Another unique voice-entry application for computers is that of *speaker identification* or *voice verification* as it is sometimes called. During the opening sequence of the preface, Dr. Smith was requested to speak his name followed by the word "cyclone." As he followed the instructions given by the computer system, his spoken word "Smith" was compared for frequency and harmonic content against a previously stored template for his name. The word "cyclone" had been randomly selected by the computer from a prestored vocabulary of his speech. This precaution was used to prevent a false entry by simply recording a spoken entry sequence and then playing it back. Again, in this case, as in the previous comparison, the spoken word "cyclone" was compared in terms of frequency content and rhythm against an identical word previously spoken by Dr. Smith.

The voice verification or speaker identification process can be compared closely to that of fingerprint matching. Since the harmonic content of each voice is primarily determined by the shape of the throat and mouth for each individual, voices are unique. The voiceprint matching theory assumes that no two individuals will have identically shaped throats and mouths (not to mention the effects of the lips and vocal cords on the final speech output). Although this means of speaker identification is being used by numerous secure facilities for research (Texas Instruments Incorporated has had one in operation for several years), actual voiceprint matching has yet to become a legal facility for use in the court system.

The procedure of speaker identification is another of the applications of voice entry that cannot be easily duplicated or replaced with other technologies. In particular, the ease of identification using only the vocal characteristics allows hands-free operation of secure entry systems. This leads to another interesting possibility, which is now being used to a limited extent in the U.S. This speaker verification system provides for phone-line voice verification of the identities of a bank's clients. Few other ways of positive identification would be as accurate over a phone line with the possible exception of access codes.

Conversational Applications

Uses of voice recognition for conversational applications is obviously still in the future. Very few people would gain personal satisfaction by sitting down at a console and holding a lengthy conversation with a machine, no matter how novel the encounter might be. However, as you might expect, the human-to-computer interface with true conversation will eventually evolve as the listening and reasoning facilities of machines are improved. And, as the conversational computer comes into existence, the Turing test will be satisfied.

In his original proposition on intelligent machines in 1950, Alan Turing (1912–1953) proposed a scenario where a computer operator would sit in a room in front of a computer terminal and through keyboard entries carry out an intelligent conversation with the entity at the other end of the line. Turing's hypothesis was that if the operator could not tell whether he was talking to a machine or another person at a similar terminal, then that machine was in fact a true Turing machine having the equivalent of human intelligence. As the technology for voice synthesis and recognition evolves, a vocal Turing machine is almost certain. Exactly what these conversant machines will talk about is still anyone's guess. However, a marriage of voice synthesis and recognition with some *current* artificial intelligence programs would provide a computerized psychiatrist with *today's* technology. In the future, conversational machines might be placed in information booths to provide untiring information service.

One application which is sure to appear as the cost of conversant systems drops is the computerized telephone caller. This system, which would have doubtful value for society, would routinely call and converse with each and every telephone number about some product or merchandise to be sold. At that point, each of us would certainly want to have the same system at *our* end of the line to talk back to their computer. Can you imagine the confusion when each of the computers tries to decide if it's talking to a person or a computer? Prepare for tiny clouds of electronic smoke when this happens.

Since the field of voice recognition is still awkwardly young and in many ways a neophyte to the applications of life, many problems associated with this technology must be solved before it becomes a truly acceptable means of man-machine interface. The next section will discuss a few of these problems and how they relate to our rather illogical human world.

Automated Speech Recognition Considerations

The remainder of this book will discuss the problems and technology associated with the implementation and application of voice recognition. However, just to get you started thinking, let's look at some of the more difficult hurdles to overcome when trying to achieve accurate voice recognition capabilities.

Connected-Speech Problems

Fortunately for the advancement of the field of voice recognition, not all applications will require the capability for connected-speech recognition. Many uses will find that single word or separated word responses will suffice. As a matter of fact, in the previous four applications mentioned, all but the last one (conversational applications) could be performed without connected speech. This type of voice recognition is known as *isolated word* recognition. Its implementation requires only that single isolated words be spoken and recognized, thereby eliminating problems of contextual or semantic interpretation. Vocal responses such as yes and no can certainly be recognized without much trouble by most of today's voice recognition equipment. Systems with large vocabularies capable of storing several hundred words allow for recognition of spoken numbers, names, and numerous commands. In each of these cases, the user must condition himself to speaking very clearly with definite pauses of speech or silence between intervening words. This presents no major problems for the trained speaker; however, it does tend to slow the data entry time compared to an equivalent connected-speech entry.

Connected-speech recognition systems, which are still somewhat over the horizon but *are* in development, will allow the user to speak normally without emphatic pauses between words. At first, this capability does not appear extremely different from that of isolated word recognition, but think about how the computer might try to interpret the following connected-speech statement: "Change the 'to' in line 222 to the word 'too'. " If you were to try that vocal command on one of today's speech recognition systems, which have limited connected-speech capabilities, you would have to wait a while before your command was obeyed, if at all. Why? Well, the recognition of and compliance with such a phrase requires a number of steps before the computer can correctly proceed. A relatively simple flowchart of how the process might be achieved within a connected-word recognition system is given in Fig. 1-1. The first problem encountered by the system in trying to separate words from each other occurs in a comparison of templates of the words stored in memory. Since there are very few, if any, pauses in the sentence, the recognizer must rely on pattern matching with known words to isolate each spoken word. The result of the first template matching pass might resemble the sentence as translated in Block A of Fig. 1-1. Hypothetically, if the computer could translate this sentence, then its first decision must lie in which line to examine. Since there would normally be a short pause following the utterance of line 222, the recognizer will most likely use this as its first search parameter. Since

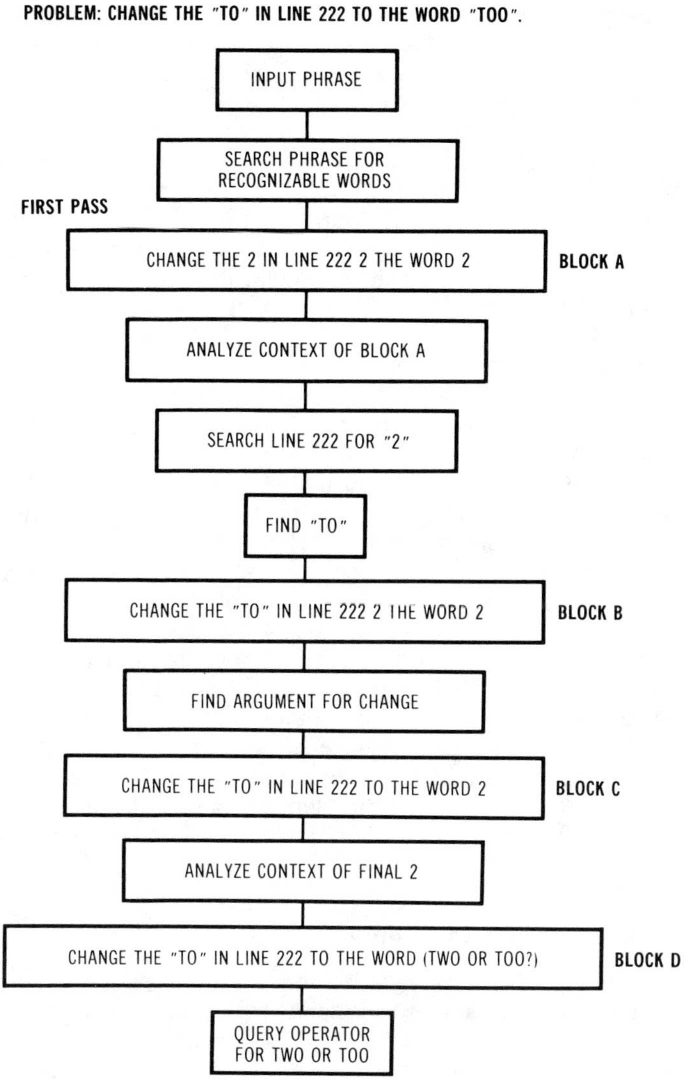

Figure 1-1.
The connected-speech process problem.

the speaker has identified the mysterious line through inference as having only one "to," then the computer must realize that it will find one *and only one* identical word within that line. Then the applications program, which might be a vocal-input word processor, scans line 222 for "to," "2," or "too." If after scanning the line of text the system found more than one of any of the search words, then, of course, it would have to ask you to explain which word to change. But, assuming that there *is* a single word "to" in line 222, then the word recognizer would have its first clue as to what the command really means. The first round of contextual analysis would yield the newly translated sentence in Block B of Fig. 1-1. The system must then continue to lexically parse the verbal command by knowing that the command "change" has associated with it two arguments: the "from" argument and the "to" argument. Having interpreted this part of the command, the phrase in Block B is converted to that shown in Block C. If we continue the hypothetical analysis of the input statement, then the recognition system would probably try to identify the correct form of the word in the command. A truly smart system would realize that since "word" is specified, the final "2" cannot be the number but must be one of the three words "too, two, or to." And, since the order has been made to change the identified word "to" to something else, then that word is eliminated. The resultant argument for the command "change" must then be either "too" or "two." At this point, the system would probably have to punt and query the operator as to which of the two words to use. The final process would be that shown following Block D in Fig. 1-1.

The process of continuous speech recognition as shown in the previous illustration is necessarily rather complicated because humans do not always speak in a logical manner. In fact, fortunately for us, we have a sense of creativity about our hearing so that we tend to fill in the real meaning of what we hear in most cases. This is probably one of the most difficult tasks for a listening computer. It requires a capability approaching that of true artificial intelligence as described in later chapters. As we leave this problematical example of connected-speech recognition, remember that the primary problem encountered was not that of just understanding the words spoken, but more of understanding what was *meant* by the words spoken.

Speaker-Dependency Problems

In the speech recognition process by computer, the primary means of distinguishing between different spoken words is by frequency discrimination and rhythm analysis of the audio spectrum. The recognizer, in effect, has "signatures" of spectral frames stored that it compares against an incoming spoken word. If there are significant differences between the incoming word and the signatures, the word is rejected as being nonidentifiable. The net effect of this confusion is that recognition accuracy for one particular speaker may be very high, approaching 95% to 99%, while very low (around 60% to 70%) for another. Conversely, to us as human listeners, there is no problem at all in discerning the same word spoken by a very large group of people. This difference exists because we have the mental processing power to make adjustments for subtle differences in speech tonality and rhythmic patterns.

To the recognizing computer, the subtle differences become the fatal flaw in speaker-independent speech recognition. The solution to the speaker-dependency problem lies not in increasing the recognition system's acuity, but in increasing its ability to recognize variations of the same spoken word. This capability should eventually develop as the algorithms for processing and matching speech patterns improve.

The real crux of the speaker-dependency problem in speech recognition is trying to make a very logical computer respond to a variety of sounds for which there seems to be no logical connection. If we expand our view of speaker dependency to a wider scope, then not only do we have differences in voice frequencies, but we begin to see a wide variety of accents and dialects that must also be recognized with equal accuracy. For us as humans, the recognition and accurate interpretation of words from any number of varied speakers (including foreign accents) is a rather trivial task. Then why should it be so difficult to program a computer to respond with the same accuracy as our ears and brain?

One possible reason might be that in our thinking process, we have the capability of filling in unknown quantities with a form of pattern supplementation. An example of how our eyes can do this is given in Fig. 1-2. A seeing computer (which is another book) might view this figure as a collection of graphically disconnected lines. However, as we visually assimilate the sparse figure, we mentally supplement the available visual information with our template-matching process to produce the first six letters of the alphabet. As we listen to speech from human speakers, we perform a similar process that very rapidly finds, for each word spoken, the closest match in our own mental vocabulary. Then after perceiving the entire spoken utterance, if we have missed a word or two, we fill in those words through context supplementation. Because of our extremely large learning base in our natural language, speaking and listening is one of our easiest tasks.

We *can,* however, begin to get a feeling for the complexity of the task of understanding connected speech from a variety of speakers by listening to a normal conversation between people in a language other than our own. For instance, if a language such as Spanish is not your second or first tongue, then switch your television set to a Spanish cable channel and see if you can pick out each individual word that is being spoken. You probably cannot! As you attempt to learn a foreign language such as Spanish, you may be able to translate fairly well in the

Figure 1-2.
The mental supplementation process.

early stages *if* the speaker slowly enunciates each word with unnatural pauses between them. The process is very similar to that of isolated word recognition. As you become more comfortable and fluent with the language, you should be able to gradually carry on a *connected-speech* conversation with little trouble. We might make a rather abstract analogy by saying that the computer's natural tongue is machine language. As we teach it our own form of communication and language, it undergoes the same process that we undergo when we learn a new language. The big difference here is that we have the innate capability for acquiring a very large number of languages. The computer recognition system on the other hand must be programmed in *how* to learn the language. The truly identifiable dichotomy in all of this discourse is that of a difference in intelligence between man and machine. This distance is becoming shorter as computer science searches into the field of artificial intelligence with ever increasing determination.

Artificial Intelligence Inferences

In the previous section, the discussions on how we learn a language and how the computer must be taught to learn a language is intruding into a field of computer science known as *artificial intelligence* (AI). At the present time, this field ranks high on the list of sciences that approach those straight out of science fiction. If you are relatively unfamiliar with this area of computer research, then there are some excellent suggested reading materials mentioned at the end of this book for further reference. Chapters 6 and 7 of this book also contain information on the field of artificial intelligence pertinent to the subject of speech recognition.

You might ask, "Why is the field of artificial intelligence being featured in a book on speech recognition?" As you will soon see in the next few chapters, the task of inputting voice to a computer is a relatively simple one, requiring little more than a microphone and a handful of electronic components. The closest biological equivalent to this would be an electronic substitute for our ear. The signals from the microphone (ear) are a series of electrical impulses that are fed to the computer (brain) for subsequent language processing. If our analogy is correct, then the brain holds the key to speech recognition; in the case of the listening computer, these capabilities exist through complex highly sophisticated software.

The software of choice for artificial intelligence is not BASIC or Pascal or FORTRAN but rather a somewhat obscure exotic language called LISP. Features of this language make it ideal for the interpretation of natural language understanding. This is crucial to the field of speech recognition. Programs have been written that interpret natural language from a *keyboard* and allow a user to carry on a more or less normal conversation with the computer. In later chapters, we will examine how programs written in LISP, when eventually interfaced with speech recognition equipment, should in the future give our computers the capability of conversational speech recognition.

Finally, since the science of artificial intelligence is so closely intertwined with that of speech recognition research, its use is paramount to the capability of connected-speech recognition. Research in this area will eventually bring about powerful computers similar to the HAL 9000 in Arthur C. Clark's *2001: A Space Odyssey* (preferably without the malevolent attitude). As we proceed in this direction, our programming safeguards will hopefully ensure that our computers do not turn against us as that one did.

In summary, the scientific field of speech recognition and voice processing is still relatively young. In terms of their projected futuristic capabilities, our computers are now toddlers. Continuing through this book, you will find the major considerations and technologies required for speech processing and recognition. The chapters logically follow the process from its origination to the final translation into computer actions. Since the origin of speech is our mouth, its characteristics and the associated acoustics will be our first subject for examination.

CHAPTER 2

Characteristics of Speech Acoustics

To start your thinking off in the right direction for speech acoustics, I would like to propose a question. If a speaking person stands two feet away from a hearing individual and speaks in a normal voice, will the intended recipient of the message understand it? Although that question appears to be a relatively benign one, the true answer to it must be a qualified "no." By answering the question in that way, I admit that I am playing the part of the devil's advocate, but only to emphasize a few characteristics of speech transactions that we normally take for granted. If you answer that question with "What does this question have to do with speech recognition by a computer?" remember that we have within us an almost perfect speech recognition system. We would do well to have our computers emulate this capability. The point is, that if there are circumstances that prevent *our* understanding of a spoken message, then these will surely influence the understanding of the same message by a less-than-perfect hearing computer.

Now, before you dismiss this discourse as an author's lunacy, let me give you the reasoning behind my qualified "no" answer. The missing element in the description of the above verbal intercourse was the environment in which it occurred. Suppose that I place the two subjects in an airless chamber (it turns out they don't need air to live) and then ask the same question. Since the message originating at the mouth relies on air as a transmission medium, there could be no hearing because the verbal message never left its place of origin. In fact, without air, the vocal cords could not vibrate nor generate any sound at all! Thus, the message is not heard or understood.

All right, maybe that *was* an unrealistic set of conditions since humans tend to have trouble surviving a vacuum. Let me propose a few realistic scenarios that you must agree *will cause problems.* Suppose the speaker is American and the listener is an aborigine from Australia. Still a bit unfair? Okay, then let's qualify the previous question by saying that the conversation must occur with a transmission medium *and* in the same language. We still have a qualified *no.* Now, let me place the two hypothetical subjects, both speaking English, at the side of a major airport runway. If, at the time that a 747 jet airliner begins its takeoff roll, one subject speaks to the other, chances are that the speech will still not be perceived correctly. In this particular case, although the transmission medium and language channels are correct, the external noise environment is so high that the message is overshadowed by the roar of the jet engines.

Even if we were to allow the jet to take off and disappear over the horizon so that the two test subjects were left standing near a relatively quiet runway in a moderate 20- to 30-mph wind, a repeat of the message transferal attempt would probably not work. In this case, although the surroundings are relatively quiet, the noise created by the wind impinging on the ear of the listener could be sufficient to effectively prevent an accurate understanding.

If we proceed even further into our quest for accurate message transferal and place the two subjects in a quiet enclosed environment, we should then have a better chance of getting a yes answer to the original question. But, suppose the two subjects are still two feet away from each other, standing against the common wall of two large empty rooms with a small connecting doorway. If the message transfer is attempted in this case, the echoes created will most likely prevent a truly accurate understanding by a listener. If we finally allow the two hypothetical test subjects to move to the doorway, facing each other, and then attempt a transfer, we will have finally reached our yes answer.

Although the previously mentioned environmental constraints may be extremely exaggerated in your own view of the situations, their introduction should serve to remind you that each of these types of circumstances may be encountered to a lesser degree during speech recognition by a computer. And, their influence on a less-than-perfect hearing computer will certainly be more disastrous toward an accurate message transferal. In the following sections of this chapter, the characteristics and problems associated with the previous message transmissions will be discussed in more detail.

Speech Properties

The transference of messages through conversation is undoubtedly the most commonly used form of communication between intelligent beings. Fortunately for us, it is also one of the fastest and most accurate means we have available to use. In fact, we rely on spoken communications so heavily that if we are deprived of the power of speech, we quickly become frustrated. To illustrate that point to yourself, simply try to go about your normal daily routine for just one hour without speaking. If you manage to do that, then at the end of that hour, you will probably have developed a crude sign language as a substitute, or you will have acquired a pencil and paper. Imagine the bizarre possibility of another intelligent life form existing on some distant planet without a surrounding atmosphere. Since communication through sounds would be an impossibility without a transmission medium, other forms of communications would have evolved. These beings might be as conversant with their body gestures and feature reconfiguration as we are with our sounds. If the planet also existed in darkness, without sight, then forms of communication might have developed using touch or even mental telepathy. However, getting back to reality, we do have the transmission medium for speech and it appears that we certainly have learned how to use it.

Exactly what is speech? What physically occurs when we make the common gesture of conversation with a fellow human being? The answer to these questions is certainly not trivial. The characteristics of speech communications and their associated semantic content are extremely complex. To simplify our understanding of the process, we will first concentrate on the voice and its properties.

Voice Frequencies

As you begin to generate a spoken message, a great number of things happen almost simultaneously. First, the message is generated within your brain as the intended carrier of information to the recipient. Fig. 2-1 gives a very simplified flow diagram illustrating one possible way of describing the speech process. Following the generation of the message in the brain, the control parameters for the vocal tract are then formulated from memory and speaking begins. While the true order in which the sequence of events occurs may be open to debate (say the word "computer" and decide for yourself), the functions given in the flow diagram will generally occur sometime during a spoken message. Actually, the true order or sequence that is followed strongly depends upon each word being spoken. Words starting with the letter "m" for instance have a nasal beginning; thus, the mouth is not opened until after lung contraction and glottal vibrations are started. The first sounds simply come through the nose.

In all, there are probably close to 40 distinct sounds that make up our spoken language. These are referred to by linguists as *phonemes*. They in total comprise a set of distinguishable mutually exclusive speech sounds that may be found in most any spoken language. A typical set of the phonemes used for the English spoken language is given in Table

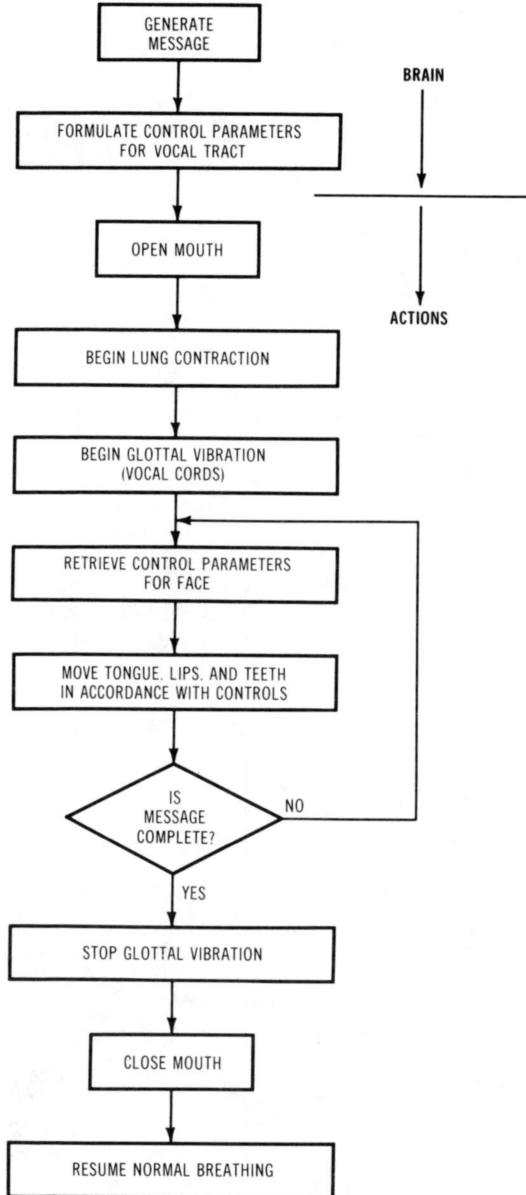

Figure 2-1.
A conceptual view of the speech process.

2-1. These independently identifiable phonemes obtained from the General American (GA) dialect are distinguishable from each other primarily by the spectrum of frequencies generated by the vocal tract during their production.

The phonemes have spectral characteristics that may not be initially obvious. Some belong to a group of phonemes referred to as *contin-*

Table 2-1.
Minimum Phoneme Set From General American Dialect

Phoneme Type	Phoneme	"as in"
Vowels*	ah	father
	ae	tap
	aw	talk
	ā	bay
	eh	step
	uh	run
	ee	beep
	i	lift
	oh	tone
	o̅o̅	moon
	oo	book
	er	stir
Consonants		
Fricatives (Voiced)*	v	very
	t̲h̲	there
	z	zebra
	zh	beige
Fricatives (Unvoiced)*	f	fast
	th	thing
	s	seek
	sh	show
	h	hit
Plosives (Voiced)	g	get
	d	dither
	b	base
Plosives (Unvoiced)	k	cat
	t	two
	p	poke
Nasals*	n	no
	m	me
	ng	ring
Glides	y	you
	w	will
Semivowels*	l	last
	r	real

*Continuants

uants. These phonemes in particular, because of a lack of vocal tract motion during their utterance, have a stable and constant frequency spectrum throughout their enunciation. Continuants are sustained sounds. Included within this category are all of the vowels, fricatives, nasals, and semivowels. The remaining classes of phonemes, the plosives and the glides, are considered to be noncontinuant dynamic sounds that normally couple to the surrounding phonemes in a manner resembling *diphthongs.*

Diphthongs exist as a class of speech sounds characterized by extreme vocal tract motion when coupling other phonemes together. They are generated as the mouth moves from one phoneme position to the next during speech. If we could speak true phonemes in a concatenated manner without any attempt to join these sounds, then the diphthong would not exist. However, since the response time of the muscles within our throat and mouth tends to slur the movement from one spoken phoneme to the next, we naturally generate a great many diphthongs within our speech patterns.

The primary frequency characteristic of the diphthongs and glides shown in the phoneme table is a dynamic frequency spectrum over the pronunciation. As an example, if a very small portion of speech spectra were taken during a continuant utterance, it could probably be identified from its spectrum as a specific phoneme. However, if a short segment were taken from a diphthong, plosive, or glide, a specific phoneme probably could not be identified.

Before we proceed any further into the discussion of frequency spectra of speech, let me illustrate exactly what I mean when I say *identifiable frequency spectra.* As we generate speech, the initial sound comes from a vibration in our vocal cords known as a *glottal vibration.* This sound, which is generated by the vocal cords rapidly opening and closing with small puffs of air, generates a frequency spectrum similar to that shown in Fig. 2-2. The waveform spectrum shown here is that which would be measured if a wide-range microphone were placed directly in the throat above the vocal cords but below the resonating structures of the vocal tract.

The spectrum of the glottal pulse is made up of harmonics of the pitch period, which is the fundamental range of frequencies produced by the vocal cords. Although the spectrum carries a very strong component near the pitch frequency (about 50 Hz), it is very rich in harmonics and thus has frequency components extending past 5 kHz.

Taken by itself, the frequency spectrum of the glottal vibration tends to yield very little information as a speech signal. However, if the recording microphone is moved to the outside of the vocal tract near the lips, then the speech spectrum takes on a different appearance—it now carries true speech information. The physical effect that occurs in this process is that of *resonance.*

As the glottal vibration passes through the chambers of the vocal

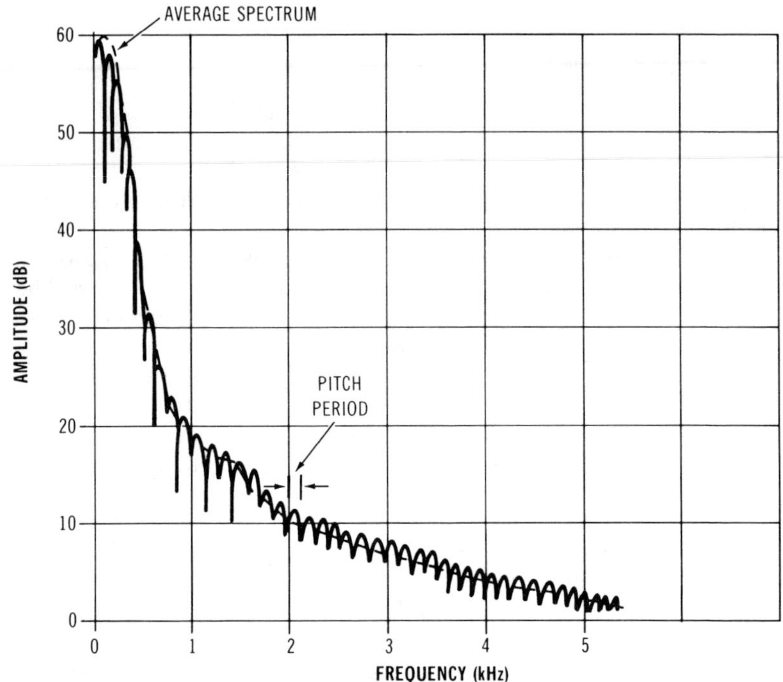

Figure 2-2.
The glottal pulse spectrum.

tract, certain volumes tend to resonate with varying frequencies in a manner analogous to the tones produced by a pipe organ. An illustration of the resonators in the vocal tract is given in Fig. 2-3. Although this is a very simplified illustration of the effects of the nose, throat, and mouth upon the glottal spectrum, it agrees well with the analogy to the chambers of a musical pipe organ. As you might expect, since there are three resonant chambers, there will be three primary frequencies of resonance emphasized in the glottal vibration spectrum. These major frequency resonances are known as *formant* frequencies. Although normal human speech can be shown to have more than three primary formant frequencies, those above the third formant contain very little relative energy and may be effectively discarded when considering the total speech spectrum. This is what effectively occurs as you speak over a telephone to another person. The mechanism that causes the loss of the higher formants is a low-pass filter in the telephone electronics; the filter only passes frequencies below approximately 3 kHz. A graphical representation of a frequency spectrum showing the formant frequencies of speech is presented in Fig. 2-4. A correlation between this spectrum and the resonators in the previous figure would show that the

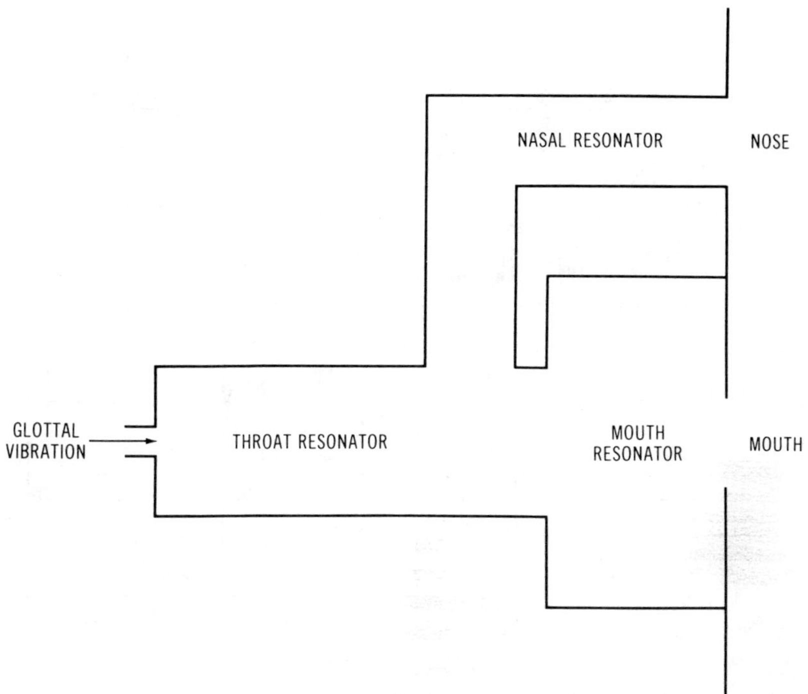

Figure 2-3.
Vocal tract resonators.

lowest formant (F1) is formed by the throat resonance. The next formant frequency (F2) is typically associated with the nasal resonator, and the third (F3) is associated with the mouth resonator.

Since we have now found that there are definitive features associated with portions of speech, we may begin to formulate some conclusions about the placement of the formants as information-carrying identifiers. Although the exact positioning of the formants in the speech spectra from randomly chosen speakers vary, the relationship and ratio of the formant frequencies remain in identifiable categories. If this did not happen, then we would not be able to dependably recognize spoken words. A significant process utilized in speech recognition becomes evident if we begin to relate the position of the formants in the speech spectrum to individual phonemes. This is our first tie between the frequency spectrum of speech and true intelligence carried within a spoken message.

An appropriate method of forming the correlation between the spoken phonemes and the closely tied formant frequencies would be to gather a very large number of randomly selected speakers and then

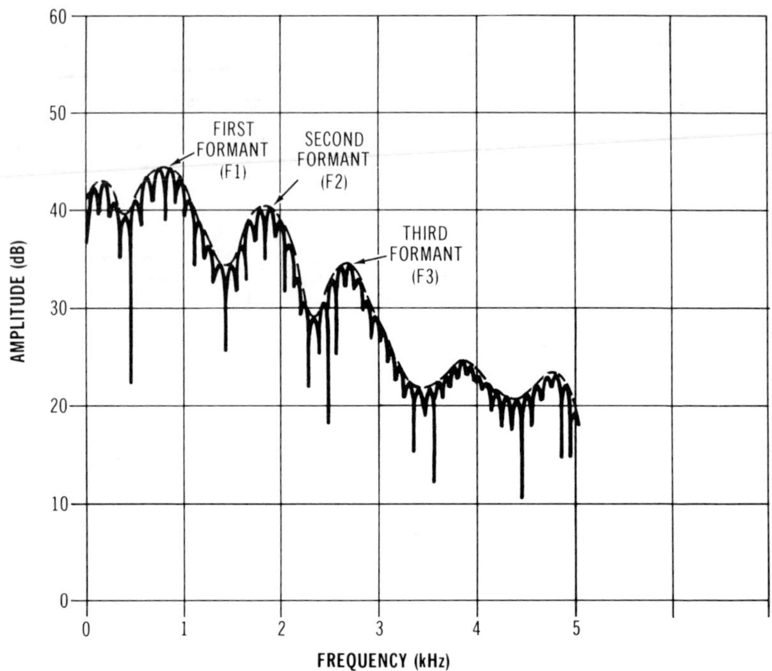

Figure 2-4.
Speech spectrum with formants.

individually analyze the frequency spectra of their speech. Fortunately, this time consuming task has been performed a number of times by speech researchers. The results of one such compilation by I. B. Crandall and Sir Richard Paget in 1925 is given in Table 2-2. One observation of the values given in this table indicates that for the nasals and semivowels, there exist resonant frequency ranges specific to each sound. This is not to say that the resonance actually covers the entire frequency range but, for a selected number of speakers, the particular

Table 2-2.
Characteristic Resonances of Nasals and Semivowels

Sound	Throat Resonance (Hz)	Nasal Resonance (Hz)	Mouth Resonance (Hz)
l	250–400	600	2000–3000
r	500–700	100–1600	1800–2400
n	200–250	600	1400–2000
ng	200–250	600	2300–2600
m	250–300	600	900–1700

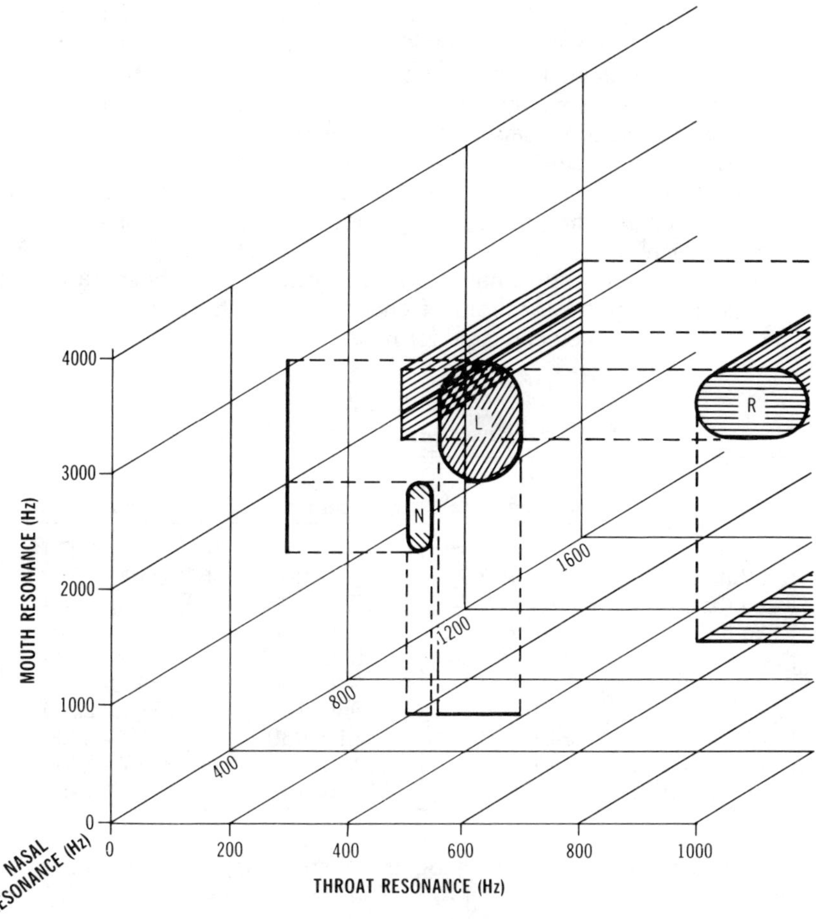

Figure 2-5.
Resonance areas for consonant sounds.

resonance varies from the lowest to the highest in the sample population.

Another observation that provides some insight into speech recognition is that while some of the sounds in the table share common frequency resonances for the throat, nose, or mouth, none of them have exactly overlapping resonances. A more understandable way to view these resonances and their mutual exclusivity might be to plot the regions of resonance in three dimensions as shown in Fig. 2-5. This plot is not really difficult to envision if you assume three axes with the throat resonance across the bottom horizontal axis, the mouth resonance in the vertical axis, and the nasal resonance extending away from you. (Only three of the sounds are plotted for sake of graphical clarity.)

Table 2-3 contains the major vowel sounds with corresponding formant frequency resonances. These vowel formant parameters, like the previously given consonant resonance parameters, can be shown to be mutually exclusive sets for each sound. A visualization of the placement of the formant frequencies in the spectrum is more easily understood when the formant frequencies are plotted in three dimensions. Fig. 2-6 is a graphical representation of some of the values in Table 2-3. Although the ranges of resonance for each formant have been narrowed for visual clarity, the centroid of each vowel "sphere" is the median frequency for the vowel related formants.

Table 2-3.
Formant Resonances of Vowel Sounds

Vowel	F1 Resonance (Hz)	F2 Resonance (Hz)	F3 Resonance (Hz)
e̅e̅ (eat)	210–330	2230–2350	2950–3070
i (bit)	330–450	1930–2050	2490–2610
eh (bet)	470–590	1780–1900	2420–2540
ae (bat)	600–720	1660–1780	2350–2470
ah (top)	670–790	1030–1150	2380–2500
aw (ball)	510–630	780–900	2350–2470
oo (book)	380–500	960–1080	2180–2300
o̅o̅ (moon)	240–360	810–930	2180–2300
uh (tug)	580–700	1130–1250	2330–2450
er (nerve)	430–550	1290–1410	1630–1750

In this three-dimensional plot, the first formant (F1) resonance is across the bottom horizontal axis. The vertical axis is the second formant (F2) frequency. Finally, the third formant (F3) resonance is in the axis extending away from you. Notice that the scales on each of the axes are different in order to provide additional separation between the phoneme characteristics. As a learning exercise, you might want to try to position the remainder of the vowel sounds in the three-dimensional coordinate system. If they were all plotted in the given figure, it would be even more optically confusing because of the effects of visual shadowing and interference.

One other important feature of the formant distribution in spectral speech analysis concerns their intensity or amplitude. It may be apparent from the given tables and graphs that the amplitude of each formant resonance area is of equal intensity. This, however, is not the case. Since the glottal vibration spectrum has an almost exponentially decaying slope, the corresponding formants generated through vocal tract resonances will also have similar decaying characteristics. As a rule of

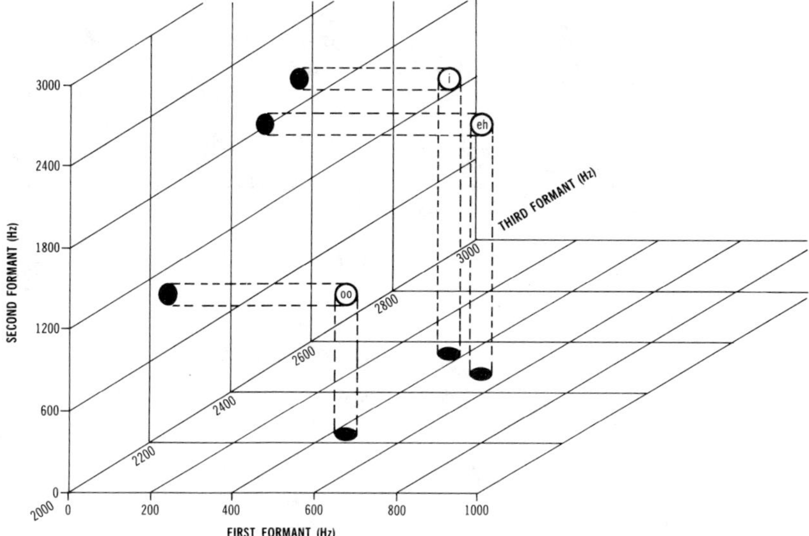

Figure 2-6.
Vowel formant resonances.

thumb, the first formant (F1) will always be the strongest of the three vocally generated formants. The second formant resonance will typically be anywhere from one-half to one-tenth of the value of the first corresponding resonance. The third formant may be as little as one-half to one-thirtieth of the amplitude of the second formant. These relative amplitude values are more easily described in terms of decibels (dB). An example of the formant amplitude differences found in a large group of speakers using the previous vowel table frequencies is given in Table 2-4. Notice that the amplitude of the first formant for each phoneme is taken as the reference amplitude for each comparison. Although there also exists an amplitude difference in the first formants *between* phonemes, the overall variation is relatively small (somewhere around 1 to 5 dB).

Before leaving the subject of voice frequencies, we must examine those phonemes that are generated by vocal tract excitation other than glottal vibrations. These phonemes are in the classes of *fricatives* and *plosives*. Their major discernible characteristic is a high frequency noise sound generated by the rapid passage of air through a constricting orifice such as the lips, tongue, or teeth.

The type of sound being discussed here is that which you make as a final sound when pronouncing the letter "s." It closely corresponds to a hissing sound. In terms of frequency content, the fricatives have a sustained high frequency noise characteristic that broadly spreads over the

Table 2-4.
Relative Vowel Formant Amplitudes
(Referenced to First Formant)

Vowel	F1 Relative Amplitude (dB)	F2 Relative Amplitude (dB)	F3 Relative Amplitude (dB)
$\overline{ee}$ (eat)	0	-20	-24
i (bit)	0	-20	-24
eh (bet)	0	-15	-22
ae (bat)	0	-11	-21
ah (top)	0	-4	-27
aw (ball)	0	-7	-34
oo (book)	0	-11	-33
$\overline{oo}$ (moon)	0	-16	-40
uh (tug)	0	-9	-26
er (nerve)	0	-10	-15

speech spectrum from 3 kHz up as high as 30 to 40 kHz. These fricative spectral lines, when viewed on a spectrograph, do not usually exhibit formant frequency-type resonance since they are generated toward the front of the vocal tract near the teeth and lips. The unvoiced fricatives as a rule have very little speech energy below 3 kHz, while the voiced fricatives contain formant-like humps combined with a blurring of spectral energy above the 3-kHz region.

As we turn our attention to the plosive sounds, which differ from the fricatives in that they are noncontinuant, we again see the characteristic high frequency noise from a restricted air passage. However, the plosives are rather abrupt and characterized by a brief absence of speech sound before their utterance. This can be seen if you pronounce "debate." The word has three plosives embedded within it. In the first and last plosive, the "d" and "t," the air passage is halted momentarily by the tongue against the front part of the roof of your mouth near the teeth. The interruption of speech in the "b" plosive is caused by the closure of your lips before the pronunciation of that sound. In each case, as the air closure is released, the pressure build-up behind that restriction produces a slight explosive burst of air. The frequency content of this popping-like sound is a very low intensity burst of noise, un-resonated in the case of the "b" and just slightly resonated in the case of "d" and "t."

The remaining plosives can be examined by speaking "ago" and "package." The most predominant characteristic of the plosive in continuous speech is the very short interruption of sound preceding it. If a spectrogram of an entire connected speech sentence were viewed, it would be quite easy to identify the plosive sounds. The ease of identification comes from their preceding zero energy characteristic which *does not* normally occur between words in natural connected speech.

If it appears that some of the pieces of the speech recognition puzzle are beginning to fall in place, then you are very observant. Using the quantitative information given in the preceding figures and tables, a computer *could* be programmed to recognize a few spoken sounds with reasonable accuracy. But, we still have a long way to go before we see how a machine can make any sense from a spoken message.

Speech Patterns

So far in our analysis of voice frequencies we have viewed speech as a static phenomenon. This may be an idealistically simple description; however, it serves the point of illustrating the correlation between speech and the acoustic frequencies generated therein. A more practical view of speech analysis by frequency discrimination must include the dynamics of spoken sounds. There would be no problem here if our speech consisted of single continuant phoneme words. However, on the contrary, there are very few of these that we might consider in the classification of "word." Two continuant words might be "ah" and "aw." If a recognition system is expected to accept more than these few single phoneme words, then it must be programmed to accept dynamically changing spectral input.

One electronic device developed many years ago for speech visibility is known as the *spectrograph*. An illustration of how the original spectrographs operated appears in Fig. 2-7. Not surprisingly, today's spectrographs operate in much the same manner; however, they normally utilize computer graphics. Other modern spectrographs substitute digital filtering for the bandpass filter collection and thus simplify electronic circuit requirements.

The visual output from the spectrograph is known as a *spectrogram*. Since in the original concept the motorized drum turned at a fixed rate, the speech spectral information was dynamically recorded. The system was also cleverly designed so that the darkness and width of the frequency bands were dependent upon amplitude, thus giving a third dimension to the graphical output. Once this system had been developed, the speech science community was given one of their greatest tools for spectral understanding of human speech. The output from a modern spectrograph is often referred to as a *voiceprint* and provides considerable information for both human and synthetic speech research.

With this tool, it becomes a relatively simple task to investigate the spectral characteristics of the noncontinuant dynamic sounds and even the spectral properties of words, phrases, and sentences. These are all part of a characteristic of spoken speech involving the time varying

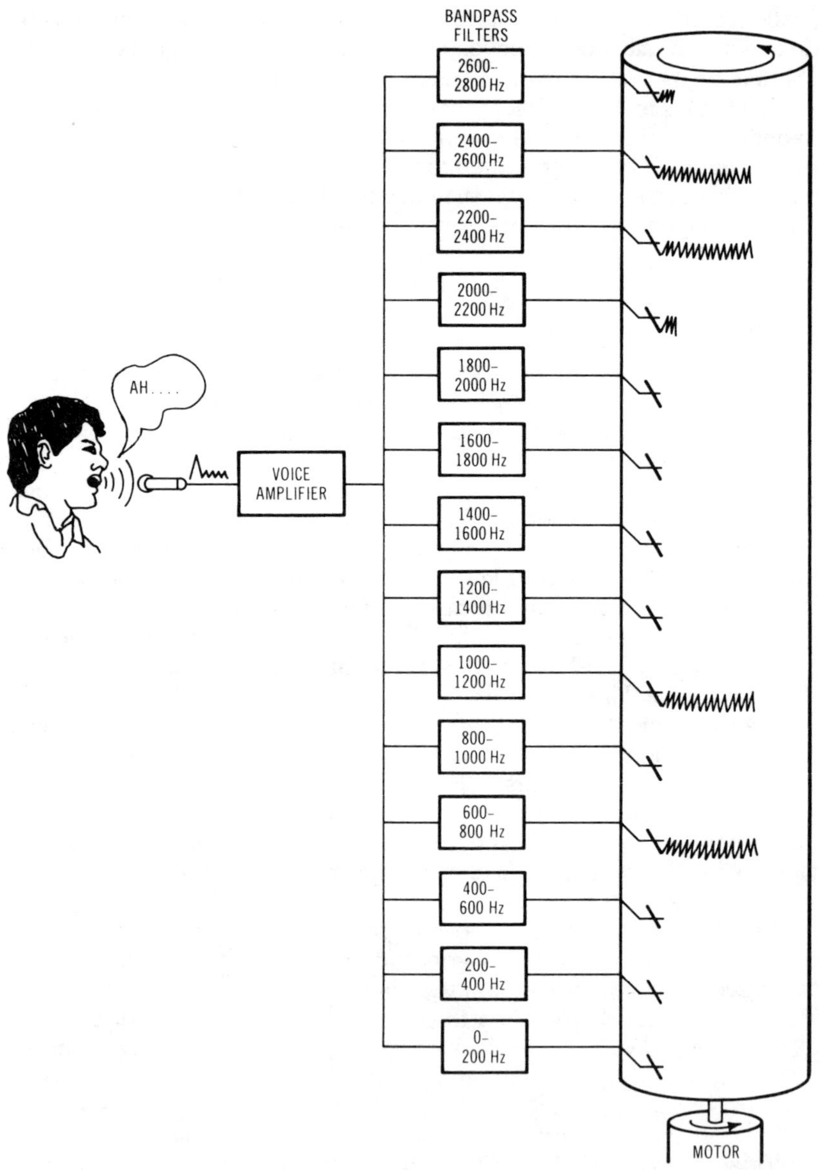

Figure 2-7.
Conceptual operation of a spectrograph.

pattern of sounds. An example of a speech pattern for the word "you", taken from a spectrogram, is shown in Fig. 2-8.

This visible representation of a spoken word reveals considerable information about the formant patterns of dynamic speech. At the beginning of the word, the phoneme glide y does truly appear quite dynamic in its formant pattern. As the utterance continues, the formants appear to drift in a downward motion forming a diphthong that couples the first phoneme y to the second phoneme $\overline{oo}$. In fact, the dynamics of the spoken sound tend to obscure the fact that there are two major phonemes being spoken for the word "you." Notice that the fourth formant (F4) is also shown in this crude spectrogram. Its amplitude, which is not shown, is of considerably less magnitude than the lower frequency formants. If our speech recognition system is to recognize this spoken sound as the word "you," then it must have the capability of not only recognizing the primary phonemes of the word, but also the coupling diphthongs which bind the major sounds together.

Another variable that enters into consideration in an analysis of dynamic speech is that of pitch variation for spoken meaning. It might be surprising to learn that the pitch frequency carries contextual information during speech, but it does! For instance, how do you know when someone is asking you a question? The primary subconscious clue that you extract from the spoken message is a rising pitch frequency at the end of the utterance. On the other hand, a normally spoken word or sentence, in most cases, ends in a falling pitch frequency. A graphical representation of the pitch frequency dynamics in either of these cases is given in Fig. 2-9. Don't be misled into thinking that these changes in pitch frequency create a corresponding change in formant frequencies. There is a change (primarily in amplitude) in the formants, but because the shape and volume of the vocal tract are not changing with pitch frequency, the positions of the formants in the frequency spectrum remain relatively stable.

We find upon examination of the dynamic sounds of speech even more pattern variations, which must be recognized if we examine the plosives or stop consonants, as they are also known. These sounds are characterized by a sudden but definite pause (about 50 milliseconds in length) in speech output before their pronunciation. For example, if you slowly pronounce "look" and observe your speech pattern, you will find a point near the end of the word where your tongue blocks the passage of air through your mouth, then releases quickly, creating a characteristic noise burst similar to an explosion. This is the reason for the name *plosive*. If you pronounce the statement "look here" you should notice that you are pronouncing two definite sounds separated by an abrupt pause. The same effective speech pattern is produced by the nonsensical phrase "loo keer." Notice that stop consonants make it impossible for a speech recognition system to separate words in continuous speech by looking for pauses.

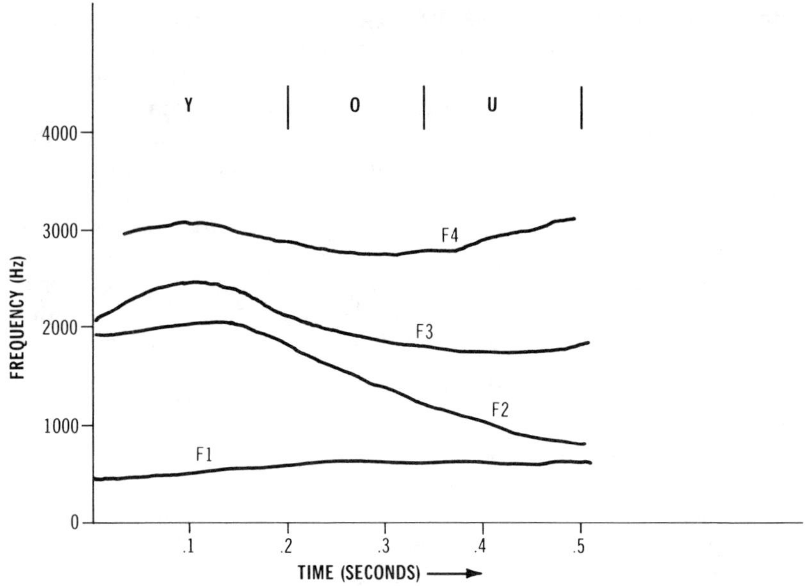

Figure 2-8.
Formant pattern for the word "you".

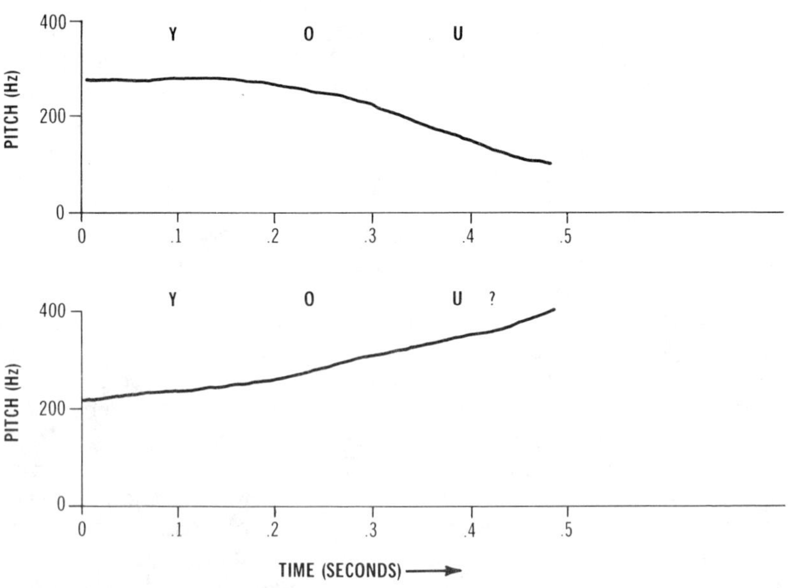

Figure 2-9.
Pitch frequency comparison for a question.

The final variable that must be considered in an analysis of speech patterns is that of stress. The *stress* being introduced here is not the type that causes hypertension, but the type that occurs during syllabification. In single words, stress is usually referred to as the "accent," denoted by the accent mark (´).

The major problems that occur during recognition of stressed words and phrases come about through the variations in shifting stress. For example, consider the word "outside". If you are leaving your house, then you might say, "I am going out side´. ". However, if something is all pervasive, then you might say it covers the "in´side and out´ side". By simply changing the placement and context of the word, its stress pattern is changed from the last to the first syllable. Don't think that this won't be confusing to a speech recognition system. Especially if it has been designed to recognize fixed patterns of spectral energy content for each word.

Other examples of stress variation can be demonstrated as words are taken by themselves and then coupled to other words or endings. Look at the stress variation between the words "solid" and "solidity." Not only has the stress pattern changed from the first to the second syllable, but the length of the pronounced vowel phonemes in the word solid have reversed.

These phonological anomalies in the English language are described as having alternating stress. They even exist in single monosyllable words. Hard to believe? Although they are not really in the alternating accent group, words such as the, a, to, for, from, and so forth can have varying amounts of stress depending upon their placement in a sentence. Another real confusion can exist for the speech recognition system as the actual phonetic sounds of words change by usage. For instance, the word "to" as an isolated utterance is normally spoken as "too". In connected speech, the same word may take on the sound "tuh" as in the sentence "I am going to town."

Variables in Normal Speech

In addition to the previously mentioned speech variables caused primarily by the spoken pattern variations in speech, there are other changes that may be equally confusing to a speech recognition system. One example you will surely run across when using a speech recognition system is that of speech spectral changes caused by germs. That's right, germs!

As odd as that sounds, have you ever stopped to realize how your speech changes when you contract a head cold or an allergic reaction such as hay fever? These influences on your vocal tract primarily block the nasal passage, thus making it very difficult to properly pronounce the nasal phonemes. For example, an attempt to pronounce a sound such as the "n" in "now" produces a word sounding like "dow". While other changes in the speech formant frequency ratios may be created by a head cold, the effect upon the nasal sounds is most pronounced.

Germs may also play havoc with a speech recognition system when they begin to interfere with proper functioning of your vocal cords. This malady, often referred to as laryngitis, affects primarily the pitch frequency of the unfortunate person's speech. This effect along with hoarseness can shift the entire pitch range of speech up or down far enough in the frequency spectrum to obscure the expected formant ratios.

A really spectacular change in voice frequencies, which has been obvious to deep sea divers for quite some time, occurs when a speaker uses some substance other than the atmosphere to vibrate his vocal cords. The effect to the diving community is so severe that men working for prolonged periods of time in the deep sea environment sound like Donald Duck. The mechanism behind this weird sounding speech is a markedly increased vocal cord vibration due to the mixture of helium and oxygen in the breathing environment. Since the gas helium is considerably less dense than our atmosphere, the vocal cords vibrate much more quickly, thus raising the pitch frequency of speech into the formant frequency ranges. The results of this change produce highly resonant first formants with a severely distorted proportion to the remaining formant structure. This exaggerated influence on the normal speech frequency characteristic is also present to some extent when the speaking subject is breathing any mixture of gases other than pure air.

The aforementioned changes to normal speech are certainly not all that may occur. An ideal speech recognition system should be able to compensate for these speaker-induced speech variances. Exactly how it should do this is still a matter of considerable research.

In addition to internally created speech variations (internal to the speaker, that is), the speech recognition system must also cope with changes in speech that occur after the sounds have left the speaker's mouth.

Perceptual Difficulties

Perceptual difficulties can be caused by acoustics, noise, and microphone quality. We'll examine each of these.

Room Acoustics (Echoes)

The opening question of this chapter produced a number of explanations for difficulties in receiving an accurately spoken message. One of these acoustic disturbances was the echo. Although an acoustic change in speech may not severely affect a speech recognizer in some instances, there will surely be situations where it will.

The acoustics within a room may create changes in the spectral characteristics of voice frequencies because of room resonances. Since any closed volume will have inherent resonant frequencies, their emphasis when interfering with a speech signal may create abnormal formant frequency ratios. The condition produced by the room upon speech is often referred to in acoustic terms as "room presence." The overall effect upon speech is a time-varying destructive and constructive interference with the original speech wave to produce amplitude and phase distortion at the microphone.

Two basic changes are produced by a room during presence modification. The first is caused by the time-delayed return of the original signal from a reflecting surface such as a wall or glass window. As the reflected wave returns with much less amplitude, and delayed in time, it interacts with the originally spoken waveform to create a new composite speech spectrum. Objects such as glass windows produce almost ideal reflecting surfaces for the entire frequency spectrum. The acoustic reflections from these surfaces very closely resemble the originally generated frequency spectrum. On the other hand, the reflection from the rough surface of a wall, for instance, tends to be poor in the higher frequencies but strong in the lower frequency range. The entire phenomena is related to the granularity of the reflecting surface when compared with the acoustic wavelength in the atmosphere. This is exactly why soundproofing materials for homes and offices have a very textured appearance. The general idea is that if the wavelength is small enough in air to pass into the opening or aperture, then it will bounce around more times before finally being reflected back to the original source. And, on each bounce, the reflected waveform loses energy owing to the additional path length.

All of these rather worrisome distortions to a spoken message can be at least diminished if the speech recognizer utilizes a noise cancelling microphone placed close to the speaker's mouth. Most recognizers in use today, in fact, have a microphone mounted at the end of a small boom attached to a head set worn by the speaker. The reason for this is to prevent room acoustics from interfering with the desired spoken waveform. In situations where the speaker cannot wear a microphone and cord, the room must be acoustically nonresonant *and* nonreflective for accurate speech recognition. Placement of the microphone is quite important in this situation to avoid coupling to existing room resonances. Even directional microphones may be utilized as an attempt to separate the original speech wave from room-generated echoes and resonances.

An alternative exists for large areas where speech recognition must be accurate at any position within the room. This system would consist of a head-mounted microphone, attached to a small transmitter worn by the speaking subject. A block diagram of such a system is shown in Fig. 2-10. The electronic wireless microphone shown in Fig. 2-10 is

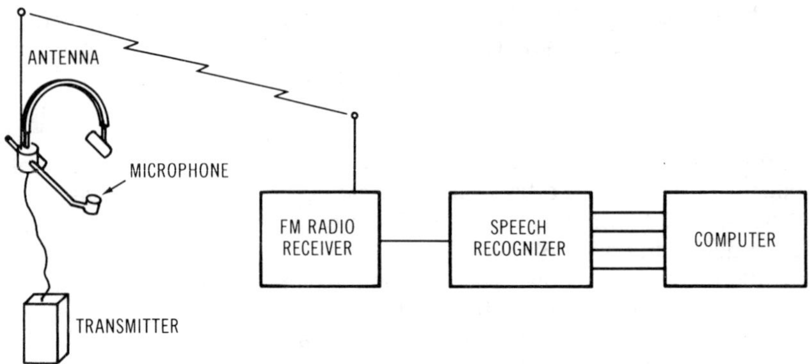

Figure 2-10.
A wireless voice-recognition system.

available from a number of sources since it is intended to be used as a wireless extension to a public address system. If the receiving apparatus is connected to the speech recognizer rather than to a PA system, then the speaker may have voice control over the computer from considerable distances.

Ambient Noise

If the user of a speech recognition system is operating the device anywhere other than in a quiet room, there is a possibility of noise interference with the spoken waveform. Even without external noise, the system is susceptible to wind noise through closely mounted boom microphones. And, believe it or not, the wind noise comes from the mouth during the intended spoken message.

Remember the previous discussion of the plosive and fricative phonemes? These were described as having puffs of air like small explosions. If the microphone is placed directly in front of the speaker's mouth, then it is very susceptible to being bombarded by these tiny wind gusts. The acoustic effect on the microphone is not unlike banging it with a rubber hammer. The best way to deal with this problem is to surround the microphone with an acoustically transparent sponge material that quickly dissipates the wind velocity of the plosive utterances but allows the normal acoustic vibrations to pass through to the microphone element. That is why most of the boom microphones in use today have a small round-shaped ball microphone. Most of the diameter of the microphone is a foam material for the reduction of wind noise.

Other external noise sources such as cooling fans in computers, air conditioners, telephones, and other people talking may also cause problems with a recognition system's accuracy. The best way to prevent these sounds from interfering with a hearing computer's operation is to use, as before, a head-worn microphone placed in close proximity to the mouth. The rule of thumb in microphone placement specifies that the actual microphone element be positioned approximately one-inch from the lips off to one side to move it out of the plosive wind-burst region. Fig. 2-11 shows the normal head-worn boom-microphone position used for optimum voice frequency response.

Another technique to cancel external noise is to filter the audio signal before it reaches the speech processing circuitry. Because the desired voice frequencies have a relatively narrow range from around 200 to 3000 Hz, the audio spectrum may be filtered through a bandpass filter to reject acoustic signals out of that frequency range. If the interfering noise signal has a known spectral characteristic, then filters may be inserted in the speech processor to block the undesired frequencies. The technical details of speech filtering systems are presented in Chapter 4.

In general, the environment of a speech recognition system should include a room with relatively low "presence" to eliminate echoes. Ambient noise levels within the room should be kept to a minimum during operation of the speech system. And, for most accurate operation, a head-worn boom microphone should be used to ensure a constant amplitude acquisition of the desired voice signal.

Microphone Quality

Probably the most influential factor in the electronic acquisition of speech signals is the type of microphone being used. Although one's tendency might be to place a $5.00 microphone on a $500 to $1000 recognition peripheral, it is not very wise. That act would be equivalent to placing a $10.00 set of stereo speakers on a $1000 stereophonic high-fidelity system. A cheap poorly made set of speakers will produce

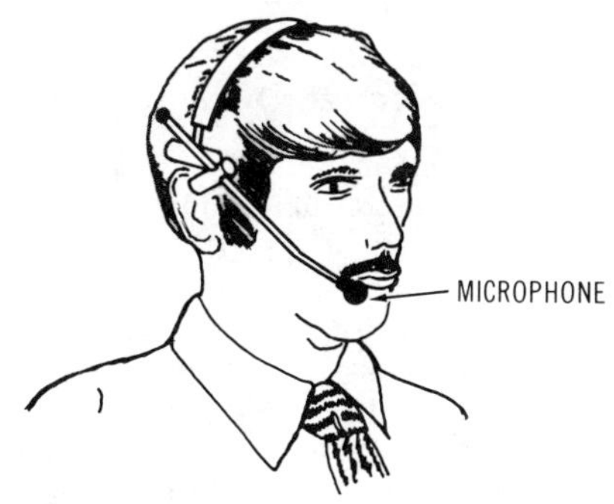

Figure 2-11.
Head-worn boom-microphone placement.

lower fidelity and higher distortion along with a limited dynamic range. A poorly designed microphone will do exactly the same for a speech recognition unit. Obviously, this consideration should be near the top of your list of comparisons when assembling a speech recognition system.

The available microphones which you will find on the market today include four major categories. The four types which differ considerably in cost and performance are:

1. The electret microphone
2. The dynamic microphone
3. The crystal microphone
4. The carbon microphone

So that you may more easily see the differences between these types of microphones, their primary characteristics are compared in Table 2-5. Each parameter of comparison in the table is of some importance in assembling a speech recognizer. The two most important parameters in this list are the frequency response and distortion comparison values. Based on these comparisons alone, the choice of microphone should be directed toward either the electret or the dynamic. If you are planning to use a voice recognition system for incoming telephone conversation, I'm afraid that you will be stuck with the carbon-type microphone because that is the type that most telephone systems use today. As production costs continue to drop for the dynamic and electret microphones, they will eventually move into telephone usage.

Other considerations in the comparison table such as output level and impedance are determined primarily by the speech recognition microphone interface. If the microphone is to be a head-worn boom configuration, then weight is of considerable comparative value.

Table 2-5.
Microphone Comparison

Parameter	Type of Microphone			
	Electret	Dynamic	Crystal	Carbon
Voice Frequency Response	Excellent	Excellent	Good	Fair
Distortion	Very Low	Very Low	Low	High
Hum Susceptibility	Low	Medium	Low	Low
Ruggedness	Excellent	Good	Fair	Excellent
Noise Cancellation	Excellent	Good	Fair	Fair
Size	Small	Medium	Large	Large
Weight	Light	Medium	Light	Medium
Cost	High	High	Medium	Low
Output Level	Low	Medium	High	High
	(Voltage)	(Voltage)	(Voltage)	(Resistance)
Impedance	High	Low	High	Low

One microphone in relatively wide use in voice recognition systems is the Shure Model SM10A. Its relatively high cost of about $130 is offset by its extreme durability and relatively flat frequency response from 200 to 12,000 Hz. It is available from Shure Brothers, Inc. in Evanston, Illinois. Their phone number is (312) 866-2200.

Electrical problems may cause havoc with recognition system accuracy. The major concern is not with those that remain static throughout the use of a recognition system, but the type of disturbances that can vary throughout the operation. For instance, with a boom-type head-mounted microphone, if the operator leans forward toward a crt display to more closely view the visual output, there is a good chance that the magnetic and electric fields surrounding the display will induce noise voltages in the microphone output. Another phenomenon that can occur in the head-mounted microphone (when improperly grounded and shielded) is proximity coupling of the electronic scanning noise from a computer keyboard as the operator's hands approach and come into contact with the keys. These effects may be minimized through proper shielding and grounding of the microphone cable to the computer chassis.

The same problem may occur in the electronics of the speech recognizer if proper grounding methods are not considered. Since the computer to which a speech recognition system is attached contains a variety of harmonically rich switching signals, unless particular attention is paid to electronic noise reduction principles, the amplified electronic voice waveform within the speech recognizer will contain a multitude of whines, whistles, and beeps as the computer operates. These signals can be very devastating for a system that depends on dynamic frequency analysis for its operation.

When all is considered, there are a great many variables against getting the proper speech input signal into a recognition unit. Through careful attention to detail in both electronic and acoustic interfering signals, a voice recognition system can be assembled and used reliably for extended periods of time. If, during the normal operation of a recognition unit, the accuracy drops markedly, it would be wise to first suspect acoustic or electronic interfering signals. If those are not the culprits, the speaker has probably changed his manner or method of speaking. In the next chapter, you will observe how these subtle changes can occur.

CHAPTER 3

Syntax and Semantic Interpretation

The functions of a speech recognition system might be classed into two separable types of operations. Isolated-word recognizers, for instance, are programmed to accept single nonconnected spoken words and act on them accordingly depending on the stored instructions. These systems need no information as to the grammatical or semantic content of the received utterance. They simply look the word up in a table of stored possible inputs (the vocabulary) and follow stored commands. To a computer, for instance, "yes" would signify a positive value while "no" would denote a zero value. Commands such as "list" have singular functions, and would definitely be unambiguous to a computer-controlled recognition system.

The point at which a speech recognizer really starts to encounter problems is when it must take connected speech and resolve the internal meaning of an arbitrarily spoken phrase. The speech recognition system that might be used in a voice activated transcription system (like a typewriter) will be required to determine through the context of a passage which homonyms to put down on paper (homonyms are words which have the same pronunciation but differ in meaning and spelling). The example in the previous chapter of the four homonyms, *to, too, two,* and *2,* will surely occur quite often because the word "to" is one of the most commonly spoken words in the English language. Other homonymic pairs include bare and bear, red and read (notice that read can even be pronounced two ways), write and right, no and know, and so on.

The problem of resolving homonyms can be quite sticky. How, for example, would you expect a voice-activated typewriter to resolve the difference in meanings between the two homonymic phrases:

I know that you will write. What is wrong?
I know that you will right what is wrong.

Although the two messages have the same phonetic structure throughout, the meanings are entirely different. The intelligent system must decide purely from the semantics of the passage where to punctuate and how to spell the words *right* or *write*. (It must also resolve the homonym *know*.) You might say that the voice-activated typewriter could stop the speaker in cases of homonymic ambiguities and request a decision, but this would prove to be very irritating to the user, particularly since almost any phrase that we can generate will include phonemic or homonymic sounds equivalent to other word sounds.

In a more extreme case, the computer-based speech recognition system, which must intelligently understand or react to a given passage, must not only determine the context within the phrases, it must also formulate conclusions about the general meanings of entire passages such as paragraphs. Consider the following speech transaction with a computer as an example:

"Find the BASIC program named *Resolve* in the disk file and load it. Search the program text for the longest line. Print it."

As *you* read that statement there is probably little confusion about what is actually meant by the command. If you were given the same command, then you would probably print the longest line in the BASIC program *Resolve*. The computer, on the other hand, must make a decision about what is to be printed. At least three or four choices exist. The computer might print the entire disk file and bury you in paper. If your recognition system has slightly more intelligence, then you might get a listing of the entire BASIC program *Resolve*. If you are less fortunate, then your printer might print "it" and be confident that it has done its assigned task. A truly intelligent program would, of course, print the longest line in the BASIC program from the disk file that you requested. How will it know to do this? It all starts through some rather complex grammatical analysis.

Grammatical Analysis

For a speech recognizer to begin making sense from a spoken phrase, it must perform the same grammatical analysis that you and I do each time we interpret a written or spoken message. To understand how this process occurs, we should have a relatively strong grasp of the knowledge of grammar. Although some people may have a better knowledge than others, we all have a subconscious template for proper grammar stored from our early school days. Since it is very possible, if not probable, that you have forgotten the technical details of grammar since then, a refresher course is in order before we attempt an analysis of language structures.

Normal dissection of English phrases is accomplished by two separate means. The first considers individual words within sentences as the parts of speech or *class* to which each word belongs. The various parts of speech are as follows:

1. Nouns
2. Pronouns
3. Verbs
4. Verbals
5. Prepositions
6. Conjunctions
7. Adjectives
8. Articles
9. Adverbs
10. Interjections

When we analyze the parts of speech as they appear within a phrase or sentence, we perform an operation known as *parsing*. A sentence such as "The operator spoke a message into the computer" can be parsed according to the previously given parts of speech in the following manner:

Article	Noun	Verb	Article	Noun	Preposition	Article	Noun
The	operator	spoke	a	message	into	the	computer.

Notice that each word can be identified as a particular form or class of word. By parsing a sentence in this way, the true meaning of the sentence is not interpreted. This might most easily be simulated by the following groups of sentences.

A worker is laying brick. He is a mason.
A worker is hammering nails into wood. He is a carpenter.
A worker is laying pipe for plumbing. He is a plumber.
A worker is installing wiring for electrical outlets. He is an electrician.
A worker is surveying a lot for a fence. He is a surveyor.
A worker is putting shingles on a roof. He is a roofer.

Taken individually, these descriptive sentences relate to specific operations that are occurring as a larger process; that of building a house. If we begin to back off from the smaller picture and see the separable processes as part of a whole, then we can functionally identify the groups of workers with larger functions. We might even say that several workers are building a bedroom while another worker builds the kitchen. Simultaneously, other small groups of workers are constructing the garage, bathroom, and living room.

To back off from a sentence in the same manner, we find that the parts of speech can be classified as to their function in a sentence. This type of global parsing is known as syntax parsing. The sentence used in the previous example may be syntactically parsed in the following manner:

Subject   Verb Direct Object   Adverbial Phrase

The   operator spoke a   message into   the   computer.

As we syntactically parse a sentence or phrase, the following elements of syntax must be remembered:

1. Subject
2. Verb
3. Auxiliary Verb
4. Direct Object
5. Indirect Object
6. Object Complement
7. Subject Complement
8. Predicate Noun
9. Predicate Adjective
10. Phrases
11. Clauses

The analysis of a sentence in these terms gives us more of a hint about the true meaning of the message. We know, for example, that the *subject* of a sentence is usually the *doer* while the *object* might be classed as the thing or person to which something is being done. Of course, the verb states exactly what action or state of being is occurring.

Syntax analysis of a spoken message yields slightly more information about the meaning than the original grammatical analysis. However, once the functions of a sentence have been identified, the computer may begin to process the syntactically translated phrase in terms of semantic evaluation. This process will be described later in this chapter. As we continue on the crash course of grammar, let us back up slightly and review a few elements of the parts of speech.

Nouns

There are basically four types of nouns: common, proper, collective, and abstract. They may refer to either persons, places, or things. Common nouns relate to general descriptions such as "dog." A proper noun might be "Rover." A collective noun connotes many things grouped together as in "animals." Finally, abstract nouns, such as "hunger," are those that exist only in thought.

Nouns have several types of classifications, which include gender, number, and case. The gender of nouns refers to the sex (which is not always immediately obvious without the knowledge of the semantic relationship of the noun). For instance, *man* is a masculine noun while *woman* is a feminine noun. Neuter nouns, such as house, computer, and book, are those that contain no reference to sex.

The number of a noun refers to whether it is singular or plural, and indicates a quantity of one or more than one. Finally, the *case* of a noun relates to its usage within a sentence; and may be considered *nominative* (*Rover* bit the mailman), *objective* (He saw *Rover* bite the mailman), *possessive* (*Rover's* teeth bit the mailman), and *vocative* (*Rover*, come here).

So, here we are back at Dick and Jane except that the dog's name has been changed from Spot to Rover. Unless you happen to be an elementary school grammar teacher, then these terms are probably long forgotten in your memory. However, remember that if you intend to understand and create speech recognition within a computer, then *you* must teach the computer how to understand grammar. Although you might change the names of the elements of speech as you create the understanding computer, they must all be there in some form.

Pronouns

Pronouns consist of those replacements for nouns such as I, you, he, we, they, etc. Possessive pronouns include those that indicate ownership: my, your, his, our, their, etc. Other pronouns that are used in place of nouns are: this, that, which, all, some, somebody, both, and so forth. To the computer, the pronoun should signify a question to be resolved as to the identity of the pronoun reference. This is deeply intertwined with contextual interpretation of phrases and can present a very significant confusion for the speech recognition system. (Remember "print it"?)

Verbs

These are probably the most easily identifiable features in grammar. They normally invoke a thought of action although they may also show a state of being as in "I *am* here." The *verbs* of a sentence normally give a natural language recognition program considerable clues about the semantic interpretation of a phrase. They also may leave a number of questions—or include hidden meaning in their usage. For example, the phrase "I fell" says not only that the subject moved from a higher to a lower place, but that the subject might have been injured during the action. From this example, it may be said that identifying the words and associated word phrases are only clues to the puzzle of phrase interpretation.

There are two types of verbs, transitive and intransitive. Transitive verbs express action that is performed on some person or thing. These types of verbs always require a direct object. Intransitive verbs express action or states that do not require a direct object. Both transitive and intransitive verbs have the properties of tense, voice, mood, person, and number, which are detectable through both the inflexion (that is, the change in form) of the verb and its context.

The first property, tense, should be a key element for computer recognition in connected speech because it implies the passage or expectation of time. Tenses include six types:

1. Present tense   *I speak.*
2. Past tense   *I spoke.*
3. Future tense   *I will speak.*
4. Present perfect tense   *I have spoken.*
5. Past perfect tense   *I had spoken.*
6. Future perfect tense   *I will have spoken.*

The second property, voice, tells whether the action is being done by or on the subject. When the action is done by the subject, the voice is active. When the action is done on the subject, the voice is passive. "I spoke" is active; "The sentence was spoken by me" is passive.

The third property, mood, tells about the feeling behind the verb. Verbs have three moods: indicative, subjunctive, or imperative. The indicative mood expresses or asks a fact, the subjunctive expresses an uncertainty, and the imperative expresses a command. "You are to go" is indicative, "If you were to go" is subjunctive, and "Go!" is imperative.

The fourth property is person, of which there are three. They are named, aptly enough: first, second, and third. When the subject of a verb is the speaker, then the verb is in the first person. When it is the person being spoken to, the verb is in the second person. And when the subject is someone or something that is not a participant in the discussion, then the verb is in the third person. "I eat" is first person, "You eat" is second person, and "He eats" is third person.

The last property is number, which simply tells whether the verb refers to one (singular) or several (plural). "He eats" is singular, and "They eat" is plural.

Notice that the form of the verbs often changes according to the tense, voice, mood, person, and number that the verb expresses. These changes in form, known as the inflexion of the verbs, are important clues to a computer concerning the meaning of the verb. One way for a computer to recognize all forms of a verb is for the computer to have a table of every possible form in its memory. Another way would be to have the computer try to match the incoming verb with forms of verbs that it generates from "principal parts" tables. Principal parts are the forms of a verb from which other forms may be generated by using the rules of conjugation. For instance, the principal parts of "speak" are the present indicative form "speak," the past form "spoke," and the past participle form "spoken." All the other forms—"will speak," "had spoken," and so forth—can be derived from the principal parts. With principal parts, the computer would use less memory for storing the different forms of the verbs, but it would take more time in generating the different forms of verbs for comparison with the incoming word.

Adjectives

We all know what adjectives do; they modify nouns. In fact, it's hard to create a descriptive sentence without the use of some adjective. "I have a *fast* computer" uses *fast* as the adjective. There are eight different kinds of adjectives but, in general, they all transfer additional descriptive meaning to an item being discussed. They also imply a knowledge of numbers in their usage. If I said that I had the *faster* computer, then I imply that there are two computers in question. If I were to say that I had the *fastest* computer, then I imply at least three computers in the comparison.

Adjectives can also be used as predicate adjectives as in the sentence "His face was red." They become object complements when used in this way: "I consider computers *smart.*"

Adverbs

These are modifiers of verbs, adjectives, and other adverbs. They, like the adjectives, impart additional meaning to a phrase. If we add an adverb to a previously examined phrase, we gain additional information: "I fell *here*" tells where I fell. If I add another adverb to make "I fell here *softly*" then I impart information concerning the severity of the fall. A third adverb can be added to indicate timeliness as in "I fell here softly *yesterday.*" Adverbs may also be used in comparisons like adjectives by a mechanism similar to that used in adjective comparisons: "My computer runs *faster* than yours" or "My computer runs *fastest* of all."

Prepositions

These are nominally combining words used to create prepositional phrases. For instance, "The man *with* the fastest computer always finishes first" contains the preposition *with,* which conveys information about the man. A sentence like "The computer only understands when you speak *in* English" conveys considerable information about the intended spoken message with the prepositional phrase "in English."

Conjunctions

These types of speech are those tiny words that link parts of sentences together. They consist of words like *and, or, but, either,* and *neither.* Logically, they have deep significance for computer understanding because they relate almost directly to Boolean operations. For instance, in the phrase "The car is red and green," there is a substantially different meaning than in "The car is red or green." Another rather obvious example is "*Either* the car is red *or* it is green." How about "If the car is red then paint it green." Look familiar? If X = red car and Y = paint car green, then the phrase translates directly to computer logic in "If X then Y".

Verbals

The verbal elements of speech will be used to a great extent in computer semantic analysis. These are often considered to be the base words of those used when normally speaking. The most common verbal is probably the infinitive form of the verb. A sentence like "I could see that he was coming" has two infinitives associated in its meaning: *to see* and *to come*. As we shall see later, the computer will have a much easier time in understanding what is happening in a sentence by reducing verbs to the infinitive form.

Other verbals include *gerunds* which are generated by adding "ing" to the ends of verbs, and *participles* which are similar to gerunds. These elements of speech may be utilized in place of verbs or adjectives in sentences to convey meanings related to actions or ideas. For instance, "the thinking computer" says the computer does think. It might be parsed as "the computer which to think." Semantic analysis will almost always reduce the gerunds and participles into infinitive forms for more simplified thought processing.

The Final Exam

Those of you who have persistently continued to read through the whirlwind grammar course should be commended. Although you most likely have gained no new overwhelming knowledge of English, you will be slightly more familiar with the terms when they are encountered in the discussion of semantic phrase interpretation later in this chapter.

In closing the grammatical analysis part of this book, I will give you a test to check your parsing skills. Each sentence in the test has more or less the same meaning; however, they are created using different parts of grammar.

1. The red block sits on the blue block.
2. The block with the red color is sitting on the blue block.
3. The block which is colored red sits on the blue block.
4. Sitting on the blue block is the position of the red block.
5. The red block is positioned to sit on the blue block.

That wasn't too bad for you, was it? The same group of phrases should also be accurately interpreted by a speech recognition computer as having the same basic meaning. Although you yourself might not use all of these positional descriptions in describing the placement of two colored blocks, if we allow a large enough group of people to describe the same scene, then we will have at least this many types of descriptions. As a result, the computer should react with equal accuracy to each. Another speaking variance which may be encountered in a large group of speakers is that of geographically dependent speech changes.

Dialects

Suppose you have designed and created an intelligent voice-operated clothes washing machine that uses voice input for its control. You have gone to great pains to ensure speaker-independent operation through characterization of phonemes and speech duration from 1000 randomly chosen speakers within your city. The words you have selected for voice activation include *wash, rinse, dry,* and *spin.* As you begin to distribute the product throughout the United States, you find that in some centralized areas the machine will not operate properly for the *wash* cycle. However, in other regions of the United States, your machine is reported to be working perfectly. What would you suspect to be the problem?

This problem is at first very mystifying because in certain localized regions of the United States only one vocal function of the system is inoperative. What you would find if you traveled to those regions and talked to the local residents would be the solution to the problem. Even though everyone in the United States writes the word "wash" with the same four letters, some areas pronounce the sounds as "wah-sh" while other regions say "war-sh." There is the culprit. The geographic difference in pronunciation for the same word is known as *dialect.*

Consider the problem that the telephone company might have if it tried to automate the Touch-Tone® telephone dial for voice activation. Since the same voice-recognition system would be used across the United States during long distance calls, it would have to respond equally well for all dialects. Can you see the problem? Just the "star" push button would be a monumental problem in itself. In the Massachusetts region, this key would be pronounced "stah," while in the south, it would have a sound more like "stawer." In regions of the southwest, it would be something like "stah-wer."

These noticeable changes in speech sounds are not occurring in the formant level of speech interpretation. Speakers with identical formant frequencies for given words, which would be perfectly acceptable for speaker-independent recognition given the same dialect, become completely incompatible when analyzed at the *phonetic* level with differing dialects.

Touch-Tone is a registered trademark of AT&T.

Problems in speech recognition may occur at even higher levels of speech due to dialects because of local historical influences. For instance, the place where you go to put gasoline in your car is referred to as a gas station in the northern part of the United States while it becomes a filling station in the southern part. Similarly, a small inland body of water might be called a lake in many parts of the United States, but it is a resaca in southern Texas. A fresh-water running stream takes on the forms of branch, creek, run, and bayou in different areas across the United States. Even the word "creek" has two major pronunciations. In many parts of the northern United States this word is pronounced "crick," while in other parts, it is pronounced more phonetically in keeping with its spelling creek.

The problem of dealing with different dialects will certainly be a thorn in the side of speaker-independent recognition systems. If words having dialectal differences cannot be compensated for in speech-recognition systems, then they should be avoided.

Accents

These vocal characteristics may create severe problems with speech recognizers. Very large numbers of citizens within the United States are currently immigrants or descendants of immigrants and may retain a characteristic accent of their original country. These people should also be expected to be able to use speech-recognition systems as well as long-term natives. This is certainly no easy problem considering the number of language influences upon regional speech. If you speak in the General American dialect to a person with a foreign accent, then you may notice the accent but have no trouble in understanding the content of the conversation. What you might not realize during the conversation is that as each word is spoken, you are mentally searching through your vocabulary for the closest sounding word based on the context of the statement or even on a complete story. The key to solving this problem in a computer speech-recognition system is found in extremely flexible pattern recognition algorithms during sentence and phrase parsing. These concepts will be discussed in later chapters.

Special Languages

In this section the author would like to go out on the limb a few feet and recommend, or at least introduce, a few radical solutions to the enormous problems of understanding spoken English. The general concept behind these departures from normal thinking is if English is too complex for accurate connected speech interpretation by computers, then why not choose a more logical language that *will* work. In support of this concept, let me remind you that our first programs for the computer were not written in connected English but rather in a very concise, logically constructed computer language. We are still using logically imbued languages for computer programming such as FORTRAN, Pascal, APL, and BASIC. We all use these languages with no antagonism toward the computer because we must program it in a language that it understands. Why should we not create a similar spoken language that it will understand equally well?

Loglan

One such language was introduced many years ago in the June 1960 edition of *Scientific American* magazine. In the article, James Cooke Brown, the author, boldly introduced a newly created synthetic logical language known as *Loglan*. His hypothesis behind the creation of the language was this: The structure and logic inherent in a language spoken by a people may causally determine a limit to their reasoning power.

In his attempt to create a new spoken language, he followed pathways unlike those used to create other synthetic languages such as Esperanto. His goal was, in fact, to form a spoken communication system without ambiguity with a strong foundation in Boolean logic. Since its creation, it has had up to 200 followers. It was reported that in 1977 Brown and several other Loglan disciples "engaged in several hours of free, spontaneous discourse completely in Loglan."

The use of a synthetic language for accurate computer speech recognition has an elegant simplicity. The architecture of the language was designed for direct phoneme to text conversion with no spoken ambiguities in phonetics or semantics. In its original intent, the language took the phrase "pretty little girl's school" and showed that the ambiguous English phrase required numerous unique Loglan phrases for its representation. The tremendous power of such a logical language is immediately evident. Given the logical structure of the language, the speech-recognition computer can map spoken Loglan directly to written Loglan with no semantic ambiguities. Now, before everyone runs out to the local bookstore to buy a copy of a book on Loglan (there isn't one yet), let me illustrate a few of the features of Loglan as taken from the 1960 edition of *Scientific American*. The language contains an alphabet having only 22 letters. Since each letter is mapped directly to a sound in all spoken cases, there are also only 22 phonemes: 5 vowels and 17 consonants. The allowable Loglan alphabet with the associated fixed sounds is given in Table 3-1.

Upon initial examination, the sounds of the Loglan alphabet are a small subset of the corresponding letter sounds in our phonetic system.

Table 3-1.
The Loglan Alphabet

Letter	Sound	As In
Vowels		
A	ah	odd
E	eh	ebb
I	$\overline{ee}$	eat
O	oh	oboe
U	$\overline{oo}$	moon
Consonants		
B	b	byte
C	sh	shook
D	d	digit
F	f	fast
G	g	get
H	h	hit
J	zh	beige
K	k	kite
L	l	list
M	m	mom
N	n	no
P	p	pick
R	r	risk
S	s	so
T	t	tick
V	v	vivid
Z	z	zoo

Remember that the beauty of this language lies in its invariability. If you see a letter within any Loglan word, then it will always be pronounced the same. During the creation of Loglan, Brown also attempted the feature of universality by structuring each word in the new language based on the equivalent words in the eight most prevalent world languages: English, Chinese, Hindu, Russian, Spanish, Japanese, French, and German. In Loglan, the English word "blue" translates to "blanu," as does "lan" in Chinese and "blau" in German. Short connective words are also alphabetically short, ranging from one to three letters. Most normally used words are in the five-letter form similar to "blanu" but may be compounded by simply concatenating the appropriate word roots. For instance, given the word "earth" in Loglan as "dertu," we might create the phrase "blue earth" as "blandertu." Another very important feature for speech recognizers which is inherent within a language like Loglan is the pronunciation of the *punctuation* marks as sounds. Rather than assuming commas or periods or question marks, they are actually spoken as part of the text. This significant feature removes the decision of sentence structure and length from the task of computer speech recognition.

Finally, a characteristic of Loglan that is of paramount importance during speech recognition is its logical structure when assembled into phrases and sentences. This is accomplished in the language architecture by relating a word's placement or relative position in a sentence of its meaning. A very similar relationship is found in structured computer languages such as Pascal and APL. If you view a longer Loglan phrase and parse it into its meanings, you will find that the resultant ideas translate almost directly into computer statements. Imagine the ease of semantic analysis with such a well-structured communication medium.

If you want to know more about the language of Loglan, I refer you to the original article in *Scientific American*. The interest group, which is known as the Loglan Institute, was last known to exist at 2261 Soledad Rancho Road, San Diego, California 92109. If the thought of learning a new synthetic language with which at most 200 other people are conversant doesn't inspire you, then let me propose another linguistic simplification for your perusal. In this synthetic system, only the names have been changed.

Unifon

Around the same time that James Cooke Brown was formulating Loglan as a synthetic language, across the United States, in Chicago, an economist named John Malone was creating a linguistic simplification. His progeny, dubbed Unifon (*Uni* for one; *fon* for sound), is a phonographic system containing a 40-character pictographic alphabet that maps directly to 40 invariable speech sounds. Since its original conception, the Unifon alphabet has undergone several mutations, primarily to improve the esthetic quality of the alphabet. A relatively recent article which describes the Unifon alphabet and its metamorphosis may be found in the August 1981 issue of *Science Digest*. The author, John M. Culkin, described in this exposition the features and advantages of the Unifon alphabet. A more recent publication by the same author in the August 1982 issue of *Science Digest* relates the use of Unifon to computer-oriented systems.

The current Unifon alphabet as modified jointly by Malone and Culkin is shown in Fig. 3-1. It contains a total of 16 vowels and 24 consonants to effectively describe the modern English sounds used in everyday speech. Since the translation of English to Unifon is performed by simply mapping sounds and symbols, there is relatively little semantic interpretation involved in the process. The real advantage of using a system such as Unifon for computer-speech representation is in one-to-one, sound-to-symbol mapping. (It does not, however, simplify the computer's task of understanding the context and semantics in-

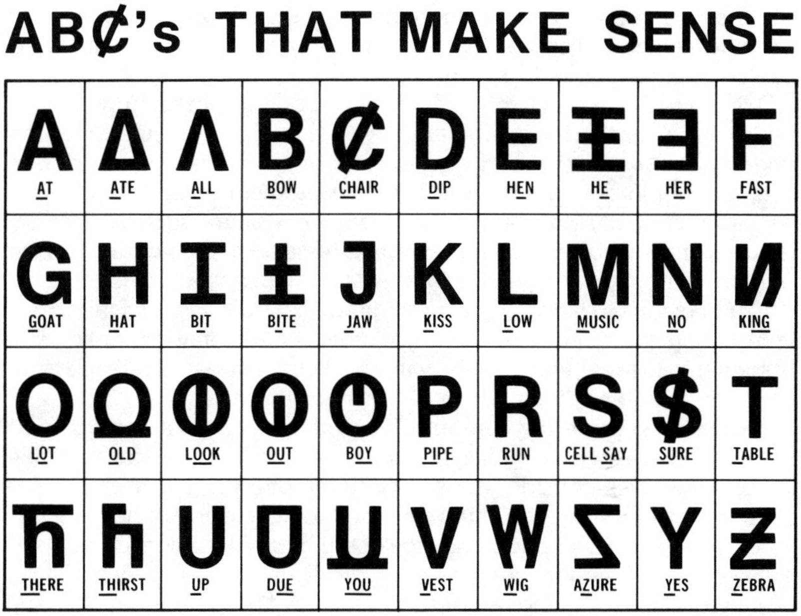

ABȻ's THAT MAKE SENSE

A AT	Δ ATE	Λ ALL	B BOW	ȼ CHAIR	D DIP	E HEN	Ⱶ HE	Ǝ HER	F FAST
G GOAT	H HAT	I BIT	± BITE	J JAW	K KISS	L LOW	M MUSIC	N NO	Ɲ KING
O LOT	Ω OLD	Φ LOOK	Φ OUT	⊙ BOY	P PIPE	R RUN	S CELL SAY	$ SURE	T TABLE
Ꚍ THERE	ħ THIRST	U UP	∪ DUE	⊔ YOU	V VEST	W WIG	Σ AZURE	Y YES	Z ZEBRA

Figure 3-1.
The unifon alphabet (Courtesy John M. Culkin and John Malone).

volved in phrase interpretation.) As an example, the simplified representation in Unifon of the two homonymic words fore and four is:

$$FΩƎ$$

That bothersome trio of homonyms, to, too, and two, are all represented by the Unifon equivalent:

$$T⊔$$

If we take an average phrase like "computer speech written in Unifon" and translate it to its Unifon orthographic representation, we will have the symbolic phrase:

KUMPUTƎ SPIȼ RITEN IN UNIFON

The process of changing the English-spoken sounds into Unifon is really quite fun. You can take any sentence from this book and easily, by speaking the sentence, translate it into Unifon. The unifonic representation of the sentence once translated has no pronunciation ambiguities. If a computer, having a phoneme-type synthesizing capability for computer-generated speech were given the phrase in Unifon, it would map correctly to spoken English.

This is a real advantage if you have ever worked with an English text-to-phoneme synthesizing program. Even though these rule-following programs are very powerful and may observe English pronunciation rules ranging in the thousands, there always seem to be a few words that are incorrectly pronounced. If a written system, such as Unifon, had universal acceptance, then the text-to-speech problem would be solved.

In a previous paragraph, I mentioned that the use of Unifon for representing spoken English does not provide additional semantic clues to spoken phrases. How, then, will an abstract construct like Unifon assist in computer speech-recognition performance?

In situations where the computer must semantically interpret a command or idea, there is really no advantage to using a concept like Unifon. However, consider the simplification of a voice-activated typewriter if it no longer has to determine the proper spelling of homonymic words. A voice-transcription machine could be easily designed and used like a court reporting machine to phonetically transcribe speech directly to printed Unifon. A visionary machine, which I will name "The Typing Talkwriter," is conceptually shown in Fig. 3-2. The hand-held transcrip-

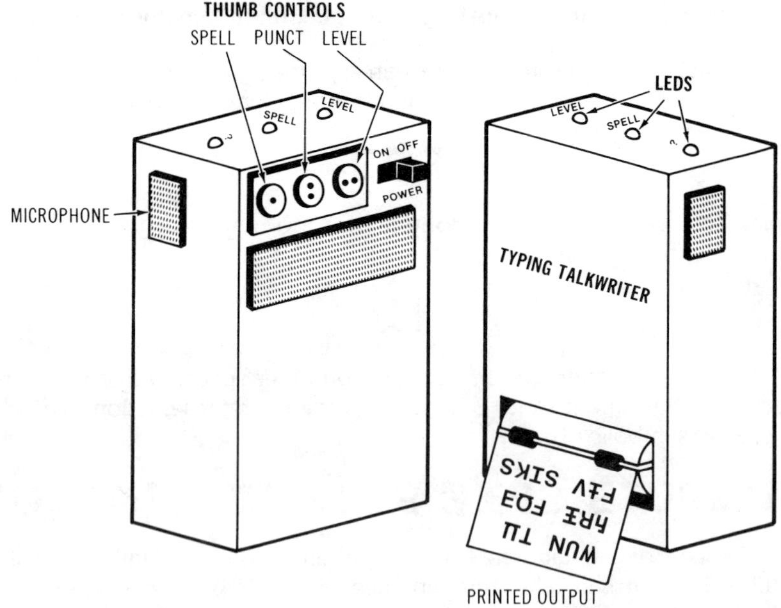

Figure 3-2.
The Typing Talkwriter.

tion device with a Unifon output provides a printed record that may be read and understood by individuals fluent in Unifon. If we allow, in our fantasy, for another machine to exist that can optically read the Unifon characters, then this larger machine can take the Unifonically printed text, derive the correct spellings of the words from context, and then print the orthographically correct English equivalent text. The entire two-process system would very closely simulate a voice-activated type-writer with an intermediate phonetically readable code resembling the P-code concept used in Pascal programming languages.

If machine transportability is considered, think what might happen if the Typing Talkwriter were given to a person having French or German as their natural language. As they begin to dictate into the device, it would transcribe their foreign speech directly into Unifon without regard for the originally spoken language. Talk about a universal machine! This is just one more example of what may be accomplished if we permit a compromise in our linguistically complex written and spoken English.

Does It Hear What I Mean?

A voice-recognition computer must be able to interpret phrases, and deal with both word symbolisms and syntax errors.

Phrase Interpretation

Unless a voice-recognition computer intends only to transcribe a spoken message, then it must possess some means of intuitively extracting the meaning from the spoken messages. For a computer to be able to attempt this complex procedure, it must be endowed with some knowledge of natural language processing. And that is no simple task! Not only does it involve the science of computers, it extends into philosophy, linguistics, and the science of semantics. Considering that entire books have been written on natural language processing, the coverage in this book will be a rather cursory review of the procedures used in natural-language processing.

Okay, what's so difficult about processing natural language? Well, put this way, if ten of the fastest Cray-1 computers were put to work in parallel on determining the semantic meaning of a story as simple as "Mary Had a Little Lamb," they could not possibly understand the total meaning as fast as you or I. However, there are methods of interpreting context and the semantics of spoken messages with reasonable accuracy and speed.

In general, a language-understanding program must be capable of handling five types of problems associated with natural language: (1) the syntax problem, (2) the semantics problem, (3) the inference problem, (4) the generation problem, and (5) the integration problem. What the speech-recognition computer must sequentially do as it solves each of these problems in understanding speech is to most accurately determine the intended motive behind the message, the intended emotive content, and finally the true meaning of the message as spoken. It may not be entirely obvious that a phrase may contain ambiguous information which the computer must resolve as having inherent "real-world" inferences. An example of this phenomenon is given in the sentence "We saw four white horses driving home today." A human analysis of the phrase yields no ambiguity because we all know that horses cannot drive. However, unless a language-understanding computer has been given intrinsic information about horses and cars, it will most likely logically assume that what we saw today were four white horses *driving* home.

If we examine the semantics and syntax of the phrase using the accepted tree-branch analysis of the sentence structure, then we may generate a descriptive graph like that shown in Fig. 3-3.

The processes that the computer might perform in analyzing a spoken phrase would be very similar to the associative inferences in this figure. For example, a number of conclusions must first be drawn about each syntactical element in order to create the overall intent of the phrase. "We" is determined to be the subject of the phrase with an inferential dictionary meaning the *speaker and others*. Thus, the computer has an idea of who "we" are. The verb of the sentence is subsequently parsed into the infinitive form "to see" with a past tense usage modified by the

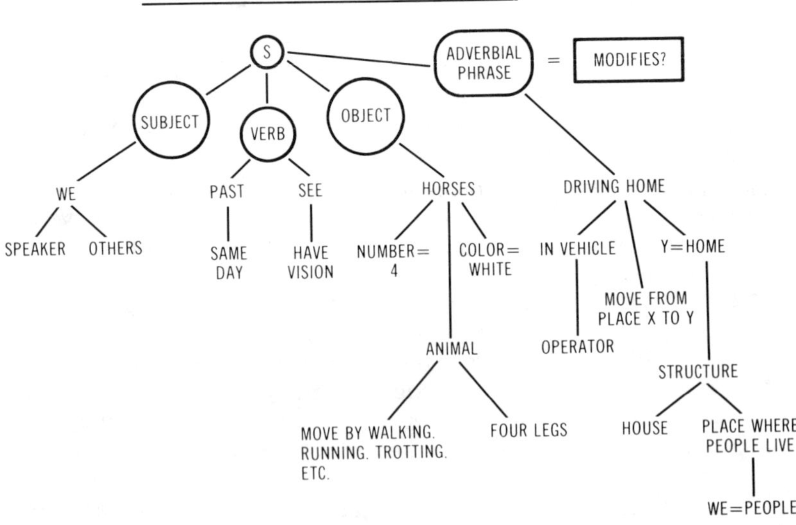

Figure 3-3.
An associative property list evaluation of a phrase.

adverb *today*. This inference gives temporal data to the computer about the time of occurrence of the event. If "horses" is assumed to be the object of the phrase, then the two adjectives "four" and "white" give the physical properties of the object. The object also has associated with it a property list which indicates that horses are animals having four legs which normally move by walking, running, trotting, etc. Other properties for "horse" which might be contained within the association list (in computer memory) include large, feeds on hay, used for pulling heavy objects, and likes sugar cubes. The final analysis in the sentence involves the adverbial phrase, "driving home." This phrase can be parsed into knowledge inherent nodes which associate as being in some sort of a vehicle as the operator, and moving from place X to place Y. The object of the gerund in the adverbial phrase "home" is parsed as the letter Y condition for the "driving to" property of the gerund. The computer does not know X, but it may inquire. Also associated with the object "home" are intrinsic properties telling the computer that the home is a structure, typically a house, and a place where people live. This also recursively refers back to the "we" as the subject of the phrase to infer that the home is where we live.

Having parsed the phrase to a fairly deep semantic level, the computer is left with an unresolved inference in the adverbial phrase. The computer's dilemma is whether to associate the modifying phrase with the verb "saw" or the object "horses." The *intelligent* natural-language computer will make a quick comparison between the two possible references for the modifier to see if there is an apparent incongruity in the comparisons. Since the property characteristics of horses includes only motivation by foot (under animals), then this feature is identified as a paradox in the property list associated with a possible reference to "horse." Thus, the perceptive computer system will quickly link the modifying adverbial phrase to the verb to complete the semantic interpretation of the phrase.

Having been given the preceding phrase, the computer now has stored in its reference knowledge an idea that closely relates to the original message. Suppose you queried the computer with "What color were the animals we saw today?" The computer's response would be "white." If you continued the interrogation with "Who saw them?", you should get a response similar to "You and other people." Similarly, "Where were we going?" should yield the answer "To the place where you and the other people live." Notice in the above hypothetical conversation with the computer, that it truly appears to *understand* the spoken phrase. Its inferential responses to the given questions show the required intelligence level necessary for accurate speech understanding systems.

The procedure explained in the interpretation of the previous phrase is typical of what must occur in a connected-speech–recognition system. The *key element* to realizing why there is such a difficulty in this process lies in the fact that our words to us are simply logical symbols for ideas. Let us examine this concept in more detail.

Word Symbolisms

As you read the word given at the very end of this sentence, take a mental snapshot of your thoughts immediately following your recognition of the word: "automobile." Think about it. If we could replay the flood of information brought forth immediately after you perceived the word, we could generate a list of properties about automobiles that would fill many pages of text. Possibly the most brief description of the object you generated during the process was a mental picture. Did you see the car from the side or from the front or rear? What color was it? Was it the kind that you have parked in your garage? More than likely these questions would be difficult to answer given that brief examination of your mental flash. You might even find that what you mentally pictured was a generic automobile without specific identifiable qualities. Those can be added later whan I say "Cadillac automobile." Now your picture has more detail. As you walk around your mental Cadillac and admire the polish and smoothness of the finish, what do you think is going on in your mind?

Words are obviously used by us to represent those ideas that are contained as mental images within our perceptive mechanism. There is a great task involved in transferring the same ability to a computer.

Using current state-of-the-art techniques, words and word symbols may be generated through extended property lists for association. An ideal computer language created primarily for this purpose—that of processing lists—is known as LISP. LISP is the language of choice for programs in artificial intelligence. Since the language is based upon associative lists of properties and even lists of lists of properties, it makes the symbol characterization of words a relatively simple procedure. And because a computer running in LISP can process each word under examination in terms of associative properties, the apparent intelligence and knowledge of real word elements can be quite impressive.

The language of LISP is quite complex and too lengthy for a proper description in this book. Almost all major programming in natural-language understanding is currently being written in this language. If you can imagine a language that easily allows lists of properties to be linked to other lists and subject elements called *atoms*, then you can see how the previous phrase interpretation might be simply represented in this language. Not only does it allow physical properties of objects to be linked to their "word" names, it allows ideas and abstract concepts to be elegantly bound together. For instance, think about the meaning behind the word *persuade*. If I said that I will persuade you to read this book, you certainly understand what I am saying.

Consider the abstract ideas contained within the word. First of all, *persuade* is something I do. I do this act to cause you to become influenced so that you intend to read the book. Thus, the word "persuade" symbolizes the thoughts "do," "cause," "become," and "intend." Look at the properties that are associated with an idea as simple as "hurt." They are "do," "cause," "become," "not," "feel," and "well." An abstract idea like "kill" has the semantic structure decoded which yields "do," "cause," "become," "not," and "alive." This semantic procedure could be carried on *ad infinitum*. However, remember that the dissection of simple words in this manner is the key to transferring the necessary level of intelligence into the computer for speech recognition and understanding.

Syntax Errors and Their Disasters

No matter how careful the designer of a speech-recognition system may be, there will be instances where ambiguities will occur. That postulate can be confirmed because the same error commonly occurs during human conversation. The only difference is that if you hear something that to your mind seems nonsensical, then you would simply say, "What did you say?" The problem becomes even more acute when a computer operator begins talking to a computer in phrases that do not necessarily have surrounding phrases for context supplementation.

As evidence, suppose you are interacting verbally with a computer to edit a previously written program and issue the command "repeat lines 100 through 500." If the computer recognition system has a 95% accuracy in understanding, then 5% of the time it will get the words wrong. More often than not, rather than realize it cannot find the word correctly, it chooses an inappropriate word or phrase for its result. If it happens to choose as its translation of your spoken phrase "delete lines 100 through 500," then you are simply out of luck.

As speech-recognition computers are given greater physical powers such as controlling robots, then these recognition errors can be dangerously disastrous and possibly even hazardous to your health. What, for instance, would you expect to happen if, when verbally operating a powerful robot system that had been ordered to lift you, you ordered it to "Please put me down." Do not be too surprised if, rather than the expected action, the robot responds with "Okay, dummy. You wear glasses, you've got a long nose, and you're just plain ugly. You don't know how to operate robots, and you certainly are a glutton for punishment with your ambiguous English phrases."

As a rule, the use of ambiguous phrases and words (particular homonymic type words) should be rejected for speech-recognizer vocabulary construction. If a computer realizes during semantic analysis of a spoken phrase that an ambiguity exists that cannot be resolved, then it must query the operator for verification. If we extrapolate this idea slightly, we can formulate a set of rules for hearing computers in the same vein as Isaac Asimov's original *Laws of Robotica.*

These laws for the ethical conduct of robots, when taken with a grain of editorial freedom, may be used to produce the Five Laws of Auditory Automata for hearing computers:

1. An auditory computer may not hurt or kill the operator!
2. It may not hurt itself without *verbal confirmation* from the operator. This includes:
   (A) Formatting or erasing disks.
   (B) Deleting or modifying files.
   (C) Deleting or modifying programs.
   (D) Clearing memory.
   (E) Releasing or adding peripheral devices.
   (F) Activating or deactivating peripheral devices.
   (G) Modifying its own architecture.
3. It may only make inferences about statements which are spoken directly to it. (This may be assured by preceding each spoken computer command with a reference name, like "Hal.")
4. It may not attempt to carry out verbal orders if the resultant action or inaction will violate Rules 1, 2, or 3.
5. It must give computing priority to verbal commands over internal computations.

Remember that these are only proposed rules. Computer intelligence and capabilities are beginning to approach levels in which ethical operation must be instilled. If we *truly* generate machines that reason and contain what we call "intelligence" for understanding natural language, then we must control the reins to that power. Particularly where the possible misinterpretation of speech and semantic content is involved.

In closing the chapter on language and its semantic interpretation, remember what has been given here is only the tip of the iceberg. If it interests you, then I suggest that you slip on a mask, wet suit, and some very large air tanks. As you dive below the surface, you will find that there is great beauty in the depth of these sciences. But, wait! A second iceberg has come into view. This one seems to have some small writing on it. I cannot quite make out what it says. Oh, yes! Now I see it. It says "Electronic Speech Processing. . . ."

CHAPTER 4

Speech Signal-Acquisition Techniques

It's time to take a break. The chapters of this book, so far, have discussed sciences that seem to lack a certain amount of precision. Each time we felt we had a firm grasp of an idea or subject, our illusion was shattered by ambiguities and interpretational difficulties. As we move our consideration toward electronic speech processing, things become more precise. In this chapter, we will begin our examination of electronic speech processing with the first element of its implementation: speech acquisition. The techniques discussed herein are those used by speech recognition systems to convert the acoustic speech signal to appropriate electronic data for eventual intelligence extraction and processing.

Two methods stand out as primary candidates for optimal acquisition techniques. The first, direct signal digitization or waveform encoding, as it is also known, is accomplished by simply digitizing the analog voltage from a microphone. The second technique, which we will call spectral acquisition, requires more complexity in the processing of analog information. Now, taken one at a time, here's how they work.

Direct Waveform Acquisition

Two methods of direct waveform acquisition are waveform encoding and delta modulation encoding.

Waveform Encoding

The speech acquisition technique known as direct waveform encoding is a relatively simple process where an analog signal is converted to a

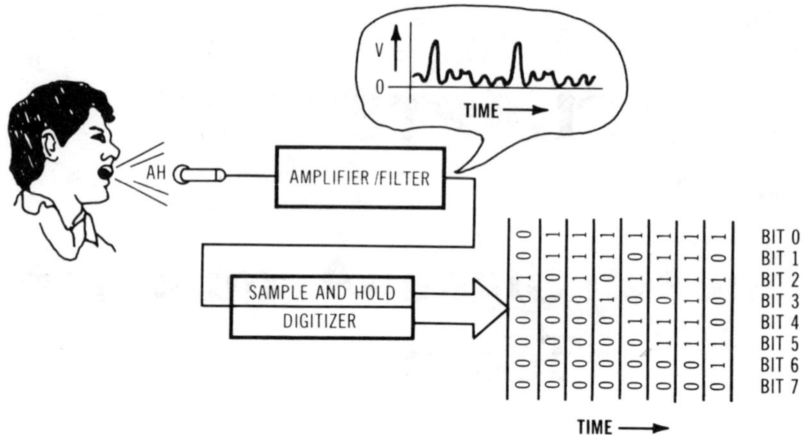

Figure 4-1.
Speech digitization.

serial string of binary data. The binary data may be either in single bit form or parallel byte form. Fig. 4-1 illustrates the speech digitization process in which the speech analog waveform is converted to a serial string of 8-bit bytes for each data sample. What is really occurring in this sequence of events is that at periodic intervals a *sample-and-hold* circuit captures a snapshot of the analog incoming voltage, which is immediately converted to a voltage-equivalent parallel data byte by an analog-to-digital (a/d) converter.

The same process may be viewed in terms of electronic blocks in the diagram in Fig. 4-2. Not only does this diagram illustrate the individual

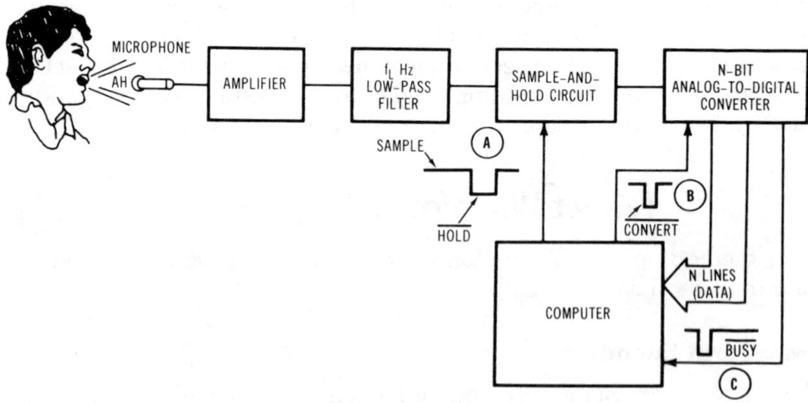

Figure 4-2.
Representation of speech waveform encoding.

blocks within the waveform encoding process, it also represents the control signals to and from the computer which govern the digital encoding process. The signal flow in this diagram is from the microphone to an amplifier that boosts the speech voltage levels to usable values for subsequent digitization. Immediately following the amplifier is a low pass filter to remove high frequencies that might interfere with the sampling process. (This will be discussed in more detail momentarily.) The output of the low pass filter (which is still an analog voltage) is processed by the sample-and-hold circuit exactly as its name implies. Upon command from the computer, the circuit that has been continuously *sampling* the input waveform briefly *holds* the current analog voltage during the digitization process. Following the release of the hold command, the sample-and-hold circuit returns to the sample or *tracking* mode.

During the time that the sample-and-hold circuit is holding the analog voltage, the N-bit analog-to-digital converter performs the actual digitization of the "held" speech waveform. Conversion times for normal speech digitizers range anywhere from 2 to 100 microseconds. Following the conversion to a digital byte, the a/d converter signals the computer that it has completed the assigned task. The controlling computer may now input the digital byte corresponding to the temporary voltage level and repeat the entire cycle until the full desired waveform has been captured.

The sequence of events is best put into perspective by observing the control signals and their time relationship during the process. Fig. 4-3 presents the three waveforms plotted in the same time frame reference to illustrate their temporal relationships. In the figure, notice that the sample-and-hold command (A) is the first control line to change levels. Following a brief delay (on the order of a few microseconds), which allows the sample-and-hold amplifier to stabilize, the computer commands the a/d converter to convert by briefly taking the *convert* command line (B) low. As the a/d converter recognizes that it has been given a command to convert, it immediately takes its *busy* response line low indicating to the computer that it is, in fact, "busy" converting. The important feature of the three waveforms is that the *hold* signal (A) stays low until the signal conversion has completed. The computer must do this through logic to ensure that the digitizer does not try to digitize a changing input signal. (If the input signal to the a/d converter were allowed to change during conversion, errors in quantization will occur which the computer will view as audio distortion.) Finally, after the a/d converter has taken its *busy* line back high again, the computer may reset the sample-and-hold circuit to its sample mode, and then delay for the next periodic conversion time out.

A few paragraphs ago, I mentioned that we would come back to the effect of low-pass filtering upon sample time. The actual need for the low-pass filter arises because speech frequencies can easily extend up to and beyond the sampling frequency. In most systems, speech fre-

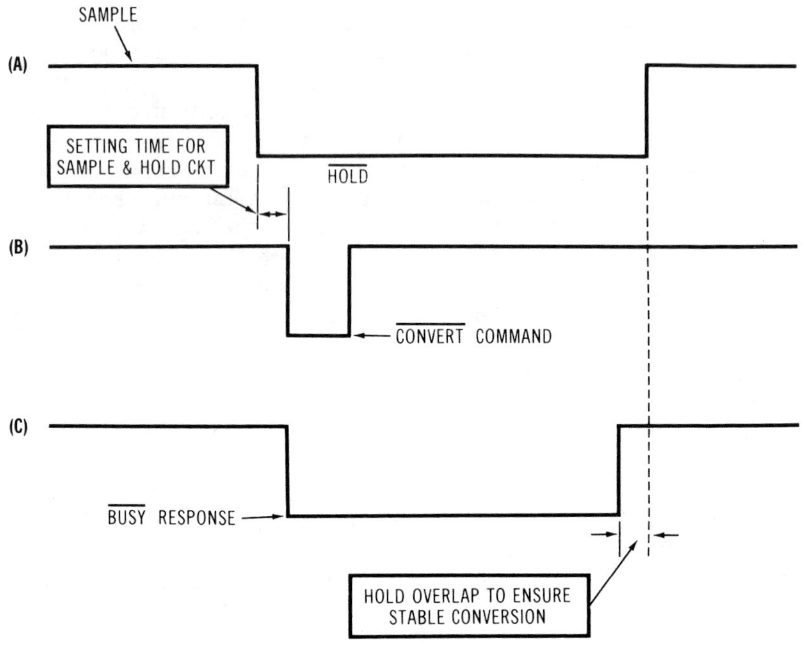

Figure 4-3.
Digitization control signals.

quencies beyond 3 to 4 kHz are redundant and provide little more information than those below that range. Now, if we can find some reason for lowering the sample rate to a minimum value, then we are putting less bytes per second of data into memory (the net effect is to allow the digitization of longer words or phrases for a given fixed size memory).

To determine a sample rate for adequate speech input digitization, we must keep in mind a powerful theory of sampled data discovered by a fellow named Henry Nyquist of Bell Laboratories many years ago. His perceptive observations of sampled analog waveforms detailed a phenomenon that occurs when the frequency of the incoming waveform reaches and extends beyond one-half of the sampling frequency. When described in words, the manifestations of the sampling theorem are quite complex. However, if we view the physical process of a changing sampling rate in Fig. 4-4, we can easily see the artifacts of an increasing sample rate.

The original signal shown in Fig. 4-4A corresponds to any incoming waveform which is—for sake of clarity—a cosine waveform at frequency f_o. The waveform in Fig. 4-4B is the sampled voltage equivalent when sampled at a frequency equal to eight times the original fre-

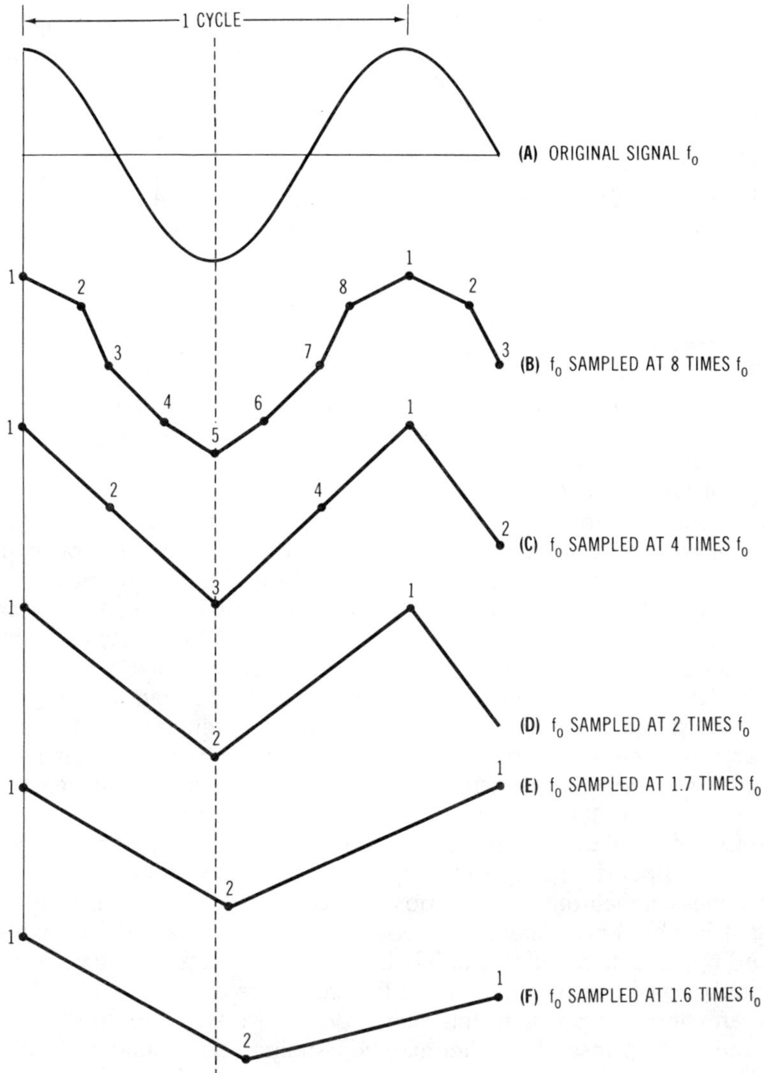

Figure 4-4.
The sampling frequency problem.

quency. It closely follows the original shape and thus yields considerable information about the top waveform. The next two waveforms in Figs. 4-4C and 4-4D are the sampled representations of the original signal at four times and two times the frequency f_o, respectively. Each of these triangular waves still contains the original fundamental frequency as part of the sampled information. The problem, which arises when sampling at less than twice the original frequency, is shown in the remaining waveforms of the figure. The original waveform when sampled at 1.7 times the original frequency (Fig. 4-4E) is the same triangular waveform as in Fig. 4-4D *but* the period of the sampled data is beginning to change. The same frequency distortion occurs to a greater extent in Fig. 4-4F as the sample rate drops to 1.6 times the original frequency. As the sampling frequency and original frequency move closer to each other, the resultant sampled data continually moves down in frequency until they are equal (f_o = the sampling frequency). At this condition, the sampled output is a dc value sampled once each period, which produces a steady nonchanging output.

The resultant effect of the sampling problem described by Nyquist is that as the original signal exceeds one-half of the sampling frequency, an artifact frequency is generated equal to the sampling frequency (f_s) minus the original frequency (f_o), which lies *in the passband* of the original frequency. Once it has been generated within the same passband as the desired signal, it may no longer be filtered out.

As a precaution to prevent the previously described undesirable condition from occurring, the sampling rate should always be held at a frequency at least twice that expected within the analog data to be sampled. For instance, if a speech spectrum cutoff frequency of 3 kHz is desired, then the sampling frequency should at least be 6.5 to 7 kHz. The higher that the sampling frequency is placed above the original frequency, the fewer *image* frequencies will be generated within the desired speech spectrum. It is also necessary to impose rather strict conditions upon the speech spectrum to ensure that it never reaches more than one-half the sampling frequency. This may be ensured by the use of a rather fast drop off low-pass filter with the passband edge near the upper desired speech frequencies (in the example: 3 kHz).

A physical realization of one possible low-pass filter circuit is given in Fig. 4-5. The 3-pole filter is a Chebyshev design having a 0.5-dB passband ripple. The rolloff rate at 3 kHz is 18 dB per octave (one octave is a doubling of frequency). Thus, if the sample rate is 6 or 7 kHz, then the amplitude response of this filter is down at least 18 to 20 dB. The frequency response of the filter may be visualized by plotting the output of the filter for a fixed input voltage versus frequency. Fig. 4-6 illustrates the performance of the filter in Fig. 4-5 versus frequency. Notice in this plot that if the speech signal is above 3 kHz, then the resultant image amplitudes within the speech passband will be reduced by the filter response level. Ideally, the cutoff slope should be almost vertical at 3 kHz; however, this is very difficult and expensive to achieve with physical filtering systems. Switched-capacitor type filters may approximate a steep cutoff slope with a simple filter design but their cost is rather high for the increased advantages.

Another consideration in the speech digitization process is the reso-

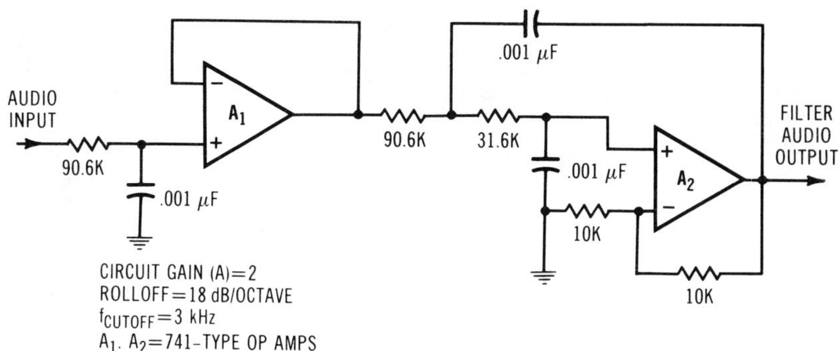

Figure 4-5.
A 3-pole Chebychev low-pass filter with 3 kHz cutoff.

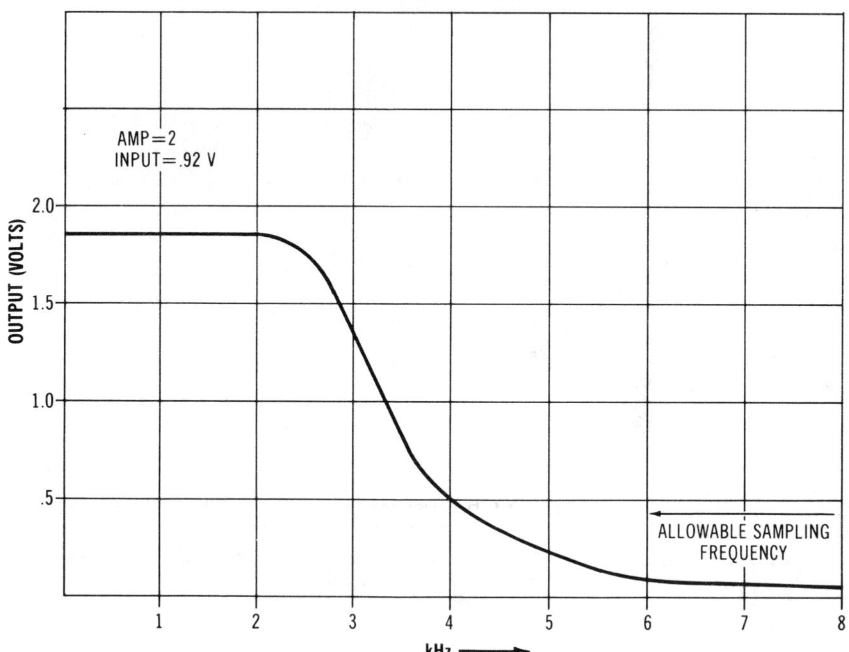

Figure 4-6.
A 3-pole 3 kHz low-pass filter response.

lution of the analog-to-digital converter. The previous figures show an
N-bit converter being used to digitize the analog values with no indication of exactly how many bits are being converted. The total number is
really left up to you; however, 8 bits is probably the most convenient.
This adds a feeling of comfort with 8-bit microprocessors because each

sample corresponds to one byte. Let me issue a *caveat* here about this normal inclination. While an 8-bit digitized signal will represent 255 levels of possible sampled signal amplitudes—and should be perfectly acceptable for normal speech—the dynamic range of the speech may present problems. Think back to the formant frequency tables in Chapter 2. In Table 2-4 from that chapter, the ratios of the formant frequencies are given, with some third formants being approximately 40 dB below the first formant frequency. This is 100 times less than the maximum formant amplitude. What this means, in the sampling and digitizing process, is that the third formant component of speech will be digitized only with a 2.5-bit resolution. This is relatively crude to say the least! Some of the fricative sounds which are very soft and weak in amplitude will have the same problem when digitized with an 8-bit resolution. For this reason, you should consider a digitization resolution of at least 12 bits to encompass the entire dynamic range of speech. Although it means that you must carry an extra 4 bits through an 8-bit computer (no problem for a 16-bit processor), you have at your disposal 4,096 levels of digitization. Accordingly, even the smallest levels of speech that may be expected will be digitized with a 40- to 50-level resolution. This relatively small concession in cost (the 12-bit over the 8-bit a/d converter) will yield considerable improvement in the digitization of the softer sounds of speech.

Although it may sound rather complicated, the process of acquiring the digital equivalent of a speech waveform is relatively simple. If the concepts of sampling rate and presampling filters are closely observed, there should be no problems. Low-cost sample-and-hold amplifiers like the National LM-398N sell for around $4.00 each and provide perfectly adequate sampling capabilities for speech recognition. Analog-to-digital converters with 12 bits of resolution are rather expensive; however, National Semiconductor also makes a relatively low-cost 12-bit converter with a conversion rate allowing up to 10-kHz sample frequencies. This converter, the ADC1210, sells for around $50.00 but provides very high-resolution speech input. Remember, the cost of the components that you put into the system normally determine the quality and accuracy of the resultant speech recognition capabilities.

Delta Modulation Encoding

This is another form of directly digitizing speech input, but its use in speech recognition systems is rare. It is mentioned here primarily to cover the field of direct signal acquisition and because there may be some creative ways of using this simplified speech input method for speech recognition.

Basically, delta modulation encoding is a form of digitization of an analog signal which retains only the information about the *change* in the signal over time. That is where the process got its name. The *delta*

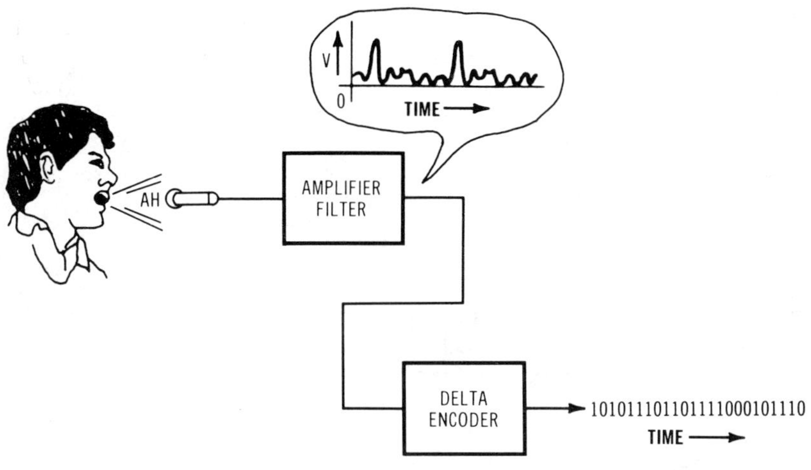

Figure 4-7.
A delta encoding system.

refers to a difference between samples. As a signal acquisition process, it is quite a bit simpler than the previous waveform encoding method, particularly when it comes to circuitry. The block diagram of a delta encoding circuit is shown in Fig. 4-7. The system is relatively simple in that it consists of an amplifier/filter to limit the speech response, followed by a delta encoding circuit. At each sample time, the encoder outputs a *single bit* to indicate whether the signal has increased, decreased, or stayed the same since the last sample. Given any point of the sample process, the computer cannot tell what actual value is being digitized. It only knows that the signal is changing from a previous value. As it turns out, this is a perfectly adequate procedure for digitizing speech. Since we are concerned primarily with the amplitude changes in time, we have no particular need to know the absolute voltage level at any sample.

The advantage to this type of encoding in addition to simplified circuitry is the need for only a single input bit to the computer. The disadvantages lie in the increased sample rate needed to adequately digitize high frequency signals. An example of how a speech signal can be digitized using only one bit is shown in Fig. 4-8. The waveform at the top represents an input signal that might come from a microphone. The center waveform is the output of a delta modulation encoder representing only the change information within the incoming signal. Notice that at the peaks of the cosine wave (where the signal goes through a relatively slow change), the delta data must alternate to produce the leveled output shown at the bottom of the figure. The correspondence between the "one" bit and the "zero" bit is very simple and direct. When the delta data is high, it corresponds to an increasing slope of

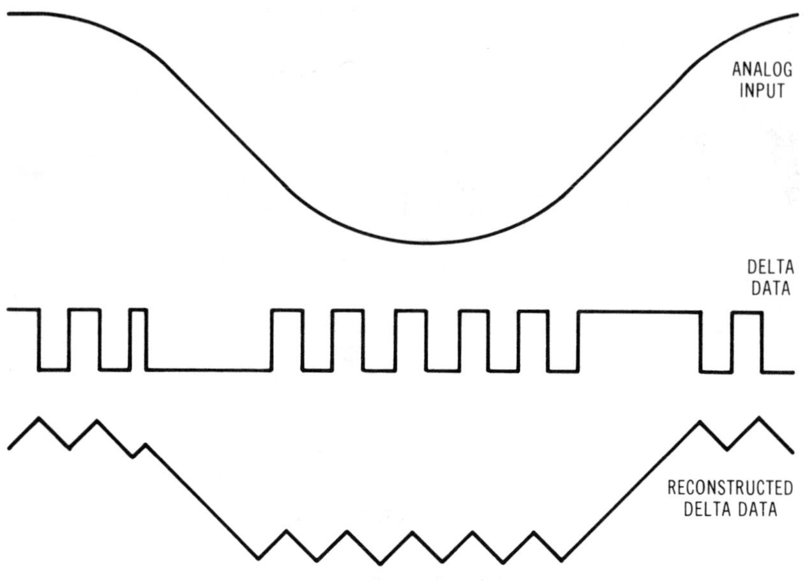

Figure 4-8.
The delta encoding process.

constant value. When it is low, it indicates a decreasing constant slope equal to the magnitude of the rising value. Thus, when the delta signal alternates, it represents a stable nonchanging incoming signal level.

As I mentioned earlier, the delta encoding process yields no real advantages and possibly even has disadvantages for use within speech recognition systems. However, the absolute waveform value may be recreated within the computer by simply adding or subtracting a fixed number from some arbitrary starting point for each clocked bit change. For example, if each clocked delta bit represents an incoming voltage change of 0.1 volt per millisecond, then a computer monitoring the delta line may internally add to a starting number (say 128) the value of 1 for each high delta data bit. Each low delta data bit would therefore correspond to a subtraction in the original 1. The resultant internal computer number after each addition or subtraction would be a relative value corresponding to the incoming signal amplitude.

As you can see, the idea of delta encoding is mechanically simple, while its concept of operation is somewhat more difficult than direct waveform digitization. There *is* a slight advantage in transmission bandwidth in using this method (approximately 3 to 6 dB), but since it requires more diddling with the numbers once they are in the computer, you will be spending more time working with the details of acquisition and less with those of actual recognition methods. There is a way that allows much simpler signal acquisition and even simplifies the computer analysis of acquired speech. Its hardware realization is more complicated, but as you will see in the next section, it takes a large burden off of the computer in processing the speech signal.

Spectral Signal Acquisition

Spectral signal acquisition can involve analog, digital, and mathematical filters.

Analog Filtering

Having seen the complexities of direct waveform encoding of speech, you might wonder if there aren't some simpler methods that involve acquiring the frequencies of speech directly, before digitization. This is certainly an acceptable method of acquiring speech for speech recognition systems, and, in fact, simplifies the computer's task of processing spectral data. How does it work? Well, assume that a fairly large bank of selective filters is placed between the microphone and the computer to limit the frequency range in each digitized signal. The diagram of such a spectral acquisition system that might be used in front of a speech processor is shown in Fig. 4-9. Does it look familiar? It should. It is very similar to the spectrograph described in Chapter 2. Using the same technique of segmenting speech into frequency bands, the computer may digitize incoming signals more slowly but with more information carried during each sample.

In the example, there are 12 frequency bands which subdivide the vocal spectrum. Following each bandpass filter is a rectifier circuit which does nothing more than produce a dc voltage corresponding to the amplitude in that frequency band. Following each rectifier there is a smoothing filter capacitor which ensures that the output changes from each rectifier vary slowly with time. This allows a slower signal sample rate because we are no longer trying to directly digitize speech, but instead we are capturing the frequency variations in speech. The smoothing filter has to be no faster than our vocal tracts can change their shapes, thus giving a time window on the order of 10 to 20 milliseconds for each complete digitization sequence.

During the acquisition sequence, the computer must sequentially select, using the analog multiplexer, each filter output and in turn digitize that value for input. Then, internal to the computer are a bank of 12 registers used to store the frequency components of speech as they are digitized. The process is really quite simple. It gives the computer information that may be used to directly access possible phoneme tables or stored speech patterns of sounds and frequencies.

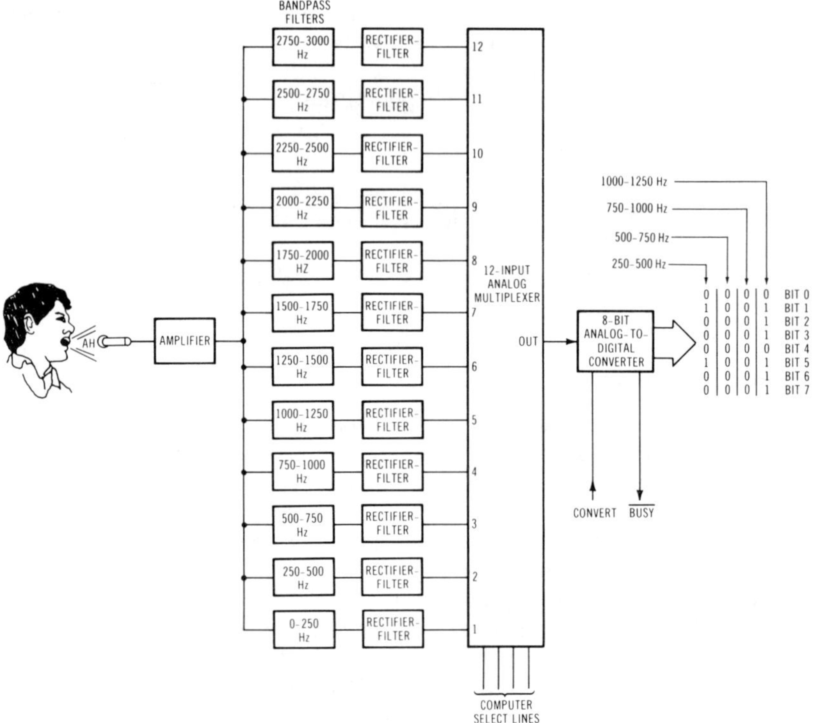

Figure 4-9.
Spectral acquisition of speech.

Since the task of digitizing all the filter outputs must be accomplished in a 10- to 20-ms window, the 8-bit analog-to-digital converter has considerable time to spend with each rectifier-filter output. Of course, the computer software is significantly simplified because the speech spectral information is digitized directly. The trade-off in hardware costs versus software complexity and running time must be considered depending on your own desires and pocketbook. For a look at the type of hardware being discussed, Fig. 4-10 shows a typical filter-rectifier combination. Remember that this circuitry has to be duplicated, for the example, *12 times.* Even though the amplifiers may not be expensive, the resistor-capacitor combinations must be highly precise to ensure nonoverlapping frequency coverage. Actually, if the filter system is to be accurate, the cut-off bands of each filter should also be very sharp and nonoverlapping. This would require extremely costly and complex bandpass filters compared to the one shown in Fig. 4-10. If you would like to experiment with different bandwidths or design your own bandpass filters, the BASIC program in Listing 4-1 gives the values for the filter circuit in Fig. 4-10 over the speech band.

FIG. 4–9 FILTER FREQUENCY RANGE	R_X VALUE
0–250 Hz	96.6K
250–500 Hz	14.3K
500–750 Hz	4.56K
750–1000 Hz	2.27K
1000–1250 Hz	1.36K
1250–1500 Hz	904 Ω
1500–1750 Hz	645 Ω
1750–2000 Hz	483 Ω
2000–2250 Hz	375 Ω
2250–2500 Hz	300 Ω
2500–2750 Hz	246 Ω
2750–3000 Hz	205 Ω

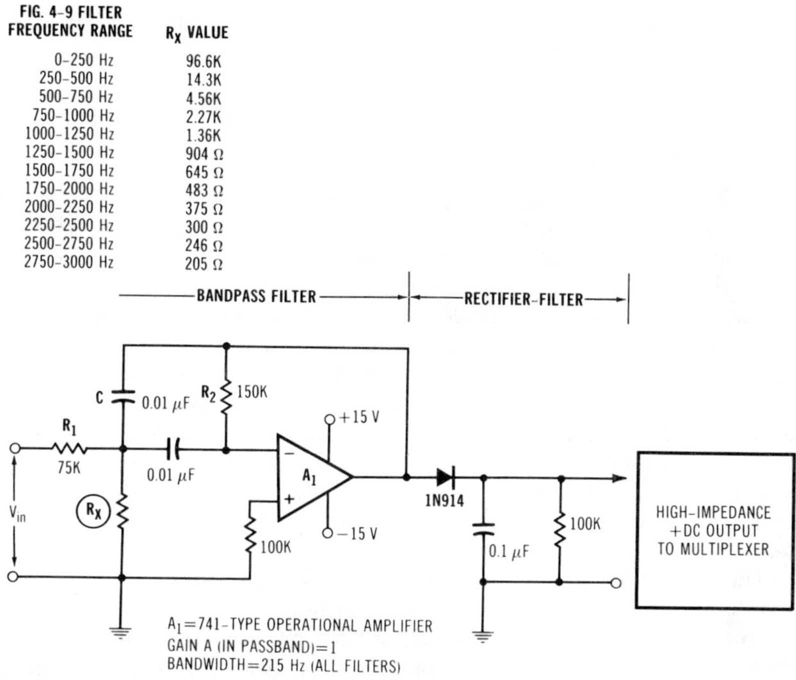

Figure 4-10.
Filter circuit for implementing spectral acquisition system.

Listing 4-1.
Bandpass Filter Values.

```
5 REM THIS PROGRAM COMPUTES VALUES FOR A BANDPASS FILTER
7 REM FROM FIG. 4-10 IN ELECTRONICALLY HEARING #22173
9 REM AND FIG. D-11 IN ELECTRONICALLY SPEAKING #21947
10 REM
11 REM CHANGE VALUES FOR C, R1, AND R2 TO ADJUST
12 REM FILTER BANDWIDTH AND GAIN.
13 REM
14 REM C=.01 UF, R1= 75K OHMS, R2= 150K OHMS
15 C=.01E-6:R1=75000:R2=150000
17 REM
18 PRINT!"FOR C=";C,"R1=";R1,"R2="R2
19 PRINT!:PRINT!
20 FOR FRQ=125 TO 3000 STEP 250
25 IFFRQ<200 THEN FRQ=200
30 RX=1/(R2*4*(3.14159^2)*(C^2)*(FRQ^2)-(1/R1))
40 PRINT!"GAIN=";R2/(2*R1),"BW=";INT(1/(3.14159*C*R2));"HZ","FR
   Q=";FRQ,"RX=";RX;"OHMS"
45 IF FRQ=200 THEN FRQ=125
50 NEXT FRQ
60 PRINT!:PRINT!:PRINT!:PRINT!"END":PRINT!:PRINT!:PRINT!
```

There is an alternative method that may be used if the analog hardware route is undesirable. This alternative utilizes the relatively new technology of digital switched-capacitor filters.

Digital Filtering

This nomenclature may be slightly misleading because the filters to be described within this section are of the switched-capacitor type, and are basically analog filters internally. However, because these devices require an external clock frequency input that sets the filter center frequency, they should be classed as truly digital filters. They are a result of a fairly recent major innovation in semiconductor technology to construct physically realizable monolithic floating capacitors with closely controlled capacitance ratios. They appear to have been first developed in the laboratories at the University of California at Berkeley and were exactly that: laboratory curiosities. Once the monolithic technology and integrated circuit construction techniques were compatible with the circuit designs of switched-capacitor filters, they became economically feasible.

The operating principle behind a switched-capacitor filter relies primarily on a technique called charge distribution. An example of a very simple section of a switched capacitor filter is shown in Fig. 4-11. In this diagram, the switch is used to connect the capacitor C_s between either voltage V1 or voltage V2. If the switch moves from position 1 to position 2, the capacitor voltage will change from V1 to V2. The change in the charge on the capacitor (ΔQ) is described by $C_s * (V1 - V2)$. As the switch begins to move faster and faster and the same amount of charge is moved for each repetition, a net current flows in the direction from V1 to V2. The current in this case may be mathematically represented by an equation that combines the two voltage values, the capacitance value, and the switching frequency F_s:

$$I_s = \Delta Q * F_s = C * (V1 - V2) * F_s$$

If we now allow the switching frequency F_s to increase beyond any possible variation in time of either V1 or V2, then the circuit may be

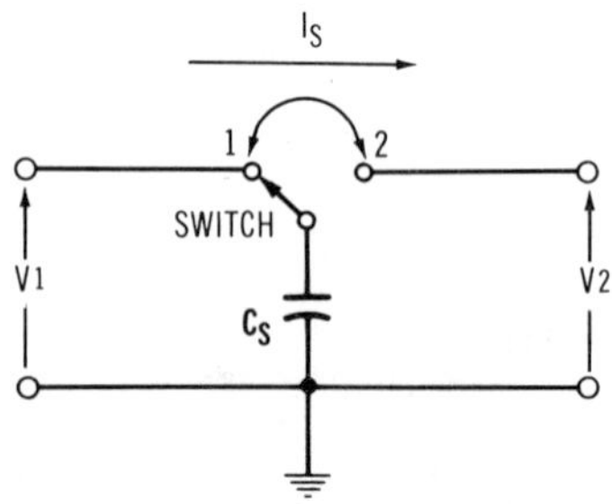

Figure 4-11.
A simple switched-capacitor
circuit.

viewed as a simple resistance having a given current flow for a given voltage difference. If we take the equation:

$$I = (V1 - V2)/R$$

and compare it with the previous equation, we see that we can also then equate the two terms:

$$1/R = C_s * F_s$$

The analogy can be carried further to the circuits of Fig. 4-12 to illustrate how the switched capacitor may be used to replace a resistance in a single-stage RC filter. The two parts of this figure are identical in function, *if* the switching frequency F_s is selected to equal an identical current flow that occurs in resistance R for the same input voltage. What is significant in this circuit is that the resistance no longer has to be placed on the monolithic integrated circuit. Since the capacitance ratio determines the RC constant of Fig. 4-12B, the circuit is much easier to produce. The mechanism also allows the filter to be tuned by simply changing the switching frequency F_s. Thus, if a large group of these filters is utilized in a complex filter structure, the entire passband of the filter system may be readily changed by simply varying the input switching frequency. Remember, though, that the key to the operation of this circuit is that the switching frequency F_s must be much higher (on the order of 50 to 100 times) than any expected input signal variation.

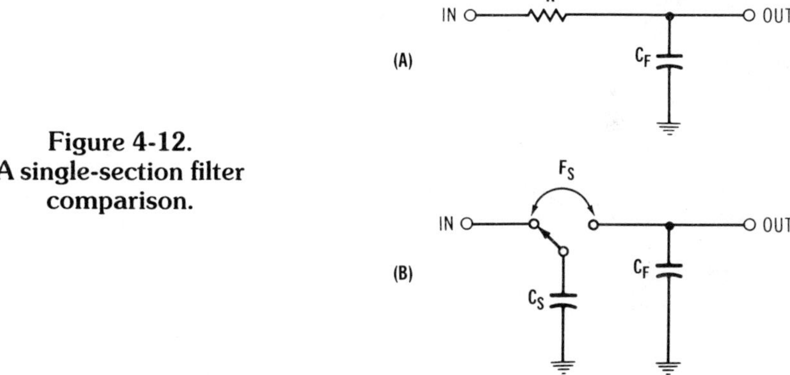

**Figure 4-12.
A single-section filter
comparison.**

The net results of the switched capacitor filter development is the rather inexpensive availability of extremely complex filters in very small integrated circuit packages. Several companies are now producing these filters, which may be used for either bandpass filtering of spectral input, or low-pass, presampling filtering. Motorola produces a fifth-order elliptic low-pass switched-capacitor filter fifth called the MC-145414. Each of these filter chips contains two fifth-order filters, which may be cascaded to produce a tenth-order elliptic low-pass filter with extremely sharp cutoff at the filter frequency. In the Motorola circuit, the sampling frequency is approximately 40 times greater than the signal frequency.

Another manufacturer, American Microsystems, Inc., produces a seventh-order elliptical filter that is programmable through either the adjustment of the clock frequency or the input of a binary code. The S3528 switched-capacitor filter provides 50-dB attenuation of the input signal at 1.3 times the cutoff frequency of the filter.

Another important manufacturer of switched-capacitor filters is Reticon, Inc., which produces a family of filter chips, including low pass, bandpass, and high pass. These may be used to construct an entire spectrum analysis system and can simplify the task of building a spectral acquisition system similar to that shown in Fig. 4-9. Reference to these manufacturers is given in the appendix.

Mathematical Filtering

This type of signal filtering is more commonly referred to as true digital filtering. However, because in most cases these systems first digitize the analog input and then mathematically manipulate the data according to sampled data equations, they may also be referred to as mathematical filters.

The technique of mathematical filtering is not limited to integrated circuit technology. With proper equations and data manipulations, digitized data in any computer may be mathematically filtered to present band-limited information for further speech processing. The general theory behind digital filters is somewhat complex. For instance, a representation of a first-order mathematical filter is shown in Fig. 4-13. The method of operation is based upon three basic computations. For a

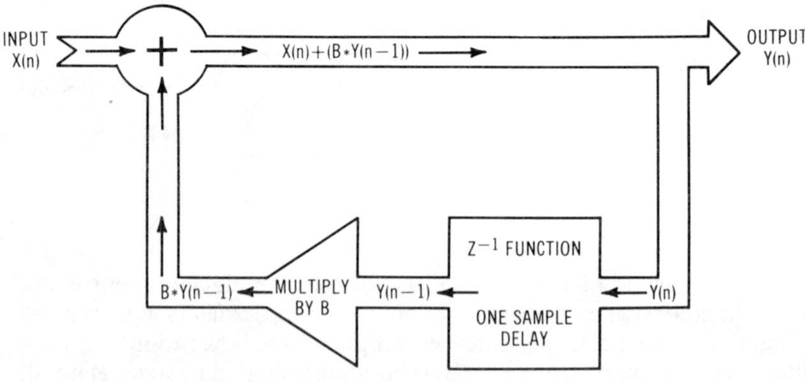

Figure 4-13.
A first-order mathematical recursive filter.

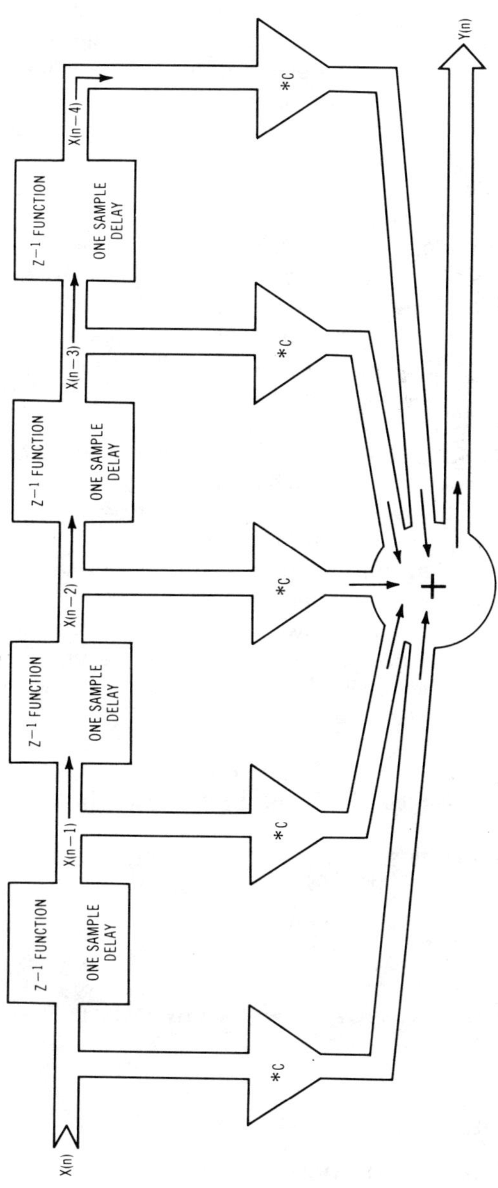

Figure 4-14.
A nonrecursive mathematical filter.

given input, X(n), the filter's output is Y(n). What occurs between the input and output is a mathematical filter process of the *first order*. This is the *simplest* type of filter in the mathematical filter family.

There are basically two types of computational filters in digital filter theory: the recursive and the nonrecursive filter. If a filter has the property of recursion, then its output is based upon previous samples of its own output. In other words, there is some type of feedback within the system. The filter in Fig. 4-13 is recursive. It is also called an IIR (Infinite Impulse Response) filter. A nonrecursive filter, on the other hand, generates an output that is based solely upon the input samples and *not* on previous values of the filter output. An example of a nonrecursive filter is shown in Fig. 4-14. This one is an FIR (Finite Impulse Response) filter. Its operation is very similar to the previous recursive filter; however, it is unconditionally stable (it has finite response) and cannot go into a mode of oscillation like the recursive filter. (That is where the name "Infinite Impulse" originates.)

The operation of these filters is based upon a series of sampled data taken in order beginning with the first through the nth. The square boxes in each of the two previous figures represent a one-sample delay. This is nothing more than backing up one previous sample from the one currently under consideration. If a series of samples is stored in memory, then the computer performs the Z^{-1} function by simply indexing one memory location backwards to pickup the previous Z^{-1} sample for each block. The multiplication triangle represents a process where the incoming number is simply multiplied by the constant value within

Listing 4-2.
First-order Digital Filter Simulation.

```
5 REM BASIC PROGRAM TO SIMULATE FIRST-ORDER DIGITAL FILTER
6 REM -- RECURSIVE TYPE --
10 DIM XN(30),YN(30)
15 INPUT "B=",B
20 FOR I=0 TO 26
30 READ XN(I)
40 NEXT I
45 PRINT!"1st-Order Recursive Filter Response":PRINT!"for B=";B
   ;" in Fig. 4-13."
46 PRINT!:PRINT!
47 PRINT!" Input","Output"
48 PRINT!"------------------------------"
50 REM NOW FILTER XN
60 FOR N=0 TO 30
65 IF N=0 THEN YN(N)=XN(N):GOTO80
70 YN(N)=XN(N)+B*YN(N-1)
80 PRINT!"X(n)=";XN(N),"Y(n)=";INT(YN(N))
90 NEXT N
100 PRINT!:PRINT!:PRINT!
150 DATA 0,0,10,10,10,10,10,10,10,10,10,10,0,0,0,0,0,0,0,0,0,0,
    0,0,0,0,0
```

that block (B in the case of Fig. 4-13, C in the case of Fig. 4-14). Finally, the "round" addition shapes add the incoming numbers together and then produce a single summed output.

The mathematical functions of Fig. 4-13 may be simulated in a computer using a BASIC program as shown in Listing 4-2. The rather simple mechanism of the computation should indicate that the filtering calculations are relatively straightforward and understandable. If we allow this program to run with varying values for B, we have the resultant outputs given in Figs. 4-15 through 4-18. Each of the response values Y(n) represents the filter response to a square pulse input of amplitude 10 with a length of 10 sample periods. In each of the figures, the filter architecture remains the same and only the multiplying coefficient B changes. Notice that as B increases from 0 through 0.8, the response time of the filter slows considerably. If we allow B to increase to a value of 1 or greater, then the filter becomes unstable and has a continually increasing output whether the input is present or not. Aha! The Infinite Response!

```
Input            Output
-------------------------------
X(n)= 0          Y(n)= 0
X(n)= 0          Y(n)= 0
X(n)= 10         Y(n)= 10
X(n)= 10         Y(n)= 10
X(n)= 10         Y(n)= 10
X(n)= 10         Y(n)= 10
X(n)= 10         Y(n)= 10
X(n)= 10         Y(n)= 10
X(n)= 10         Y(n)= 10
X(n)= 10         Y(n)= 10
X(n)= 10         Y(n)= 10
X(n)= 10         Y(n)= 10
X(n)= 0          Y(n)= 0
X(n)= 0          Y(n)= 0
X(n)= 0          Y(n)= 0
X(n)= 0          Y(n)= 0
X(n)= 0          Y(n)= 0
X(n)= 0          Y(n)= 0
X(n)= 0          Y(n)= 0
X(n)= 0          Y(n)= 0
X(n)= 0          Y(n)= 0
X(n)= 0          Y(n)= 0
X(n)= 0          Y(n)= 0
X(n)= 0          Y(n)= 0
X(n)= 0          Y(n)= 0
X(n)= 0          Y(n)= 0
X(n)= 0          Y(n)= 0
X(n)= 0          Y(n)= 0
X(n)= 0          Y(n)= 0
X(n)= 0          Y(n)= 0
```

Figure 4-15.
First-order recursive filter response for B = 0 in Fig. 4-13.

```
    Input           Output
---------------------------------
X(n)= 0          Y(n)= 0
X(n)= 0          Y(n)= 0
X(n)= 10         Y(n)= 10
X(n)= 10         Y(n)= 13
X(n)= 10         Y(n)= 13
X(n)= 10         Y(n)= 14
X(n)= 10         Y(n)= 14
X(n)= 10         Y(n)= 14
X(n)= 10         Y(n)= 14
X(n)= 10         Y(n)= 14
X(n)= 10         Y(n)= 14
X(n)= 10         Y(n)= 14
X(n)= 0          Y(n)= 4
X(n)= 0          Y(n)= 1
X(n)= 0          Y(n)= 0
X(n)= 0          Y(n)= 0
X(n)= 0          Y(n)= 0
X(n)= 0          Y(n)= 0
X(n)= 0          Y(n)= 0
X(n)= 0          Y(n)= 0
X(n)= 0          Y(n)= 0
X(n)= 0          Y(n)= 0
X(n)= 0          Y(n)= 0
X(n)= 0          Y(n)= 0
X(n)= 0          Y(n)= 0
X(n)= 0          Y(n)= 0
X(n)= 0          'Y(n)= 0
X(n)= 0          Y(n)= 0
X(n)= 0          Y(n)= 0
X(n)= 0          Y(n)= 0
X(n)= 0          Y(n)= 0
```

Figure 4-16.
First-order recursive filter response for B = 0.3 in Fig. 4-13.

The second type of filter shown in Fig. 4-14, being nonrecursive, does not have the same problem. A BASIC program simulation of this filter is given in Listing 4-3. If we allow this program to run with a C value of 0.2, then we have a filter response computed as shown in Fig. 4-19. This computed filter response like the previous filter shows a time-delayed response in the $Y(n)$ output for an $X(n)$ input equal to a 10-sample square wave of amplitude 10. This type of filtering is very closely related to a sliding average, and the filter of Fig. 4-14 represents a 5-point sliding average along the incoming digitized data.

The cutoff frequencies for these types of filters is directly dependent upon the sampling frequency and the amount of delay induced by the filter. Many books have been written on digital and mathematical filtering methods with all of their associated complexities. The references at the end of this book include some excellent advance readings in mathematical filtering methods.

As a final word on speech signal-acquisition techniques, what you have seen in this chapter are the primary types of computer acquisition

```
        Input              Output
    ---------------------------------
    X(n)=  0           Y(n)=  0
    X(n)=  0           Y(n)=  0
    X(n)= 10           Y(n)= 10
    X(n)= 10           Y(n)= 17
    X(n)= 10           Y(n)= 21
    X(n)= 10           Y(n)= 25
    X(n)= 10           Y(n)= 27
    X(n)= 10           Y(n)= 29
    X(n)= 10           Y(n)= 30
    X(n)= 10           Y(n)= 31
    X(n)= 10           Y(n)= 31
    X(n)= 10           Y(n)= 32
    X(n)=  0           Y(n)= 22
    X(n)=  0           Y(n)= 15
    X(n)=  0           Y(n)= 11
    X(n)=  0           Y(n)=  7
    X(n)=  0           Y(n)=  5
    X(n)=  0           Y(n)=  3
    X(n)=  0           Y(n)=  2
    X(n)=  0           Y(n)=  1
    X(n)=  0           Y(n)=  1
    X(n)=  0           Y(n)=  0
    X(n)=  0           Y(n)=  0
    X(n)=  0           Y(n)=  0
    X(n)=  0           Y(n)=  0
    X(n)=  0           Y(n)=  0
    X(n)=  0           Y(n)=  0
    X(n)=  0           Y(n)=  0
    X(n)=  0           Y(n)=  0
    X(n)=  0           Y(n)=  0
    X(n)=  0           Y(n)=  0
```

Figure 4-17.
First-order recursive filter response for $B = 0.7$ in Fig. 4-13.

of speech. The variant types that exist are usually based upon some form of those given here. In the next chapter, we see how a variant of mathematical filtering called the frequency-domain transform technique can produce the same results as multiple mathematical filter systems. Thus, the mathematical process can simulate a spectral signal-acquisition circuit like that described in this chapter, based purely upon computational processing of the directly digitized input waveform.

```
     Input            Output
-----------------------------------
X(n)= 0           Y(n)= 0
X(n)= 0           Y(n)= 0
X(n)= 10          Y(n)= 10
X(n)= 10          Y(n)= 18
X(n)= 10          Y(n)= 24
X(n)= 10          Y(n)= 29
X(n)= 10          Y(n)= 33
X(n)= 10          Y(n)= 36
X(n)= 10          Y(n)= 39
X(n)= 10          Y(n)= 41
X(n)= 10          Y(n)= 43
X(n)= 10          Y(n)= 44
X(n)= 0           Y(n)= 35
X(n)= 0           Y(n)= 28
X(n)= 0           Y(n)= 22
X(n)= 0           Y(n)= 18
X(n)= 0           Y(n)= 14
X(n)= 0           Y(n)= 11
X(n)= 0           Y(n)= 9
X(n)= 0           Y(n)= 7
X(n)= 0           Y(n)= 5
X(n)= 0           Y(n)= 4
X(n)= 0           Y(n)= 3
X(n)= 0           Y(n)= 3
X(n)= 0           Y(n)= 2
X(n)= 0           Y(n)= 1
X(n)= 0           Y(n)= 1
X(n)= 0           Y(n)= 1
X(n)= 0           Y(n)= 1
X(n)= 0           Y(n)= 0
X(n)= 0           Y(n)= 0
```

Figure 4-18.
First-order recursive filter response for B = 0.8 in Fig. 4-13.

Listing 4-3.
Five-Stage Transversal Simulation.

```
5 REM BASIC PROGRAM TO SIMULATE 5 STAGE TRANSVERSAL
6 REM FILTER -- NON-RECURSIVE TYPE --
10 DIM XN(40),YN(40)
15 INPUT "C=",C
18 REM OFFSET DATA TO KEEP POSITIVE SUBSCRIPTS
19 REM XN(0) THROUGH XN(3)=0
20 FOR I=4 TO 33
30 READ XN(I)
40 NEXT I
45 PRINT!"Filter Response in Fig. 4-14 ":PRINT!"      for C=";C
46 PRINT!:PRINT!
47 PRINT!" Input","Output"
48 PRINT!"----------------------------"
50 REM NOW FILTER XN
59 REM SINCE SUBSCRIPTS CAN'T BE NEGATIVE OFFSET XN AND YN BY 4
60 FOR N=4 TO 33
63 YN(N)=(XN(N)*C)+(XN(N-1)*C)+(XN(N-2)*C)+(XN(N-3)*C)+(XN(N-4)
   *C)
80 PRINT!"X(n)=";XN(N),"Y(n)=";INT(YN(N))
90 NEXT N
100 PRINT!:PRINT!:PRINT!
150 DATA 0,0,0,0,0,10,10,10,10,10,10,10,10,10,10,0,0,0,0,0,0,0,
    0,0,0,0,0,0,0,0
```

```
   Input              Output
-----------------------------------
X(n)= 0              Y(n)= 0
X(n)= 0              Y(n)= 0
X(n)= 0              Y(n)= 0
X(n)= 0              Y(n)= 0
X(n)= 0              Y(n)= 0
X(n)= 10             Y(n)= 2
X(n)= 10             Y(n)= 4
X(n)= 10             Y(n)= 6
X(n)= 10             Y(n)= 8
X(n)= 10             Y(n)= 10
X(n)= 10             Y(n)= 10
X(n)= 10             Y(n)= 10
X(n)= 10             Y(n)= 10
X(n)= 10             Y(n)= 10
X(n)= 10             Y(n)= 10
X(n)= 0              Y(n)= 8
X(n)= 0              Y(n)= 6
X(n)= 0              Y(n)= 4
X(n)= 0              Y(n)= 2
X(n)= 0              Y(n)= 0
X(n)= 0              Y(n)= 0
X(n)= 0              Y(n)= 0
X(n)= 0              Y(n)= 0
X(n)= 0              Y(n)= 0
X(n)= 0              Y(n)= 0
X(n)= 0              Y(n)= 0
X(n)= 0              Y(n)= 0
X(n)= 0              Y(n)= 0
X(n)= 0              Y(n)= 0
X(n)= 0              Y(n)= 0
```

Figure 4-19.
Filter response for $C = 0.2$ in Fig. 4-14.

CHAPTER 5

Methods of Speech Analysis

As speech data is acquired by a speech-recognition system, during the portion of the time that it remains in an analog state, it is referred to as continuous-time data. The "continuous" characteristic is best described by having a value at all points in time, thus the signal is *not* sampled data. It is also often known as an "analog" signal. Systems which deal with signals of the continuous type are known as analog or continuous-time systems. If the signals are periodically amplitude sampled, thus having only a finite number of time values, the signals become classified as "discrete-time" signals. If we examine the analog speech signals with a rather advanced mathematical technique known as Fourier Analysis, we can calculate the frequency spectrum that exists within the subject waveform.

The method of mathematically operating on either a continuous or discrete-time signal to produce the spectral components described in the previous chapter is known as the Fourier Transform. The mathematician who derived the theory behind the time-to-frequency transform was Jean Baptiste Joseph Fourier (1758–1830). He began playing with the characteristics of the sine and cosine functions in the early 1800s and found that he was able to express a trigonometric function as the sum of a mathematical series. The results of his trigonometric series derivations were published in 1822 in his work entitled *Theory of Heat*. The use of Fourier series and transforms since that time has become routine. They are now used as mathematical tools in engineering and science.

Since an analysis of continuous-time signals will do us relatively little good in a digital computer system, we will now turn our concentration toward the discrete-time system and analyze the Fourier transform in terms of its usefulness in the spectral acquisition of a speech analysis system.

There are three types of spectral analysis we will consider: Discrete Fourier Transforms, Fast Fourier Transforms, and formant analysis.

Discrete Fourier Transform

Before we can really jump into the intricate details of Fourier analysis of signals, we must set a few ground rules as to the technical terminology. First of all, consider Fig. 5-1. The figure shows a sinusoidal waveform, which we will refer to as F(t)—simply meaning a function of time—with a maximum amplitude of A. In terms of mathematical formulas, the wave may be described by the equation:

$$F(t) = A \sin \omega t$$

The frequency of the sinusoid, ω, is given in terms of radians per second rather than the normal cycles per second or hertz. This is a standard mathematical term that simply describes the circle in terms of two pi (π = 3.14159 . . .) radians rather than 360°. If we desire to express the same waveform in terms of frequency in hertz, then we must rewrite the equation in the following form:

$$F(t) = A \sin 2\pi ft$$

Thus, the frequency (ω) in radians per second is equal to 2π times the frequency (f) in hertz. Either description is just as accurate and usable as the other; however, we are more used to thinking of signal frequencies in terms of hertz so we will continuously apply the transformation $2\pi f$.

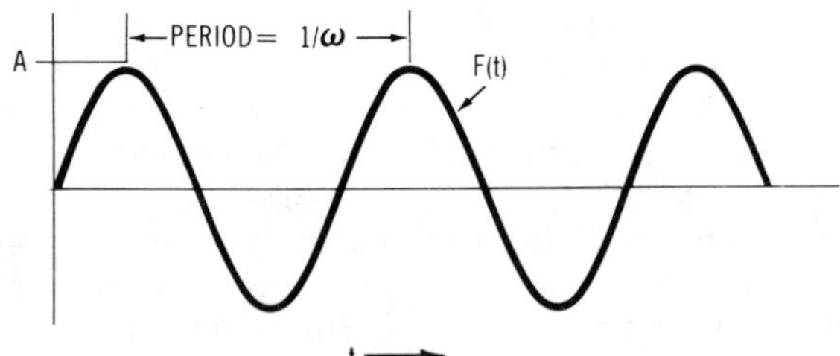

Figure 5-1.
A sinusoidal waveform representation.

Now, the Fourier analysis assumes that a signal may be represented as a rotating vector along the time axis. The plot of the equivalent conceptual Fourier waveform in Fig. 5-2 would be generated if you held a ball on a three foot string and, while walking along an axis called time, swung the ball and string around your hand in a large circle. If the

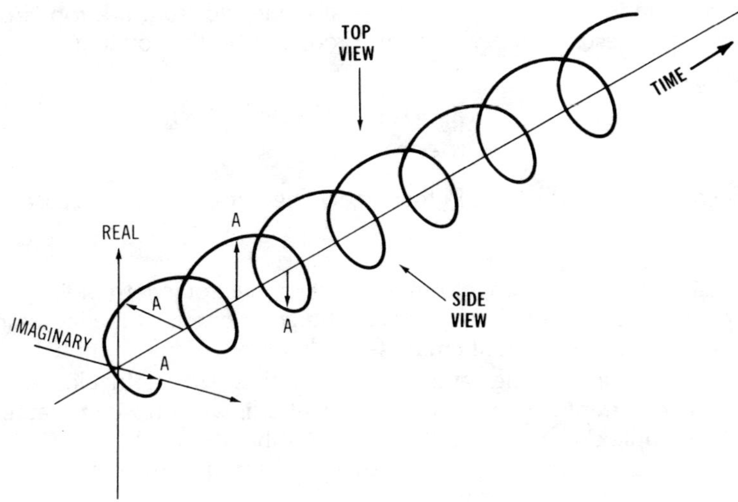

Figure 5-2.
The complex plane waveform.

waveform were viewed directly from the side, then it would appear to be sinusoidal as in Fig. 5-1. However, we have now added another dimension in the description of the waveform, thus making it a complex waveform. The vertical axis is the real axis while the axis which would normally be in and out of the page is referred to as the imaginary axis. If we can move so that we look directly down the time axis, then what we would see as a person walked swinging the ball on a three-foot string would be a circle like that given in Fig. 5-3. Remembering that we have set a string length of three feet, then the amplitude (A) of the circle diameter is 3 feet. Since the projection of the ball's shadow viewed

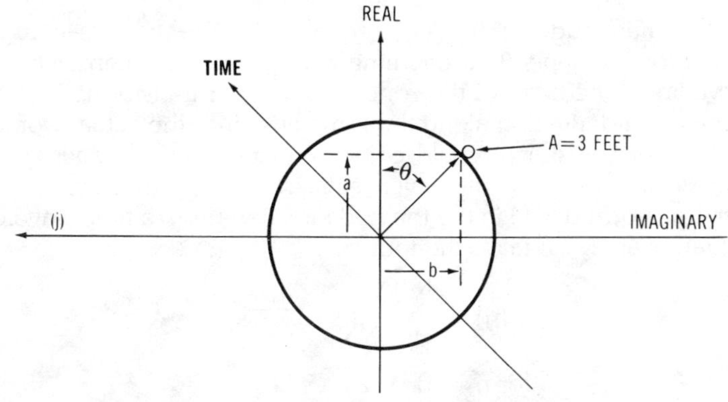

Figure 5-3.
The complex plane vector rotation.

from the side is *a* and the same projection viewed from the top is *b*, then we can describe the waveform produced by the rotating ball as being

$$a = A (\cos \theta)$$
$$b = A (\sin \theta)$$

We can also say, from the Pythagorean Theorem, that, in this case,

$$A = \sqrt{a^2 + b^2}$$

To fully describe the waveform in terms of electronic terminology, a new term must be added that signifies the component of the signal in the imaginary plane. In mathematics, you learn of *complex* numbers as being represented by the letter *i*, which equals $\sqrt{-1}$. In electronic terms, since current is represented by the letter i, we choose *j* to represent the complex plane vector. It also follows that $j^2 = -1$.

Now, if we can describe the rotating ball-string combination as a complex vector A*, we find that

$$A = a + jb$$

(The j multiplier indicates the presence of the waveform in the imaginary plane.) Using the previous identities for a and b, we may rewrite that same equation like this

$$A = \sqrt{a^2 + b^2} \bullet (\cos \theta + j \sin \theta)$$

According to an earlier derivation by a scientist named Euler, the following equation was derived and found to be factual:

$$\cos \theta + j \sin \theta = e^{j\theta}$$

Thus, the previous equation can be represented as

$$\underline{A} = |A| \bullet e^{j\theta}$$

where the magnitude of A, $|A|$, is equal to $\sqrt{a^2 + b^2}$. We may also substitute for the angle θ, at any time, the value ωt or alternately $2\pi ft$. Now, we are at the heart of the concept of Fourier transforms.

A continued derivation along the same lines into the actual workings of the Fourier transform would consume a number of pages greater than those in this book; however, suffice it to say that the Discrete Fourier Transform (DFT) in the forward direction (from a time waveform to frequency analysis) takes the form:

$$F(n) = \sum_{k=0}^{N-1} x(k) \bullet e^{\frac{-j2\pi kn}{N}}$$

$$\text{for } n = 0, 1, 2, \ldots N-1$$

---

*For more information about vectors and vector math, see *Calculus, an Introduction to Applied Mathematics* by H. P. Greenspan and D. J. Benney.

where,

N   = Number of samples,

$\chi(k)$ = kth sample of signal.

While the mathematical DFT equation does not really give a tremendous amount of intuitive feeling towards what is happening, we may learn more if we expand the transform into the computational form for a real piece of sampled data. Fig. 5-4 gives an example of the Discrete Fourier Transform at work. At the top of the figure is a random waveform that might be found during a speech input process. For simplicity of illustration only, four samples are taken (N=4), which means that

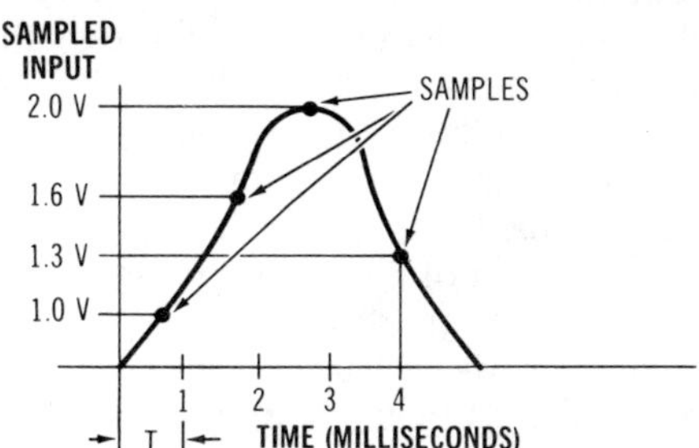

S(0) @ 1 mS=1.0 V
S(1) @ 2 mS=1.6 V
S(2) @ 3 mS=2.0 V
S(3) @ 4 mS=1.3V
SAMPLED DATA BUFFER

NOW DISCRETE FOURIER TRANSFORM

$$F(n) = \sum_{K=0}^{N-1} S(K)\, e^{\frac{-j\,2\pi Kn}{N}} \quad \text{FOR } n=0,1\ldots N-1$$

DISCRETE FOURIER TRANSFORM

THEREFORE GIVES:

$$F(0)=S(0)\cdot e^{\frac{-j\cdot 2\pi\cdot 0\cdot 0}{4}} + S(1)\cdot e^{\frac{-j\cdot 2\pi\cdot 1\cdot 0}{4}} + S(2)\cdot e^{\frac{-j\cdot 2\pi\cdot 2\cdot 0}{4}} + S(3)\cdot e^{\frac{-j\cdot 2\pi\cdot 3\cdot 0}{4}}$$

$$F(1)=S(0)\cdot e^{\frac{-j\cdot 2\pi\cdot 0\cdot 1}{4}} + S(1)\cdot e^{\frac{-j\cdot 2\pi\cdot 1\cdot 1}{4}} + S(2)\cdot e^{\frac{-j\cdot 2\pi\cdot 2\cdot 1}{4}} + S(3)\cdot e^{\frac{-j\cdot 2\pi\cdot 3\cdot 1}{4}}$$

$$F(2)=S(0)\cdot e^{\frac{j\cdot 2\pi\cdot 0\cdot 2}{4}} + S(1)\cdot e^{\frac{-j\cdot 2\pi\cdot 1\cdot 2}{4}} + S(2)\cdot e^{\frac{-j\cdot 2\pi\cdot 2\cdot 2}{4}} + S(3)\cdot e^{\frac{-j\cdot 2\pi\cdot 3\cdot 2}{4}}$$

$$F(3)=S(0)\cdot e^{\frac{j\cdot 2\pi\cdot 0\cdot 3}{4}} + S(1)\cdot e^{\frac{j\cdot 2\pi\cdot 1\cdot 3}{4}} + S(2)\cdot e^{\frac{-j\cdot 2\pi\cdot 2\cdot 3}{4}} + S(3)\cdot e^{\frac{-j\cdot 2\pi\cdot 3\cdot 3}{4}}$$

Figure 5-4.
The Discrete Fourier Transform (DFT).

only four discrete frequency bins will be computed during the total transform. Normally, this number would be on the order of anywhere from 16 to 1024 points, thus giving a relatively high frequency resolution for spectrum analysis. The equations designated F(n) at the lower portion of Fig. 5-4 represent each of the four frequency bins output by the Discrete Fourier Transform. Since the sampling time is one millisecond per sample, and we are taking four samples, giving a total sampled time of four milliseconds, the resolution of each frequency bin is 250 Hz. Thus, F(0) is the amount of energy in the lowest bin that corresponds to a dc level (0 Hz). F(1) is the energy in the first bin at 250 Hz, F(2) is 500 Hz, and F(3) is the energy at 750 Hz. While the equations in Fig. 5-4 do not easily yield to computer computations, they may be broken down through the previously mentioned Euler equality into equations similar to that given in Fig. 5-5. The computations are continued by reducing the trigonometric identities to their numeric values. The rest of the computation is then simply multiplication. The resulting answer for F(0) is 1.475 volts, which represents the power content of the waveform in the 0-Hz frequency range.

A continuation of the calculation into the first, second, and third frequency bins will yield somewhat more complicated mathematical results. This is because as the value n goes from 0 to $N-1$, the sin $(2\pi kn/N)$ part of the equation becomes greater than 0 and, consequently, there is an imaginary part to the results in each frequency bin. The answers may be taken directly as they are in each bin in terms of real and imaginary parts. If only the power spectrum value is needed, then this value may be found by taking the *magnitude* of the real and imaginary parts for each frequency. This equation is a simple process, based on the Pythagorean Theorem:

$$F(mag) = \sqrt{(real)^2 + (imag)^2}$$

That's all there is to it. The Discrete Fourier Transform is a relatively simple process that is quite complex to understand. If you continue to follow the procedure like that given in Fig. 5-5 with the remaining frequency bins from 1 through 3, then you should observe that each sine and cosine term represents a rotating vector with increasing speed, which is used as a multiplication factor across the entire sampled time. All this is accomplishing is a correlation comparison from the lowest frequency (0 Hz) to the highest (1 divided by the sample rate). The frequency resolution in each case (the step frequencies for correlation) is given by 1 divided by the product of N times the sample period T:

$$F(res) = \frac{1}{N \cdot T}$$

If you understand what is really going on, then you should quickly see that as the number of samples goes up to 64 or 256 or even to

EULER SAYS:

$$e^{\frac{-j2\pi Kn}{N}} = \cos\left(\frac{2\pi Kn}{4}\right) - j\,\sin\left(\frac{2\pi Kn}{N}\right)$$

SO:

SAMPLE 1: S(0)   SAMPLE 2: S(1)

$F(0) = 1\ V \cdot (\cos\,(0) - j\,\sin\,(0)) + 1.6\ V \cdot (\cos\,(0) - j\,\sin(0))$

(FROM FIG 5-4)

} ϕ Hz **FREQUENCY BIN**

SAMPLE 3: S(2)   SAMPLE 4: S(3)

$+ 2.0\ V\ (\cos\,(0) - j\,\sin\,(0)) + 1.3\ V \cdot (\cos\,(0) - j\,\sin\,(0))$

NOW EVALUATE TRIG FUNCTIONS: COS(0)=1 SIN(0)=0

SAMPLE 1: S(0)   SAMPLE 2: S(1)

$F(0) = \quad 1\ V \cdot (1) \quad + \quad 1.6\ V \cdot (1)$

SAMPLE 3: S(2)   SAMPLE 4: S(3)

$+ \quad 2.0\ V \cdot (1) \quad + \quad 1.3\ V \cdot (1)$

NOW ADD:

$F(0) = 5.9$ VOLTS

DIVIDE BY N TO GET AVERAGE OVER SAMPLE TIME

$$F(0) = \frac{5.9}{4} = 1.475\ V$$

Figure 5-5.
The first DFT bin computation.

1024, there are a tremendous number of computations which must be made for the discrete transform to be computed. This is the primary reason that the computation requires considerable time during execution. If the DFT is run in BASIC, the four point transform given in Figs. 5-4 and 5-5 requires somewhere on the order of 3 to 4 seconds to compute. If you attempt a 64-point transform in BASIC, then the computation time will probably extend out to 1 to 2 minutes or more.

The power of the Fourier transform lies in its ability to compute spectral values for any type of periodic sampled waveform. This can be easily seen when a sinusoidal waveform is used as the input signal and processed through the Fourier transform as shown in Fig. 5-6. If a nonsinusoid waveform such as a square wave is used as the input, then

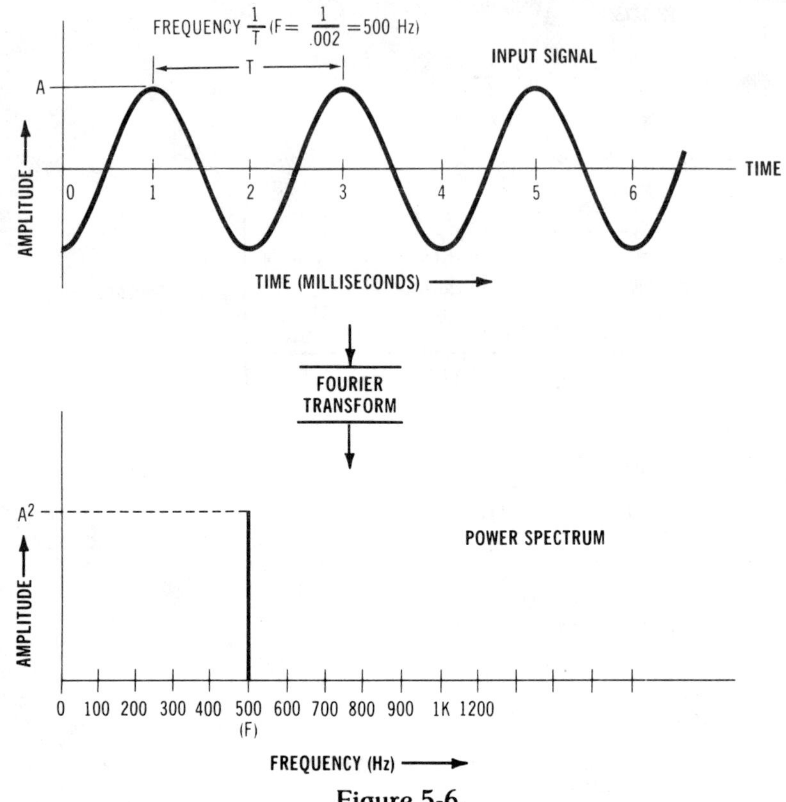

Figure 5-6.
The Fourier Transform process.

the Fourier transform will produce the inherent frequency components in the square wave as shown in Fig. 5-7.

A very simple Discrete Fourier Transform program written in BASIC is given in Listing 5-1. If you enter this into a computer which runs BASIC, then it will ask you to input the number N of sample points S(n) followed by the value of the data at each sample point. If you use the example given in Fig. 5-4, then you will see the results of the frequency analysis of that particular waveform. One important note should be emphasized here. Because of aliasing in frequency bins above ½, the sample rate within the Discrete Fourier Transform, there exists a mirror image spectrum when only real numbers are input as sampled data. In other words, in computing an 8-point DFT with N = 8, of the resulting eight frequency bins computed, only the first four are valid numbers. The top four bins are a mirror image of the bottom four frequency bins. If we were supplying complex data for Fourier analysis, then these bins would be valid. However, since our sampled speech

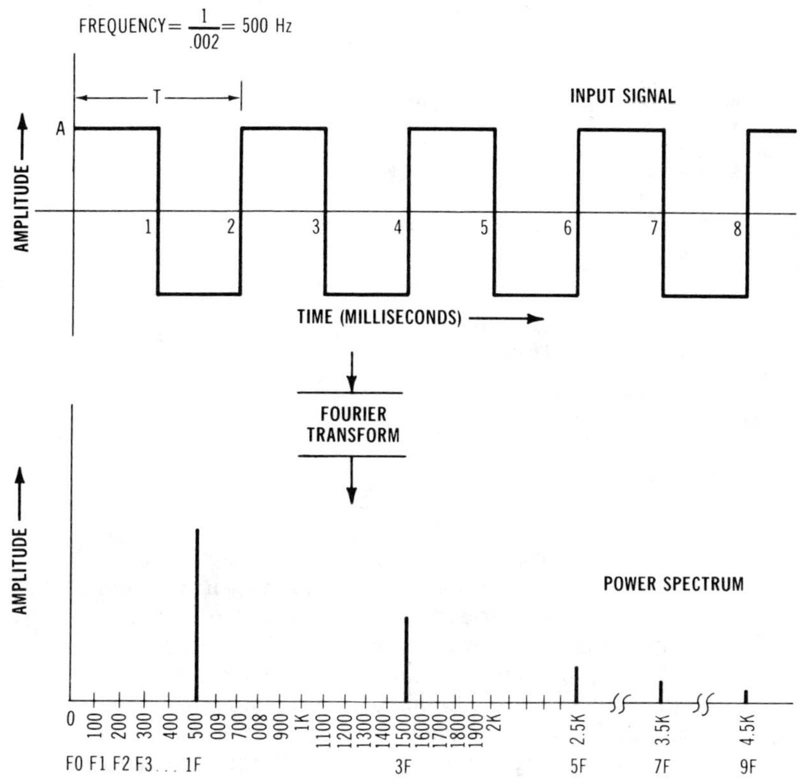

Figure 5-7.
A square wave spectrum analysis.

data will almost always be real data, we can simply ignore the top half of the frequency output bins for spectral analysis.

One problem you will quickly notice as you start to use Fourier spectrum analysis is that sometimes, with a sinusoidal wave input, the output frequency bins are not singular as shown in Fig. 5-6. Instead, what you may find with a sinusoidal input is a very course output like that shown in Fig. 5-8. The smearing of the singular frequency bin is known as *leakage* and is caused by sampling asynchronism with the incoming frequency.

While somewhat difficult to envision, the operation of Fourier spectrum analysis depends upon a periodic input waveform. The whole assumption of this type of frequency analysis relies on a waveform repeating identically as the sampling continues for each Fourier frame. This may be more easily seen in Fig. 5-9. Notice that for an eight-point transform of the sine wave shown in (a), there is a synchronization between the sampling frequency and the incoming frequency. Thus, the

Listing 5-1.
DFT Program.

```
2 REM DFT PROGRAM -- LISTING 5-1
3 REM FOR ILLUSTRATING THE DFT TRANSFORM
5 PI=3.14159
10 INPUT "N=";N
15 DIM S(N),RE(N),IM(N),PWR(N)
20 FOR I=0 TO N-1
30 PRINT"S(";I;")=";:INPUT S(I)
40 NEXT I
50 FOR B=0 TO N-1
55 RE(B)=0:IM(B)=0
60 FOR K=0 TO N-1
70 RE(B)=S(K)*COS((2*PI*K*B)/N)+RE(B)
80 IM(B)=-1*S(K)*SIN((2*PI*K*B)/N)+IM(B)
90 NEXT K
100 RE(B)=RE(B)/N:IM(B)=IM(B)/N
110 PWR(B)=SQR(RE(B)^2+IM(B)^2)
120 PRINT"F(";B;")= ";PWR(B)
130 NEXT B
140 PRINT"END DFT COMPUTATION":END
```

waveform does truly repeat for each sampling window. This particular DFT *will* yield a singular frequency bin. However, if we increase the frequency very slightly with the same sampling rate, we see the sample window in Fig. 5-9B has a problem in the assumed periodicity. Since the Discrete Fourier Transform assumes that the sampled data repeats for each window, there is a discrepancy in the sample points toward the beginning and end of each window. This appears as *a voltage step* to the transform thus giving rise to an impulse function spectrum. This causes the leakage effects around the desired singular frequency bin.

There are several ways of trying to compensate for the leakage problem and thus produce a pure spectrum result for an incoming waveform. One possible way of solving the problem would be to make the sampling period dependent upon the incoming frequency so that there is

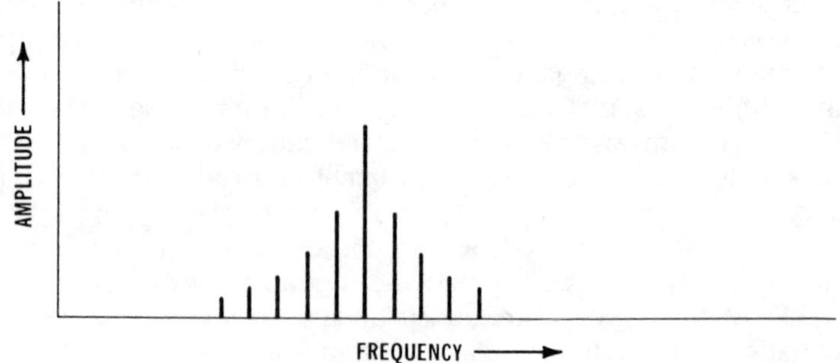

Figure 5-8.
Leakage effects on the DFT.

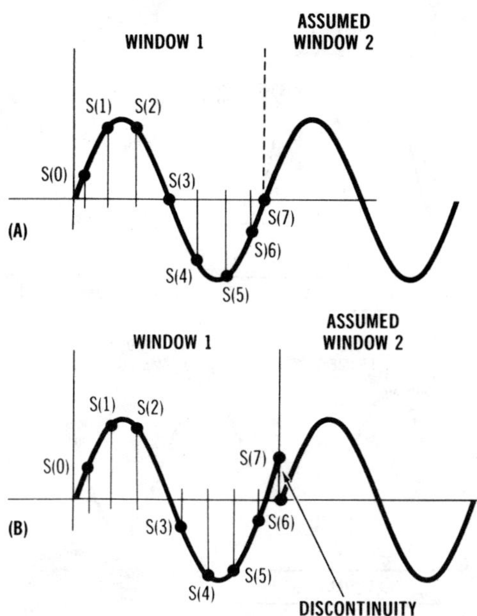

Figure 5-9.
Sampling window difficulties.

always a synchronization between them. This, in reality, proves to be very difficult. The most accepted means of compensating for leakage caused by the discontinuity at the window's edge is a mathematical process called "windowing." The process of windowing is nothing more than decreasing the significance of the sampled values toward the edges of each sampling window.

The simple process of windowing is illustrated in Fig. 5-10. What is really occurring in this figure is that the sampled data is multiplied point by point, by a fixed windowing multiplier series which begins and ends at a 0 value with a value of 1 during most of the middle portion of the waveform. The overall effect is to reduce the significance of discontinuities toward the edges of the sampled Discrete Fourier Transform frame. This particular type of window is known as a "flat top" window. Other types exist which also provide varying amounts of leakage effect reduction. Almost any type of waveform will serve as a multiplier for windowing as long as its value near the first and last samples is very close to 0 and the middle value is 1.

All in all, the Discrete Fourier Transform is quite a mathematical tool for use in speech frequency analysis. Many references at the end of this book are given which go into great detail concerning the mathematics behind Fourier spectrum analysis. Since the Discrete Fourier Transform has been around for quite some time, there has been a tremendous

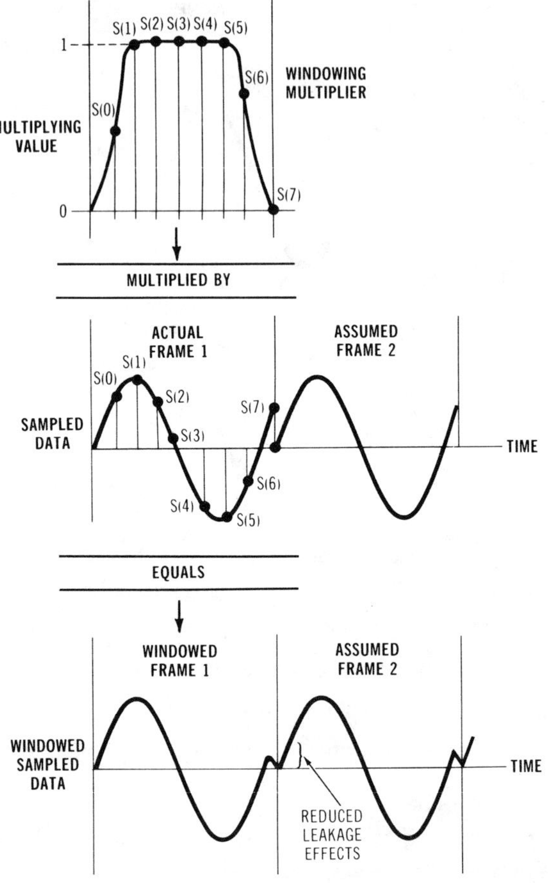

Figure 5-10.
The "windowing" process.

amount of usage and even improvements in the original mathematical frequency transform process. One of the more famous renditions of the DFT is known as the Fast Fourier Transform (FFT). There is no particular magic behind the FFT in relation to the DFT; it is just a shorthand version designed to provide faster computations. In fact, the computations involved are basically the same as those with the DFT. However, one critical restriction exists in the FFT: N must always be taken as a power of 2. So, while the DFT can operate with 1, 2, 55, 96, or even 992 samples of data, the FFT is restricted to powers of 2 like 8, 16, 64, 128, 256, etc. However, if these restraints are not prohibitive in a frequency analysis system, the Fast Fourier Transform produces the same results with considerably less time in computation for transforms exceeding somewhere between 16 and 32 sampled data points.

Without going into great detail as to the operation of the FFT, let's briefly examine the mathematical function.

Fast Fourier Transform

The first term that you will notice while reading information about the FFT, and what you will probably wonder about, is the "butterfly." As a matter of fact, it is almost impossible to find an FFT article without swarms of butterflies. Well, no these are not programs full of bugs. What the butterfly describes is a mathematical system for calculating the Fourier transform which produces the overall calculations needed. The shortened algorithm which provides the exact information produced by the DFT works because there are a fairly large number of redundant calculations performed during each Discrete Fourier Transform. These redundancies are effectively eliminated in the FFT, thus giving a much faster calculation time with equivalent results.

The nucleus of the Fast Fourier Transform, the butterfly operation, is used to multiply complex values in a straightforward manner as in the Discrete Fourier Transform. Fig. 5-11 shows the original shape of the butterly operation in terms of mathematical flow which gave the algorithm its name. At the start of the butterfly, the two input values S(0) and S(1) are processed through a kind of crisscross operation which multiplies the two values by the term $\cos \theta - j \sin \theta$ which relates back to the values in the DFT. (Remember the $\cos \theta - j \sin \theta$ operation which occurs in each frequency bin computation of the DFT?) This performs the same operation in a much more efficient manner. But, do not be deceived by the simplicity of the operation. For an FFT utilizes the butterfly many, many times during a spectral analysis operation before the final answers (the frequency bins) are computed. In support of that statement, examine Fig. 5-12 which shows the butterfly operations needed for a simple Fast Fourier Transform with four sampled points.

While this computational butterfly array looks rather formidable, it can be broken down into a series of simpler butterflies. Each of the multiplication circles $\otimes$ signifies a mathematical product of the incoming value by W with the variable k and n values equal to those applicable at that point in the computation. The summation circles $\oplus$ at each computational node simply add the incoming values and supply these to the outgoing lines.

The process of the FFT is not totally complete at the answers A(0) through A(3). The answers are, in fact, the right frequency bin answers; however, they are scrambled in order of occurrence. The unscrambling process to discover the final answers is shown in Fig. 5-13. In this

THE BUTTERFLY SHAPE

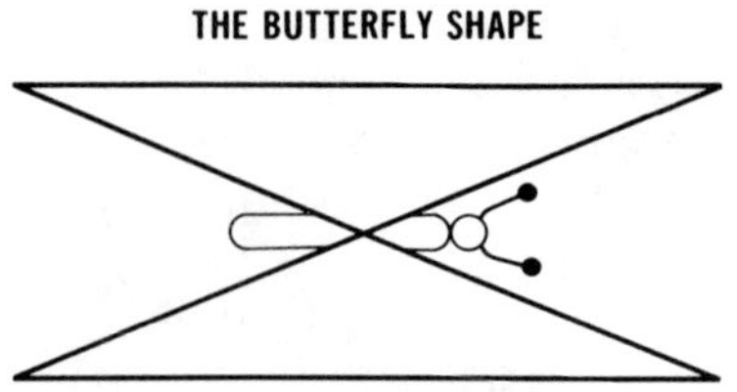

NOW MATHEMATICALLY:

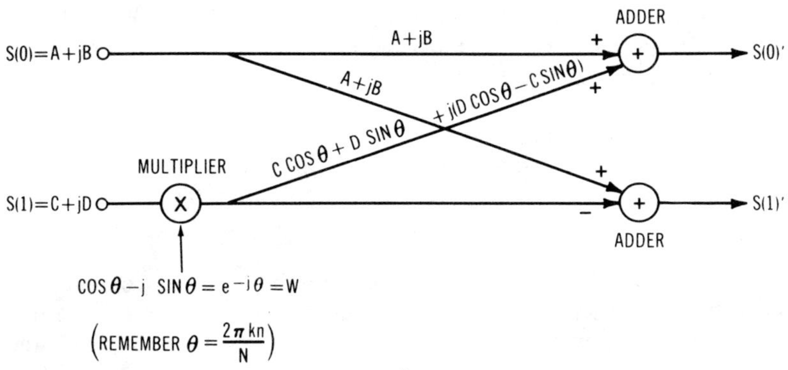

Figure 5-11.
The FFT Butterfly process.

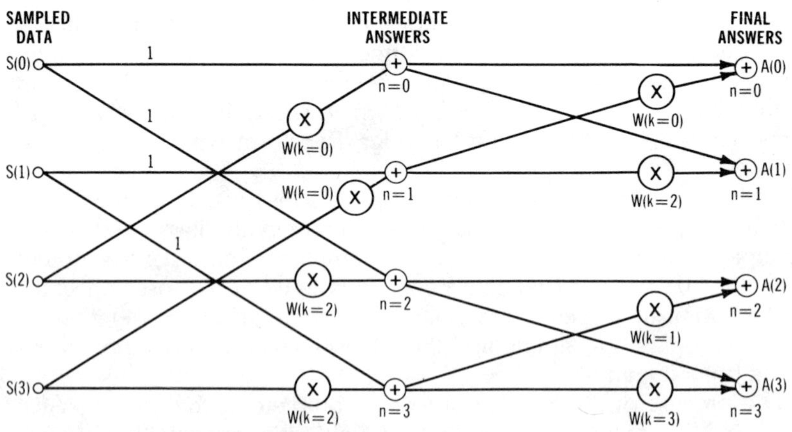

Figure 5-12.
The N=4 point FFT Butterflies.

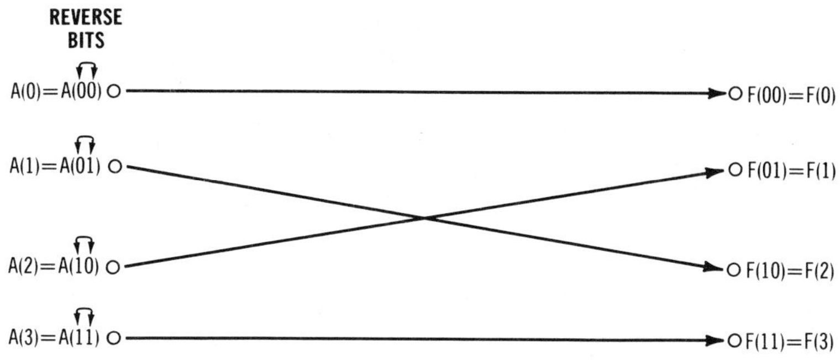

Figure 5-13.
Unscrambling the FFT by bit reversal.

process, the subscript of each answer within the parentheses is converted to its binary form and the binary representation is then flipped around the center of the number to create a mirror image. These values are then used as the final answers' subscripts. The same process is used whether there are two binary digits or eight for each subscripted answer. Thus, the frequency bin output results, F(0) through F(3), provide the equivalent Fourier transform values for an FFT with $N = 4$ with considerably fewer multiplications needed in the same computational process as the DFT.

The number of computations that might be saved by performing an FFT as opposed to a DFT can be computed by considering the number of complex multiplications and additions needed for each. In the Discrete Fourier Transform, the number of dual (multiply and add) computations is N^2 while in the FFT the equivalent number of calculations is $N \times Log_2N$. In the previous example, this means that for a transform of four points, the DFT would require 16 complex operations while the FFT requires only eight. Not a tremendous savings in calculation power or computational time. However, consider the transform with 256 points, a more commonly occurring sample size. The DFT requires 65,536 complex operations while the FFT requires only 2,048 operations. The savings are quite dramatic when the number of sample points exceeds around 64 with a ten times savings in computational speed. Transforms requiring 1,024 or 2,048 points provide a speed saving on the order of 100 to 200 times. While that doesn't seem like a tremendous amount, if we are talking about a computation which may take anywhere from one-half hour to several hours, we could be, on a 2,048 point transform, changing the computational time from two hours down to 36 seconds. That's significant enough to consider using the FFT. You can compare the speed of computation if you executed the DFT program in Listing 5-1 by entering the equivalent FFT program in Listing 5-2. Pick a sample problem with a fair number of points, say 8 or 16,

Listing 5-2.
FFT Program.

```
2 REM FFT PROGRAM -- LISTING 5-2
3 REM FOR ILLUSTRATING THE FFT TRANSFORM SPEED
5 PI=3.14159
6 PRINT:PRINT
7 PRINT"N MUST BE A POWER OF 2 - I.E. 8,16,32,64, ETC."
10 INPUT "N=";N
15 DIM S(N),IS(N),RE(N),IM(N),PWR(N)
20 FOR I=0 TO N-1
30 PRINT"S(";I;")=";:INPUT S(I)
40 NEXT I
45 I1=0:I2=N-1
50 FOR K=1 TO I2
55 Z=N
60 Z=Z/2
65 IF Z+I1>I2 THEN 60
70 I1=I1- INT(I1/Z)*Z + Z
75 IF I1<=K THEN 95
80 T1=S(K)
85 S(K)=S(I1)
90 S(I1)=T1
95 NEXT K
100 Z=1
105 G=2*Z
110 FOR K=0 TO Z-1
115 CSN=COS(K*PI/Z)
120 SNE=SIN(K*PI/Z)
125 FOR I3=K TO N-1 STEP G
130 I4=I3+Z
135 T1=CSN*S(I4)-SNE*IS(I4)
140 T2=SNE*S(I4)+CSN*IS(I4)
145 S(I4)=S(I3)-T1
150 IS(I4)=IS(I3)-T2
155 S(I3)=S(I3)+T1
160 IS(I3)=IS(I3)+T2
165 NEXT I3
170 NEXT K
175 Z=G
180 IF Z<N THEN 105
182 PRINT:PRINT
185 FOR B=0 TO N-1
190 RE(B)=S(B):IM(B)=IS(B)
200 RE(B)=RE(B)/N:IM(B)=IM(B)/N
205 PWR(B)=SQR(RE(B)^2+IM(B)^2)
210 PRINT"F(";B;")= ";PWR(B)
215 NEXT B
220 PRINT"END FFT COMPUTATION":END
```

and try both with a stop watch. You will be quite surprised at the
difference in execution speed between the programs.

No matter how much we try to shorten the calculation time for the
Fourier transform, most processors will still require execution times
ranging from a few tenths of a second up to 30 seconds. This time is
per transform. Accordingly, it's rather difficult to keep up with real-time

speech input with the sluggish mathematics involved in the Fourier transform.

Consider a speech system with a sampling rate of 8 kHz, in which you wish to compute a 64-point discrete Fourier transform. First of all, 64 samples at a sample rate of 8 kHz means that you can acquire the complete sampled data frame in 8 milliseconds—125 microseconds ($\frac{1}{8000}$ Hz) times 64 samples. So, to keep up with a real-time system, you must compute the 64-point transform in less time than is required to collect the next 64-sample points. Unfortunately, any personal computer available today would have considerable trouble computing even a 64-point FFT in 8 milliseconds. So we must search for alternate means to produce the real-time computations needed for a speech operating system. The answer to our dilemma may be found in a new generation of high speed microprocessors dedicated to computations such as these: digital signal processing (DSP) chips. The computing power of these chips is quite impressive. Typical instruction times range from 1 to 0.2 microseconds *per instruction,* which includes the multiplication time needed for the FFT butterfly operation. It is not surprising to note that even the architecture of the DSP chips is designed around such algorithms as Fourier transforms.

There are currently four major contenders on the market for computing algorithms involving the filtering and Fourier analysis of digital signals. These are available as commercial products:

> American Microsystems, Inc. AMI2811
> Intel 2920
> NEC America PD7720
> Texas Instruments TMS32010

They are all extremely fast and have architectures specifically designed to increase the speed of digital signal analysis. The comparison of the capabilities of these processors is shown in Table 5-1. While the topic of which of these processors has the most computing power may be argued at length by almost anyone, the TMS32010 seems to have the most flexible architecture and largest instruction set of the group. If you consider that you can buy one of these processors, which run at 20 MHz, for around $150, you may wonder why anyone would consider alternative methods for processing digital speech signals. (Yes, the TMS32010 *will* do a 16-bit by 16-bit multiply with a 32-bit result in 200 nanoseconds!)

The instruction set of the TMS32010 by Texas Instruments is given in Fig. 5-14. The important feature in the figure is the column labeled "CY." This refers to the number of clock cycles needed to complete the instruction. If there is a "1" in this column, then that instruction executes into 200 nanoseconds. For "2," the time required to complete the instruction is 400 nanoseconds, etc. Thus, you should notice that except for the branch operations at the bottom of the table, most other instruc-

Table 5-1.
Comparison of Digital Processor Features

Feature	TI TMS32010	NEC μPD7720	AMI S2811	INTEL 2920
Data-word size (bits)	16	16	16	25
Coefficient size (bits)	16	13	16	Variable
Accumulator width (bits)	32	16	16	28
Saturation arithmetic	Hardware	Software	Hardware	Hardware
Boolean logic operations?	Yes	Yes	No	Yes
Multiplier implementation	Hardware	Hardware	Hardware	Software
Multiplier precision (in × in = out)	$16 \times 16 = 32$	$16 \times 16 = 32$	$12 \times 12 = 16$	$12 \times 25 = 28$
Multiplication time (ns) (worst case)	200	250	300	4800
Parallel I/O (bits)	16	8	8	4 in/8 out
Instruction word (bits)	16	23	17	24
Instruction cycle (ns)	200	250	300	400
Subroutine levels	>50	4	1	None
Iteration (loop) counter?	Yes	No	Yes	No
Conditional jumps?	Yes	Yes	Yes	No
Full-speed external memory expansion	Yes	No	No	No
Instruction ROM (bits)	1536×16	512×23	256×17	192×24
Coefficient ROM (bits)	Not required	512×13	120×16	–
Data RAM (bits)	144×16	128×16	128×16	40×25
Z^{-1} function?	Yes	Yes	Yes	No
Look-up tables?	Yes	Yes	Yes	No
Package	40-pin DIP	28-pin DIP	28-pin DIP	28-pin DIP

tions execute in one clock cycle! They also look surprisingly like the instruction set from a normal general purpose 8-bit microprocessor. This ultra high-speed micro is really powerful.

Texas Instruments, in the design of the TMS32010, has opted for a non-Von Neumann architecture within the chip. In other words, the concept of the internal operations is different than most other general purpose microprocessors on the market. The difference may be seen in Fig. 5-15. This figure, the block diagram of the internal workings of the TMS32010, illustrates that there are now *two* portions of memory that may be *simultaneously* accessed through software commands. There are also *two* 16-bit buses on the chip. One bus is reserved for program control words; the other for data flow. Thus, the processor may access data memory and program memory simultaneously! This particular type of architecture is referred to as the Harvard architecture, because it was first taught there. The particular advantage of the Harvard architecture over the more standard Von Neumann architecture is the ability to access data and program memory simultaneously. Thus, a processor has the ability to perform instructions like the LTD instruction (the starred one) in Fig. 5-14. This particular instruction loads the T register of the multiplier with a 16-bit value, adds the product P register of the multiplier to the accumulator and puts that value back into the accumulator, and finally takes the 16-bit data word from the specified memory address and moves it to the next higher data memory address, all in 200 nanoseconds. That's only one clock cycle for two data memory accesses, two internal register transfers, and a 16-bit addition with a 32-bit result!

The power of the digital signal processing chip is hard to comprehend compared to the 8- and 16-bit processors that we currently have in our personal computing systems. As digital signal processors become more available and begin to have software written for them, we will have extremely fast, powerful speech processing algorithms available for use within our own computers by simply implanting a digital signal processor chip within our systems. (See Chapter 10 for instructions on adding a TMS32010 to your system.)

Most of the digital signal processors have internal ROM which may be mask programmed with factory generated algorithms. In the near future, you will be able to buy these chips with internal functions like 64-point FFTs, digital filter algorithms, and even digital modem internal programs. As these appear on the market, their use within your system will require nothing more than placing them on a data bus with appropriate input and output ports to your main 8- or 16-bit microprocessor. However, until the algorithms are developed, most of these chips will be used with external RAM to develop and generate signal processing software. The FFT algorithm is relatively easily implemented in any of the major DSP chips. The fastest ones developed will certainly gain wide acceptance in the current vacuum of available software.

TMS320 INSTRUCTION SET

INST	INSTRUCTION REGISTER (15→0)	HEX 1st	2nd	3rd	4th		CY	WD	DESCRIPTION
ADD	0 0 0 0 C I S	0	0-F	0-F	0-F		1	1	ADD TO ACC WITH SHIFT
SUB	0 0 0 1 C I S	1	0-F	0-F	0-F		1	1	SUBTRACT FROM ACC W/ SHIFT
LAC	0 0 1 0 C I S	2	0-F	0-F	0-F		1	1	LOAD ACC WITH SHIFT
SAR	0 0 1 1 0 R I S	3	0-7	0-F	0-F		1	1	STORE AUXILIARY REGISTER
LAR	0 0 1 1 1 R I S	3	8-F	0-F	0-F		1	1	LOAD AUXILIARY REGISTER
IN	0 1 0 0 0 PA I S	4	0-7	0-F	0-F		2	1	INPUT DATA FROM PORT
OUT	0 1 0 0 1 PA I S	4	8-F	0-F	0-F		2	1	OUTPUT DATA TO PORT
SACL	0 1 0 1 0 X I S	5	0-7	0-F	0-F		1	1	STORE ACC LOW
SACH	0 1 0 1 1 X I S	5	8-F	0-F	0-F		1	1	STORE ACC HIGH WITH SHIFT
ADDH	0 1 1 0 0 0 0 0 I S	6	0	0-F	0-F		1	1	ADD TO ACC HIGH
ADDS	0 1 1 0 0 0 0 1 I S	6	1	0-F	0-F		1	1	ADD TO ACC WITH SIGN-EXTENSION SUPPRESSED
SUBH	0 1 1 0 0 0 1 0 I S	6	2	0-F	0-F		1	1	SUBTRACT FROM ACC HIGH
SUBS	0 1 1 0 0 0 1 1 I S	6	3	0-F	0-F		1	1	SUBTRACT FROM ACC WITH SIGN-EXTENSION SUPPRESSED
SUBC	0 1 1 0 0 1 0 0 I S	6	4	0-F	0-F		1	1	CONDITIONAL SUBTRACT FOR DIVIDE
ZALH	0 1 1 0 0 1 0 1 I S	6	5	0-F	0-F		1	1	ZERO ACC & LOAD HIGH
ZALS	0 1 1 0 0 1 1 0 I S	6	6	0-F	0-F		1	1	ZERO ACC & LOAD LOW WITH SIGN-EXTENSION SUPPRESSED
TBLR	0 1 1 0 0 1 1 1 I S	6	7	0-F	0-F		3	1	TABLE READ
MAR	0 1 1 0 1 0 0 0 I S	6	8	0-F	0-F		1	1	MODIFY AUXILIARY REGISTER AND POINTER
DMOV	0 1 1 0 1 0 0 1 I S	6	9	0-F	0-F		1	1	DATA SHIFT IN MEMORY
LT	0 1 1 0 1 0 1 0 I S	6	A	0-F	0-F		1	1	LOAD T-REGISTER
LTD	0 1 1 0 1 0 1 1 I S	6	B	0-F	0-F		1	1	LOAD T-REG., ACC P-REG. & SHIFT DATA MEMORY
LTA	0 1 1 0 1 1 0 0 I S	6	C	0-F	0-F		1	1	LOAD T-REG. & ACCUMULATE
MPY	0 1 1 0 1 1 0 1 I S	6	D	0-F	0-F		1	1	MULTIPLY WITH DATA WORD
LDPK	0 1 1 0 1 1 1 0 K 0 0 0 0 0 0 0 0 D	6	E	0	0-1	6E0X	1	1	LOAD DATA MEMORY PAGE IMMEDIATE
LDP	0 1 1 0 1 1 1 1 I S	6	F	0-F	0-F		1	1	LOAD DATA MEMORY PAGE
LARK	0 1 1 1 0 R K	7	0-7	0-F	0-F		1	1	LOAD AUXILIARY REGISTER IMMEDIATE

Figure 5-14.   The TMS

Mnemonic	Binary					Opcode			Description
XOR	0 1 1 1 1 0 0 0 I — S	7	8	0-F	0-F		1	1	EXCLUSIVE OR
AND	0 1 1 1 1 0 0 1 I — S	7	9	0-F	0-F		1	1	LOGICAL AND
OR	0 1 1 1 1 0 1 0 I — S	7	A	0-F	0-F		1	1	LOGICAL OR
LST	0 1 1 1 1 0 1 1 I — S	7	B	0-F	0-F		1	1	LOAD STATUS
SST	0 1 1 1 1 1 0 0 I — S	7	C	0-F	0-F		1	1	STORE STATUS
TBLW	0 1 1 1 1 1 0 1 I — S	7	D	0-F	0-F		3	1	TABLE WRITE
LACK	0 1 1 1 1 1 1 0 — K	7	E	0-F	0-F		1	1	LOAD ACC IMMEDIATE
NOP	0 1 1 1 1 1 1 1 1 0 0 0 0 0 0 0	7	F	8	0	7F80	1	1	NO OPERATION
DINT	0 1 1 1 1 1 1 1 1 0 0 0 0 0 0 1	7	F	8	1	7F81	1	1	DISABLE INTERRUPT
EINT	0 1 1 1 1 1 1 1 1 0 0 0 0 0 1 0	7	F	8	2	7F82	1	1	ENABLE INTERRUPT
ABS	0 1 1 1 1 1 1 1 1 0 0 0 1 0 0 0	7	F	8	8	7F88	1	1	ABSOLUTE VALUE
ZAC	0 1 1 1 1 1 1 1 1 0 0 0 1 0 0 1	7	F	8	9	7F89	1	1	ZERO ACC
ROVM	0 1 1 1 1 1 1 1 1 0 0 0 1 0 1 0	7	F	8	A	7F8A	1	1	RESET OVERFLOW MODE
SOVM	0 1 1 1 1 1 1 1 1 0 0 0 1 0 1 1	7	F	8	B	7F8B	1	1	SET OVERFLOW MODE
CALA	0 1 1 1 1 1 1 1 1 0 0 0 1 1 0 0	7	F	8	C	7F8C	2	1	CALL SUBROUTINE INDIRECT
RET	0 1 1 1 1 1 1 1 1 0 0 0 1 1 0 1	7	F	8	D	7F8D	2	1	RETURN
LARP	0 1 1 0 1 0 0 0 — K / 1 0 0 0 0 0 0 0 Y	6	8	8	0-1	688X	1	1	LOAD AUXILIARY REG. POINTER IMMEDIATE
PAC	0 1 1 1 1 1 1 1 1 0 0 0 1 1 1 0	7	F	8	E	7F8E	1	1	LOAD ACC WITH P-REGISTER
APAC	0 1 1 1 1 1 1 1 1 0 0 0 1 1 1 1	7	F	8	F	7F8F	1	1	ADD P-REGISTER TO ACC
SPAC	0 1 1 1 1 1 1 1 1 0 0 1 0 0 0 0	7	F	9	0	7F90	1	1	SUBTRACT P-REG. FROM ACC
MPYK	1 0 0 — M	8-9	0-F	0-F	0-F		1	1	MULTIPLY IMMEDIATE
BANZ	1 1 1 1 0 1 0 0 0 0 0 0 0 0 0 0	F	4	0	0	F400	2	2	BRANCH ON AUX. REG. NOT ZERO
BV	1 1 1 1 0 1 0 1 0 0 0 0 0 0 0 0	F	5	0	0	F500	2	2	BRANCH ON OVERFLOW
BIOZ	1 1 1 1 0 1 1 0 0 0 0 0 0 0 0 0	F	6	0	0	F600	2	2	BRANCH ON I/O ZERO
CALL	1 1 1 1 1 0 0 0 0 0 0 0 0 0 0 0	F	8	0	0	F800	2	2	CALL SUBROUTINE DIRECT
B	1 1 1 1 1 0 0 1 0 0 0 0 0 0 0 0	F	9	0	0	F900	2	2	BRANCH UNCONDITIONALLY
BLZ	1 1 1 1 1 0 1 0 0 0 0 0 0 0 0 0	F	A	0	0	FA00	2	2	BRANCH IF < 0
BLEZ	1 1 1 1 1 0 1 1 0 0 0 0 0 0 0 0	F	B	0	0	FB00	2	2	BRANCH IF ≤ 0
BGZ	1 1 1 1 1 1 0 0 0 0 0 0 0 0 0 0	F	C	0	0	FC00	2	2	BRANCH IF > 0
BGEZ	1 1 1 1 1 1 0 1 0 0 0 0 0 0 0 0	F	D	0	0	FD00	2	2	BRANCH IF ≥ 0
BNZ	1 1 1 1 1 1 1 0 0 0 0 0 0 0 0 0	F	E	0	0	FE00	2	2	BRANCH IF $\neq 0$
BZ	1 1 1 1 1 1 1 1 0 0 0 0 0 0 0 0	F	F	0	0	FF00	2	2	BRANCH IF $= 0$
PUSH	0 1 1 1 1 1 1 1 1 0 0 1 1 1 0 0	7	F	9	C	7F9C	2	1	PUSH FROM ACC TO STACK
POP	0 1 1 1 1 1 1 1 1 0 0 1 1 1 0 1	7	F	9	D	7F9D	2	1	POP TO ACC FROM STACK

32010 Instruction set.

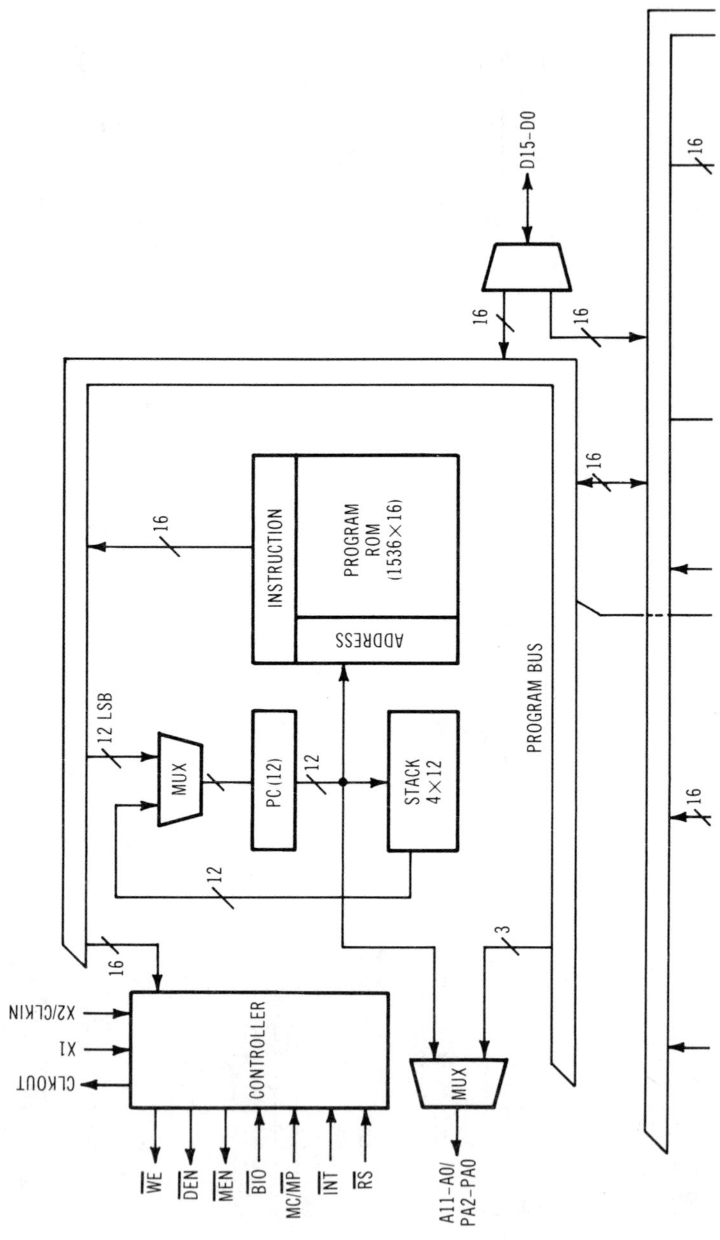

Figure 5-15.   Block diagram of the

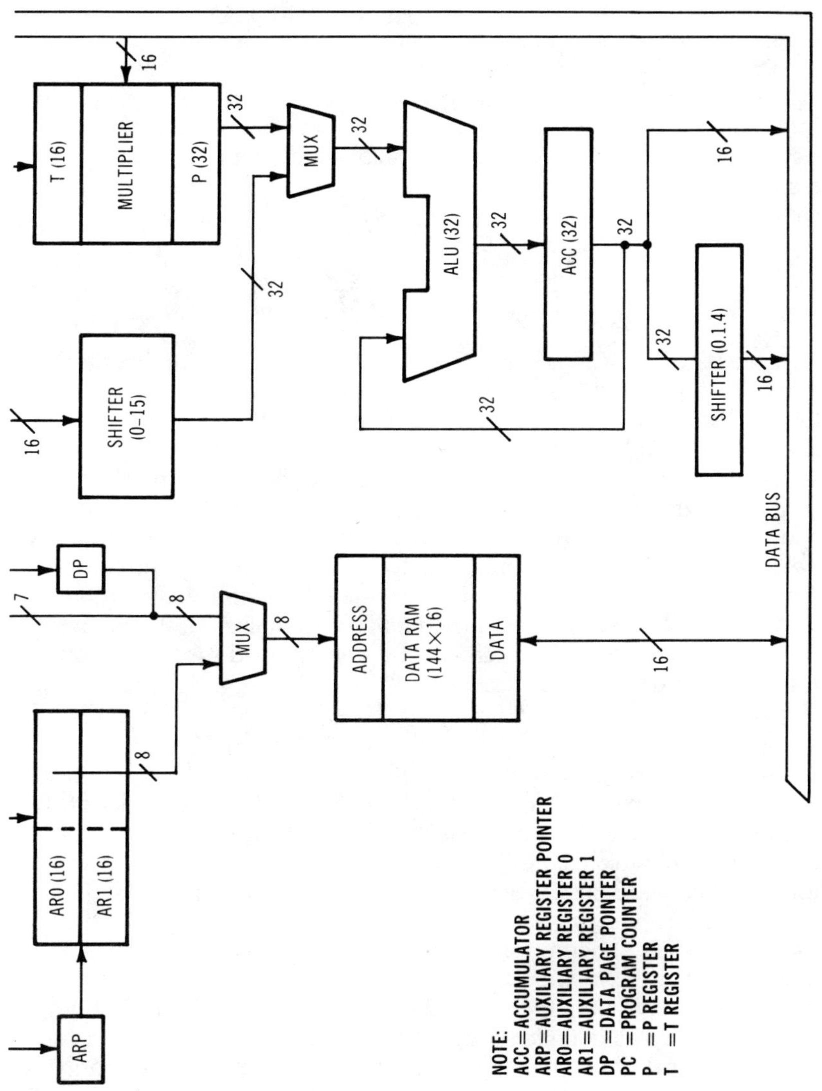

TMS32010 Harvard Architecture DSP.

The Fast Fourier Transform and the Discrete Fourier Transform are very powerful methods of quickly determining the spectral content of analog signals. Their primary use within a speech recognition system is to break the frequency components of a signal into discrete values, much as your ear does, so that they may be stored and compared frame by frame with new data. If a series of spectral data agrees with a newly acquired series, then using techniques found in the next chapter, a speech recognition system can truly provide accurate speech identification and recognition.

Formant Analysis

It may appear to be a simple matter to compute the spectral content of a speech signal and then identify the formants within the spectral features. This is not generally the case. The difficulty lies in the interspersion of the pitch frequency with the formant frequencies of speech. For instance, examine Fig. 5-16. This figure shows the spectrum of a frame of speech during the sound "uh" as in cup. As you visually examine the spectrum plot, you can easily identify the three primary frequency peaks. These humps at approximately 600 Hz, 1200 Hz, and 2400 Hz represent the formants needed to generate that particular phoneme. While it may be easy to find these peaks with your eyes, the processor has slighty more difficulty because of the intermixed peaks throughout the spectrum which occur at:

$$\text{pitch frequency} \bullet n \ (n = 1, 2, \ldots N-1)$$

There might be some rather tricky methods of having a processor search through a memory stored spectrum and try to find the peaks of the formants hidden within the peaks of the pitch; however, there is an easier method which is also more straightforward. Consider the waveform in Fig. 5-16 to be a time varying signal. The pitch frequency appears to be a very high frequency oscillation with the lower frequency formant humps superimposed on it. Going back a few sections, you remember that if we were to take a Discrete Fourier Transform of the given "uh" *spectrum,* then the pitch frequency and formant humps would show up as definite spectral lines in the newly created transform of a transform. This type of process (the transform of a transform) is referred to as a *cepstrum.* The resultant output of the spectrum of a spectrum is basically a backwards, inside-out spelling of the word *spectrum.* Since the cepstrum no longer has *frequency* as its horizontal axis because it is now a cepstrum, the conventional new horizontal axis labeling is *"quefrency."* As mentioned earlier, since the low frequency pitch period occurs quite rapidly in the direct speech spectrum, its resultant cepstrum is at the high end of quefrency. The formant related humps, which are the higher frequencies in the spectrum, now become

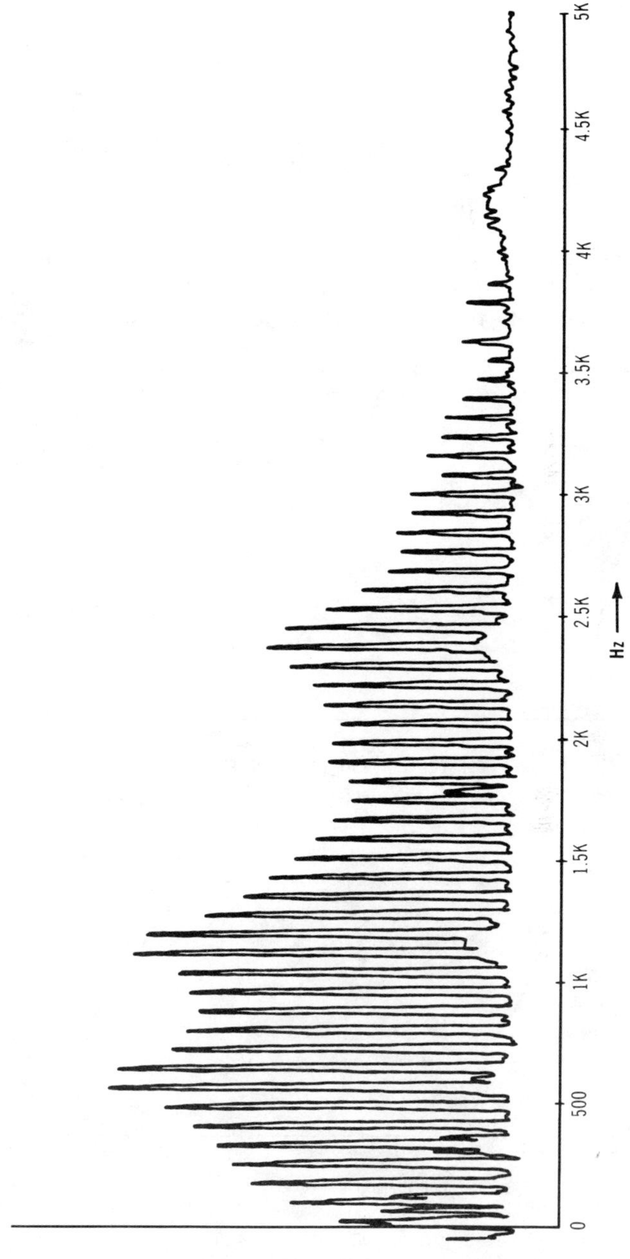

Figure 5-16.
The spectrum of "uh" with formant humps.

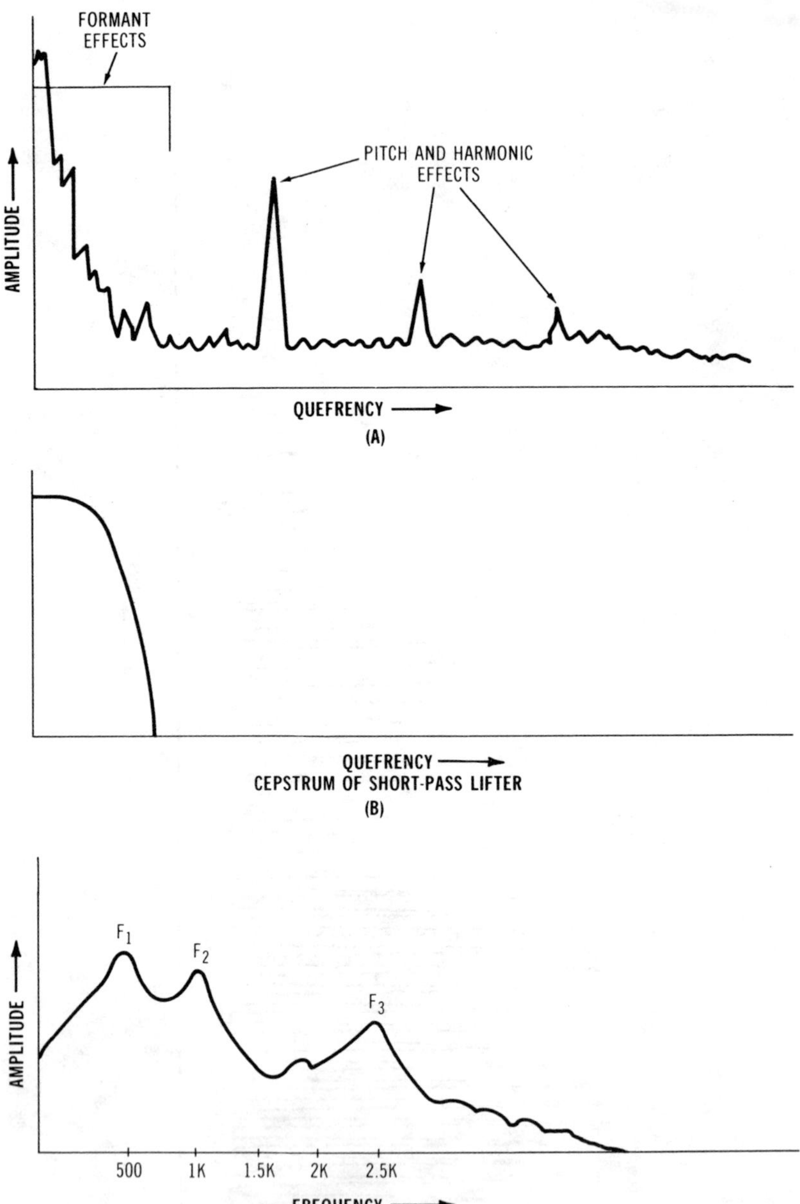

Figure 5-17.
Formant resolution through cepstrum analysis.

low quefrencies in the cepstrum analysis. This is all best understood by viewing the cepstrum of speech in Fig. 5-17. In Fig. 5-17A, the cepstrum of the speech spectrum in Fig. 5-16 shows considerable low frequency formant effects, with fundamental and harmonic peaks of the pitch frequency. The filtering process to remove the pitch effects from the cepstrum is known as—you guessed it—liftering. This is the backwards filtering required to remove the pitch quefrency effect. The resultant final cepstrum is then passed through an *inverse* Fourier transform to regenerate the frequency spectrum. The "liftered" spectrum in Fig. 5-17C clearly identifies the formant peaks within the original phoneme sound. Thus, the speech signal has been processed through quite a complex series of mathematical transformations to remove pitch effects and isolate the formant characteristics within the incoming speech.

Once the formant frequencies have been identified, then, through the process of pattern recognition and matching, it is a somewhat simpler matter to match the formants with spoken phoneme sequences. As we see in the next chapter, the process of feature extraction and pattern recognition holds the key to fast, accurate speech recognition systems.

CHAPTER 6

Feature Extraction and Pattern Recognition

If you made it through the last chapter with the equations for the Fourier transforms and did not get lost, then you should be very proud of yourself. The normal mathematics involved in Fourier transforms usually are taught in college at the senior to graduate engineering level and often take periods of six to twelve months for a full discussion. The presentation in the last chapter was necessarily brief but needed to tie the complete speech recognition process together.

In the biomedical analogy to human hearing, the portion of speech recognition that we have examined to this point covers only the *ears*. Since the latest theory on human hearing tells us that within our inner ear mechanism we have a form of crude spectrum analyzer, then what the nerve bundles carry from our ears to our brain resembles the parallel frequency bin data output by the Fourier transform described in the previous chapter.

Modern research in auditory modeling of hearing suggests that our hearing process is not completely linear with frequency. Instead, our ears tend to exhibit a frequency response which varies logarithmically over frequency, thus yielding a phenomenon referred to as "critical band" resolution. In more understandable terms, this simply means that our hearing is not constant over the audible frequency range, but rather logarithmic. At very high frequencies, our resolution is rather coarse, allowing us only a gross description of spectral frequencies. However, at the lower frequencies, our frequency resolution becomes much more detailed, giving us a fine grain structure to distinguish between the closely spaced formant frequencies found in phonemes.

The hearing process does not hinge on a single "spectral transform," but rather on time sequential transforms (periodograms) which occur during the course of a word or sentence. The information given in the previous chapter concerning Fourier transforms dealt only with spectral analysis for short periods of time on the order of a few tens of milliseconds. When we analyze speech in terms of words and sentences, we must continue the spectral analysis for periods of tenths of a second to several seconds. This procedure is a simple repetition of the short duration Fourier transform in which the spectral information is displayed vertically against a horizontal time axis. The resulting display of the sequential time spectral analysis is called a *spectrogram*. The normal axes for a spectrogram (a three-dimensional plot) are time along the horizontal direction and frequency along the vertical direction. An example of the axis system for a spectrogram is shown in Fig. 6-1. The only axis which is not easily seen from this figure is the amplitude axis which normally extends out of the page (the height dependent upon the amplitude of the frequency at any given time). A more graphic way of displaying this series of FFT frames is shown in Fig. 6-2. Another feature of the spectrogram is brought out in this three-dimensional representation: the proportional shading of frequencies in relation to their amplitude. Thus, the strongest frequencies are shaded the darkest while the weakest frequencies, which have little amplitude, have no shading at all. If the cubic three-dimensional spectrogram were viewed head-on,

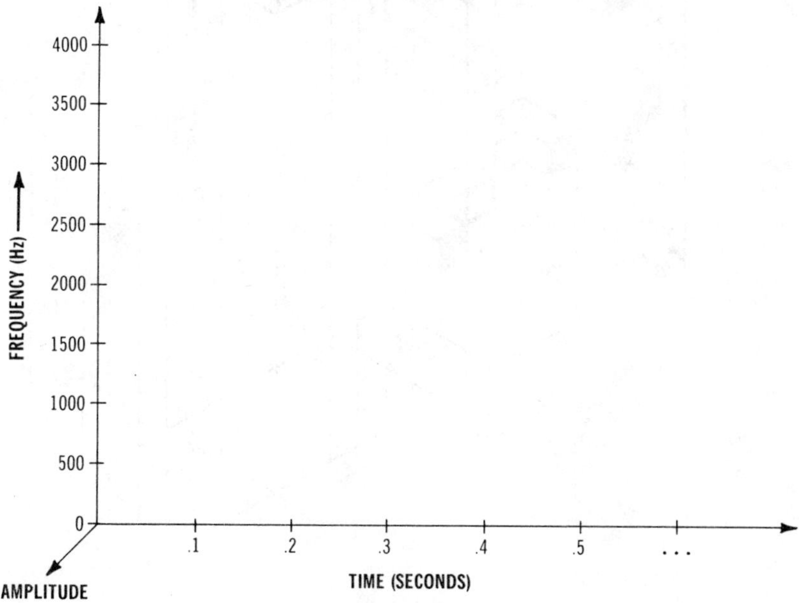

Figure 6-1.
The spectrogram axis system.

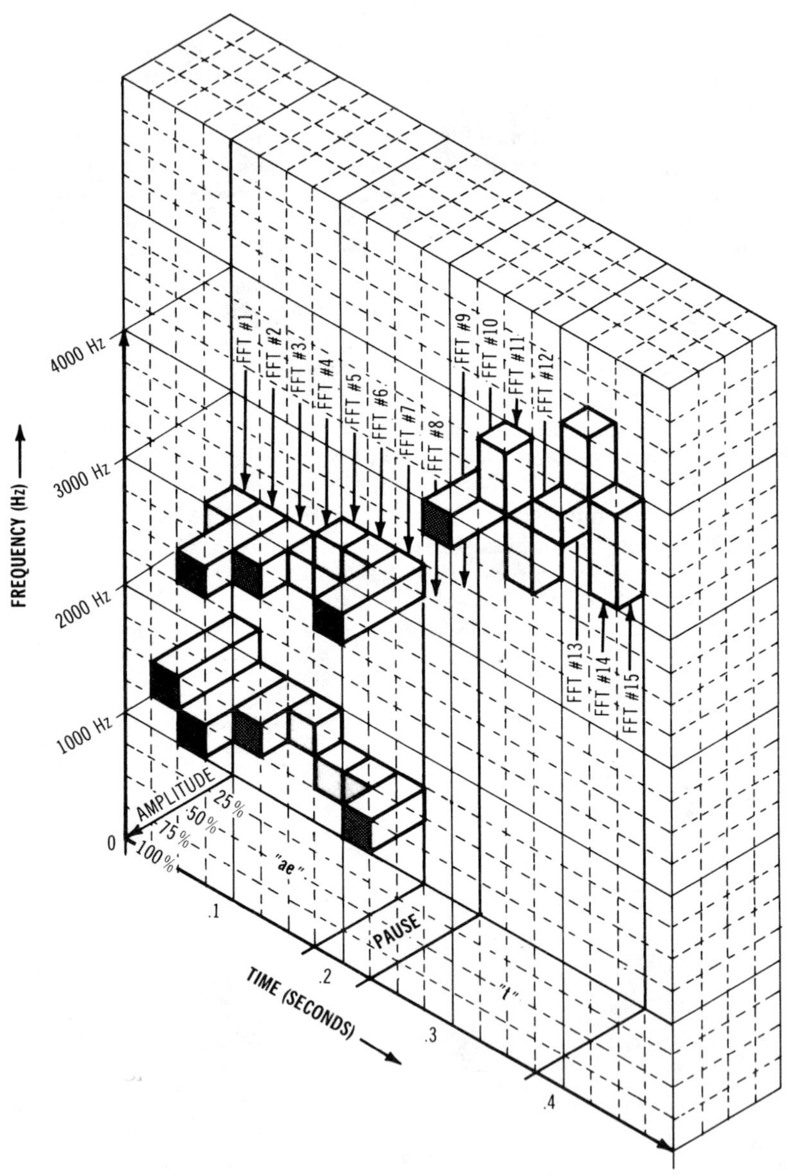

Figure 6-2.
The sequential FFT generated spectrogram.

it would begin to resemble the normal spectrogram seen in speech associated textbooks and articles. However, for the purpose of pattern recognition, this description will suffice. Consider that the figure when viewed from the side represents a number of sequential FFTs, each 16 frequency bins tall extending from 0 through 4000 Hz. This spectrogram might have been generated through a speech processing system sampling at 8000 Hz with a 32-bit transform (remember that the top half of the output bins are a mirror image of the lower half with real input data so we only get 16 valid output bins). If we look further, we see that each FFT is acquired and computed in a time frame of 25 milliseconds. By packing each FFT side by side with the previous one, a graph is generated in three dimensions which characterizes the spoken message in its entirety. The utterance for Fig. 6-2 might be the word "at" with its associated *ae* sound followed by a glottal pause of 50 milliseconds and then the fricative *t* sound. Notice that the FFTs numbered 10 through 15 produce the somewhat random distribution expected from the hissing noise in the *t* sound. The contents of this spectrogram may be used with several pattern recognition techniques to eventually determine what has been spoken.

The process of extracting the spoken information from spectrograms is performed in most currently available systems by one of two methods: feature extraction and template matching. There is even considerable disagreement in the speech-recognition community about which of these processes works better. Although there is considerable intermingling of the two types of speech recognition within each defined process (there is template matching within feature extraction and feature extraction within template matching), they will be presented in an attempted unbiased view so that you may decide yourself which class of pattern recognition your system should use.

Features

As well as we can describe a person's face by the length of his nose, the color of his eyes, the shape of his lips, we may also describe speech in terms of its features. There are only a certain number of features that may be extracted from a given portion of speech. These include pitch, timing, phonemes (or formant frequencies), and envelope contours. The method of extraction of these features from speech may be performed in a number of ways. Once they have been extracted, they are used to compare against a reference set of features to determine if the spoken message is a match to a reference vocabulary word, no match, or no decision. The process is very similar to looking at a parking lot with two grey Ford automobiles and a red Chevrolet. As you visually examine the three cars, there are similar features between the Ford automobiles other than color that immediately tell you that these two belong to the same class and are distinctive from the Chevrolet. The computer must perform basically the same matching process in comparing speech features to determine if the incoming words match reference vocabulary words. There is some of the pattern matching process that occurs in the feature based recognition; however, the matching occurs only between the features. They must first be extracted from the speech before any attempt at speech recognition proceeds. Taken singly, the features of speech can be characterized as to their importance in the following sections.

Pitch

The importance of voice pitch in speech recognition is almost a nuisance value. Consider a male and female speaking the same words. The pitch of the male voice in this case will usually be lower than that of the female voice while adding very little meaning to the recognized speech. The only knowledge that might be gained at all from pitch features is that a female or male is speaking.

In the previous chapter, the last section on formant analysis presented a means of extracting the pitch of speech from the visible spectrogram. The use of the cepstrum is the most prevalent means of finding the pitch features of any incoming speech. Therefore, if the spectrogram of speech is subjected to a series of further Fourier transforms, then a cepstrogram will be generated which shows the pitch track as a series of higher harmonic spikes through the spoken message. The resultant information from this computational process on speech would be a pitch track over time, during an utterance. The particular recognition value of that pitch track is questionable since the same word or phrase can be spoken with a rising or falling pitch, changing only the semantic value of the message. (It might identify a spoken statement or a spoken question.) So, the value of pitch feature extraction lies mostly in the ability to later identify the formant frequencies after the pitch irregularities have been removed from the spectrogram.

Speech Timing

Another characteristic of speech which may be utilized in conjunction with others to possibly help identify and classify words is the timing relationship of spoken utterances. Obviously, a person can say a word very quickly or very slowly and a human recognition subject would have no problem with the identical word. The recognition computer, on the other hand, must attempt to decide if the word has been warped in time by some speaking anomaly. The method currently used to attempt this type of speech time normalization is referred to as dynamic time-warping programs. The process of dynamic warping is really nothing more than an adaptive program which attempts to identify speed changes through a word with reference words by intentionally distorting the time sequence frames of reference. Because its use in speech-recognition systems produces more of a supporting feature than an identifying feature, the feature of speech timing cannot by itself be used to identically match stored vocabulary words.

Phonemes and Formants

The speech features classified as formant frequencies are probably the most valuable part of the speech structure in the science of speech recognition. This becomes self-evident if you realize that as you whisper a word or sentence, that you are doing nothing more than exciting the formant resonant cavities in your mouth with a hissing "white noise" sound source to generate speech. The resultant speech is easily understood as a whispered message only through the broadly resonant formant humps of the whispered message. So, a prime feature of speech is the formant tracking process which identifies and tracks all prevalent formants during any spoken utterance. This also tends to simplify greatly the task of data storage for a given message. For example, assume that a feature extraction program based upon formant frequencies yields as the resulting frequencies for the first three formants: 600 Hz, 840 Hz, and 2400 Hz. Flip back to Table 2-3 in Chapter 2 of this book and see if you can visually determine the phoneme that is being spoken based solely upon the incoming formant frequencies. As you scan down the table of formant resonances of the vowel sounds, you will come across a match at the phoneme "aw." Now, if you can transfer that process into the computer program, then you have created a feature-based recognition system. The identified formants have yielded an identifiable phoneme that may be then compared with vocabulary phoneme tables from the recognition vocabulary.

In reality, the comparison between formants and phonemes in words is not that black and white. In connected speech, the diphthongs between words tend to overshadow the sounds when spoken as isolated words. One means of conquering this difficulty is to attempt a maximum probability match between the incoming phoneme set and the reference set in the vocabulary storage. In other words, everything does not have to match perfectly. It becomes a matter of choosing which set of phonemes most closely matches those being scrutinized for recognition.

As an example of how feature-based speech recognition might work using formant frequency features, examine the hypothetical speech spectrogram in Fig. 6-3. This spectrogram was generated artificially through phoneme tables so it looks more orderly than what might be found in real speech; however, its purpose is to demonstrate the ease of feature based speech recognition. The recognition function for this spectrogram is provided by the BASIC program in Listing 6-1. This

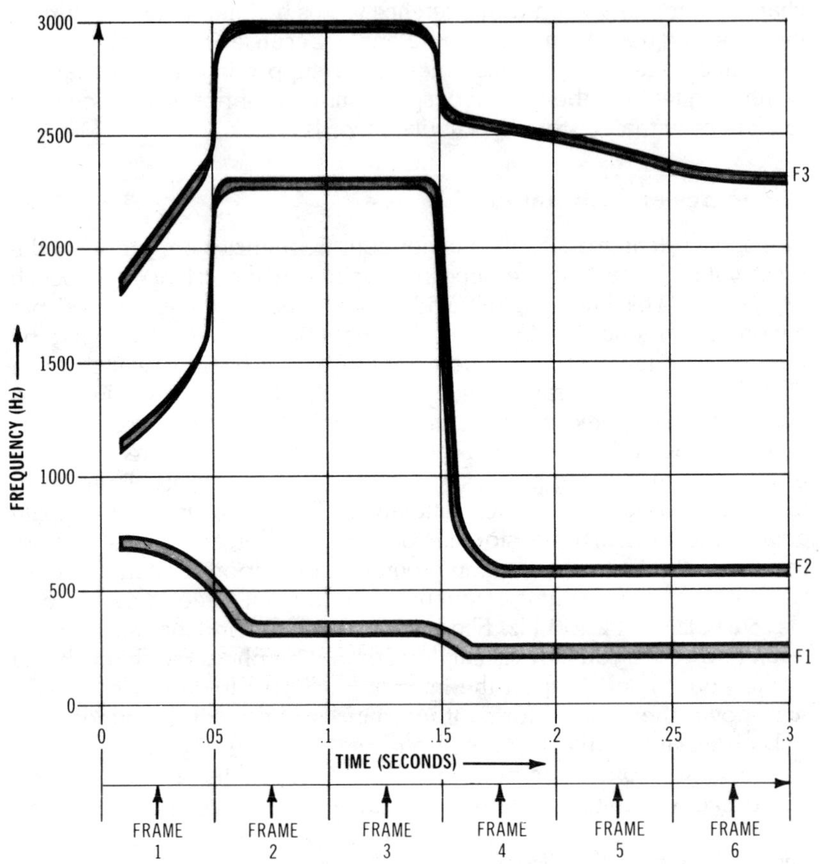

Figure 6-3.
A hypothetical spectrogram for feature-based recognition.

program, like the ones in previous chapters, should run on most computers that use a form of Microsoft BASIC. The lookup table of phonemes within the program was extracted from Tables 2-2 and 2-3 in Chapter 2 of this book. To use this feature-based recognition program, simply type in the listing and then answer questions based on the input spectrogram in Fig. 6-3. Visually, you must extract the three formant frequencies F1, F2, and F3 for input to the feature-based recognition program. Using the spectrogram plot and the frame number pointers under the plot, it becomes a rather simple matter to pick the associated frequencies at each frame number time. The process you are performing in doing this will be the same process that the computer must perform during any type of feature-based recognition. The resulting

Listing 6-1. A Feature-based Demonstration for Speech Recognition.

```
5 FRM=1
10 REM LISTING 6-1 - A FEATURE BASED DEMONSTRATION
20 REM FOR SPEECH RECOGNITION
25 PRINT:PRINT:PRINT
30 PRINT"INPUT'3 FORMANTS'OR NOISE OR PAUSE FOR FRAME ";FRM
35 PRINT"TYPE 'STOP' FOR FORMANT 1 WHEN FINISHED WITH DATA"
40 INPUT "FORMANT 1",F1$(FRM)
45 IF VAL(F1$(FRM))=0 THEN 70
50 INPUT "FORMANT 2",F2$(FRM)
60 INPUT "FORMANT 3",F3$(FRM)
70 IF F1$(FRM)="STOP" THEN 80 ELSE FRM=FRM+1:GOTO 25
80 FOR I=1 TO FRM+1
82 IF F1$(I)="NOISE" AND F1$(I-1)="PAUSE" THEN PH$(I)="(P,K,T)"
   :GOTO 1000
83 IF F1$(I)="STOP" THEN F1$(I)="":GOTO 1015
84 IF VAL(F1$(I))=0 THEN PH$(I)=F1$(I) :GOTO 1000
85 F1(I)=VAL(F1$(I)):F2(I)=VAL(F2$(I)):F3(I)=VAL(F3$(I))
90 IF F1(I)>=250 AND F1(I)<=400 AND F2(I)=600 AND F3(I)>=2000 A
   ND      F3(I)<=3000 THEN PH$(I)="L":GOTO 1000
100 IF F1(I)>=500 AND F1(I)<=700 AND F2(I)>=100 AND F2(I)<=1600
    AND      F3(I)>=1800 AND F3(I)<=2400 THEN PH$(I)="R":GOTO1000
110 IF F1(I)>=200 AND F1(I)<=250 AND F2(I)=600 AND F3(I)>=1400
    AND      F3(I)<=2000 THEN PH$(I)="N":GOTO 1000
120 IF F1(I)>=200 AND F1(I)<=250 AND F2(I)=600 AND F3(I)>=2300
    AND      F3(I)<=2600 THEN PH$(I)="NG":GOTO1000
130 IF F1(I)>=250 AND F1(I)<=300 AND F2(I)=600 AND F3(I)>=900 A
    ND        F3(I)<=1700 THEN PH$(I)="M":GOTO 1000
140 IF F1(I)>=210 AND F1(I)<=330 AND F2(I)>=2230 AND F2(I)<=235
    0 AND F3(I)>=2950 AND F3(I)<=3070 THEN PH$(I)="EE":GOTO 1000
150 IF F1(I)>=330 AND F1(I)<=450 AND F2(I)>=1930 AND F2(I)<=205
    0 AND F3(I)>=2490 AND F3(I)<=2610 THEN PH$(I)="I":GOTO 1000
160 IF F1(I)>=470 AND F1(I)<=590 AND F2(I)>=1780 AND F2(I)<=190
    0 AND F3(I)>=2420 AND F3(I)<=2540 THEN PH$(I)="EH":GOTO 1000
170 IF F1(I)>=600 AND F1(I)<=720 AND F2(I)>=1660 AND F2(I)<=178
    0 AND F3(I)>=2350 AND F3(I)<=2470 THEN PH$(I)="AE":GOTO 1000
180 IF F1(I)>=670 AND F1(I)<=790 AND F2(I)>=1030 AND F2(I)<=115
    0 AND F3(I)>=2380 AND F3(I)<=2500 THEN PH$(I)="AH":GOTO 1000
190 IF F1(I)>=510 AND F1(I)<=630 AND F2(I)>=780 AND F2(I)<=900
    AND F3(I)>=2350 AND F3(I)<=2470 THEN PH$(I)="AW":GOTO 1000
200 IF F1(I)>=380 AND F1(I)<=500 AND F2(I)>=960 AND F2(I)<=1080
    AND F3(I)>=2180 AND F3(I)<=2300 THEN PH$(I)="U":GOTO 1000
210 IF F1(I)>=240 AND F1(I)<=360 AND F2(I)>=810 AND F2(I)<=930
    AND F3(I)>=2180 AND F3(I)<=2300 THEN PH$(I)="00":GOTO 1000
220 IF F1(I)>=580 AND F1(I)<=700 AND F2(I)>=1130 AND F2(I)<=125
    0 AND F3(I)>=2330 AND F3(I)<=2450 THEN PH$(I)="UH":GOTO 1000
230 IF F1(I)>=430 AND F1(I)<=550 AND F2(I)>=1290 AND F2(I)<=141
    0 AND F3(I)>=1630 AND F3(I)<=1750 THEN PH$(I)="ER":GOTO 1000
1000 IF PH$(I)<>PH$(I-1) THEN WD$=WD$+PH$(I)+" "
1010 NEXT I
1015 PRINT"OUTPUTTING PHONEME SEQUENCE ..."
1018 PRINT:PRINT
1020 PRINTWD$
1030 IF WD$="L EE N " THEN VOC$="LEAN"
1035 IF WD$="M EE N " THEN VOC$="MEAN"
1040 IF WD$="R EE NG " THEN VOC$="RING"
1080 PRINT
1090 PRINT" VOCABULARY WORD =";VOC$
1095 PRINT:PRINT:PRINT:
1100 PRINT"END"
```

answer after inputting the desired data will be left as a surprise for you. Or you may see if you can visually figure out which word is being spoken based on the formant frequency tables in Chapter 2. The program in Listing 6-1 is really nothing more than a table lookup program for comparing values of incoming formant frequency groups. (As the program asks you for formant frequencies, simply enter the number that most accurately represents each formant frequency at that frame time.)

So if you have a computer algorithm which generates FFTs from speech input and can then very accurately predict the center ranges of the three formant frequencies, then that program combined with a program similar to Listing 6-1 will provide truly accurate speech recognition of isolated words. The vocabulary in Listing 6-1 can be expanded by simply adding the new words with their phoneme equivalent. Although the total program running time is somewhat slow, the illustration of recognition is definite.

Envelope Contours

The shape of the speech envelope, while not tremendously informative in terms of speech information, can be used as a feature for speech recognition. Since the formant based recognition system will have trouble with fricative sounds such as s, t, f, p, etc., there must be some supplementary means for identifying and classifying these fricative sounds. One possible way is through the use of envelope contour classification of the noise characteristics of each fricative utterance. While the envelope contour will not give by itself sufficient information for fricative identification, it may be used in conjunction with other extracted features to classify and identify the fricative types.

If you experimented with the program in Listing 6-1, you may have noticed that as you begin to extemporize with new speech sounds involving *noise,* that the program tends to know when the plosive sounds, p, t, and k, are spoken. It knows this because these plosives are normally produced by a noise preceded by a short period of silence or a pause in speech. To distinguish which of these plosives is the one being spoken, other features may be utilized such as envelope contours and resonance humps to determine their exact identity.

The envelope contour of a speech signal is found by simply measuring the maximum amplitude of speech over a given frame of time. These maximum values are then connected together to form a contour that quantitatively yields amplitude information about a speech signal. If a word is spoken louder than a previous utterance, then the contour will have a greater height, but the general shape should remain somewhat the same. All of these features and details of features may be utilized in a recognition system to match vocabulary words and thus produce speech recognition.

Finding the Match (or Pattern Matching)

The second class of speech recognition considered to be a valid method is known as template or pattern matching. In this process, rather than extracting features and attempting to compare these with vocabulary features, the system compares the spoken utterance in a more global form. The true mechanism of pattern matching is very similar to holding two speech spectrograms side by side and trying to visually determine if the darkened areas in each match, and thus indicate an identity between the two spoken utterances. There are several methods of doing this, but two provide the best accuracy with associated speech. These are: template searching and chain code matching.

Template Searching

A crude but effective method of template matching can be performed by simply trying to match a spectrogram of an utterance against the spectrograms of all reference vocabulary utterances. An example of how this might be accomplished is shown in Fig. 6-4. Fig. 6-4A represents

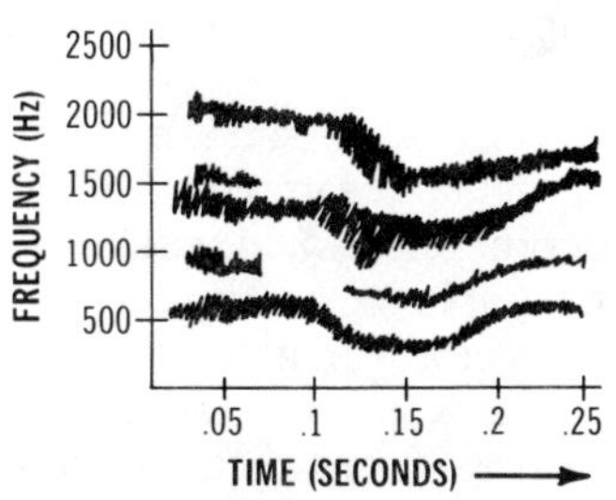

(A) Pattern for matching.

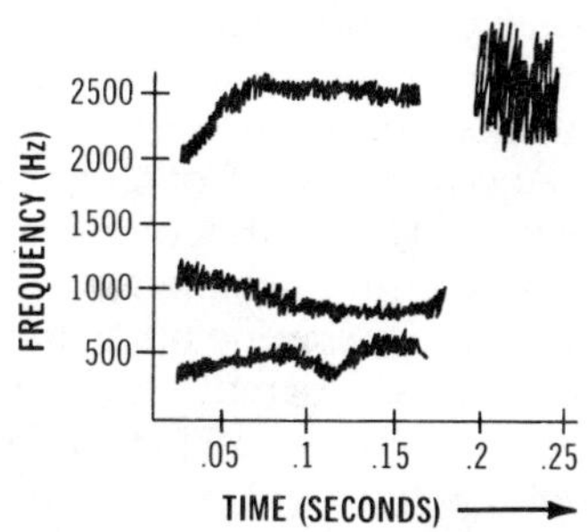

(B) Reference vocabulary 1.

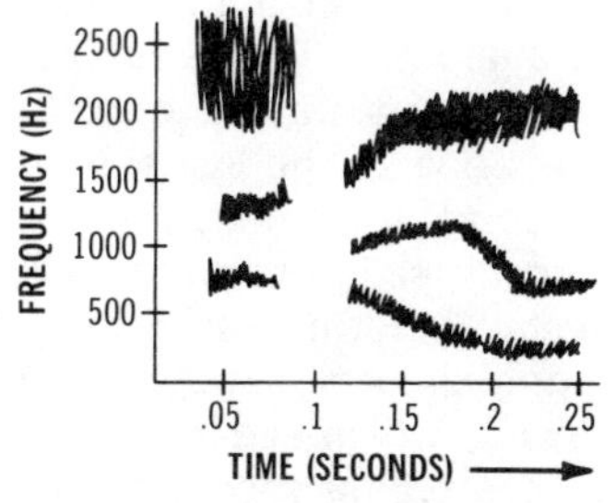

(C) Reference vocabulary 2.

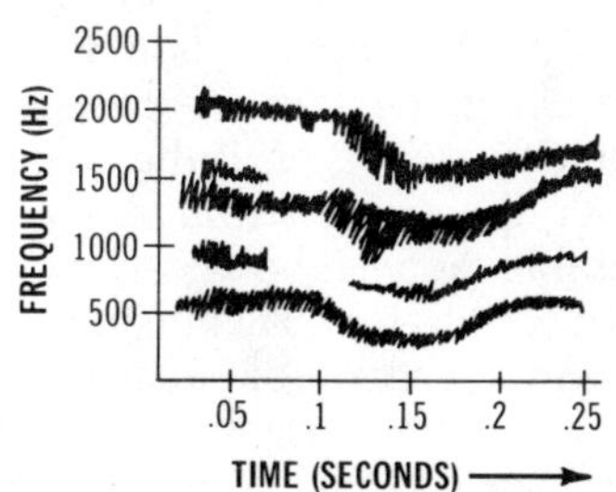

(D) Reference vocabulary 3.

Figure 6-4.
A template matching example.

the incoming spectrogram to be matched against the internally stored vocabulary spectrograms. Consider those to be as shown in Figs. 6-4B, C, and D. Since the resolution of this figure is relatively high, the storage of these spectrograms in memory would be very expensive and wasteful, but, at the same time, if you scan the incoming pattern against the three referenced vocabulary words, you might visually say that the match is Fig. 6-4D. This would be correct as the most accurate match. More realistically, the computer would break the spectrograms up into a coarser grid, for instance maybe ten by ten squares so that there are only 100 numbers in a matrix needed to compare the spoken utterances. The wasteful part of this process is that many of the numbers in the 10 by 10 grid would be effectively 0 (the white areas) so that a very large amount of storage is being wasted with no information. This is one reason for using feature-based recognition over template matching. As the number of squares is further reduced, the speed of matching the patterns will increase; however, there will be more misidentified utterances created in the process. There is also the problem of the time difference in speaking each word twice. The stored vocabulary word may have been spoken at a relatively slow rate while the incoming word has been spoken at a quicker rate. The spectrograms will look similar except they will be compressed in time relative to the referenced word. This is where the dynamic time warping mechanism becomes important in comparing and matching the given speech templates.

Another method of template matching which may be used is a direct speech waveform comparison to compare analog sampled values against stored sampled values. This can become extremely inefficient for memory storage but at the same time the complexity of the program eases. The inherent disadvantage in direct waveform matching lies in the time required to perform the match. Consider a speech input signal that is sampled at 8 kHz per second. If an average word requires one-half second to be spoken, then there are 4,000 samples to be compared for each stored vocabulary word. Given a vocabulary of 100 words, this means that for each incoming word there must be at a maximum 400,000 comparisons made. If the stored waveform is identified correctly at the start of the table, then the system appears to operate quickly; however, if the reference waveform is one of the last stored, then the operator may have to wait many seconds for a match. It is a usable system; however, variations in time and speech utterances will cause extreme difficulty in the process of direct waveform matching.

Another form of pattern matching which approximates that of feature extraction and classification relies on the principle which eliminates the storage of small values (the white areas) in comparing spectrograms. The process is known as chain coding of patterns which proves very efficient in speech recognition systems.

Chain Code Matching

This is one of the more powerful algorithms in pattern recognition. It utilizes a principle involving neighborhoods and nearest neighbors. It is a form of feature extraction; however, the features are carried as chain codes rather than formant tracks or even pitch tracks. The storage of chain codes in memory is highly efficient so this becomes an attractive alternative toward speech recognition methods.

The process of chain code generation is a relatively simple one as shown in Fig. 6-5. In Fig. 6-5A, a portion of a spectrogram is depicted which might be the upper formant frequency F3 track. Before the chain coding can begin, the computer must determine a centroid point within the darkened track toward the left end of the shape. Now, the computer must consider the spectrogram to be somewhat like an image by depicting it to be X by Y pixels for image segmentation. The intent of chain code processing is the determination of the boundary edge of the formant track under examination. The procedure is shown in Fig. 6-5B. Notice that the 0 pixel is the median point of the track chosen arbitrarily by the computer. It then begins to drop in a search for the first pixel which does not contain a neighboring pixel above the present formant track threshold value. This occurs at pixel 3 in the chain (if the search continued further, the next pixel value would be 0). At this point, the chain code generation begins by stepping arbitrarily in a clockwise or counterclockwise direction. In this model, the stepped direction is clockwise. Once a direction has been chosen, *it should be the same for all chain-coded patterns.*

From pixel 3, the clockwise step to the next pixel over threshold with the least neighbors over threshold yields pixel No. 4. Since this movement is a step to the left and down, using the chain code *legend* in Fig. 6-5C, it has a *direction value* of 5. Again, the process steps from pixel 4 to pixel 5 yielding the same direction; so again the chain acquires a 5 for the direction value. The next link in the chain is a step to the left yielding a direction value of 6 from pixel 5 to pixel 6. The process repeats until the completed chain code has been generated for the entire enclosed pattern (back to pixel 88). Thus, the chain code generated for the example pattern in Fig. 6-5 would have the form: (5, 5, 6, 7, 7, 0, 0, 1, 1, 1, 1, 2, 2, 2, 2, 2, 2, 1, 2, etc.). A more efficient manner of packing the chain code would be to describe the directional vectors in terms of two-dimensional matrices. Thus, the chain code could be set up with a group of paired numbers like (n, d). For each pair, the *n* is the *number* of direction vectors which are sequentially identical and *d* is the *direction value* of the vector or vectors. Since even our example has a large number of identical vectors together, this would save considerable time in most any pattern classification algorithm. If there are five vectors in a row with a direction value of 1, then the chain code pair for

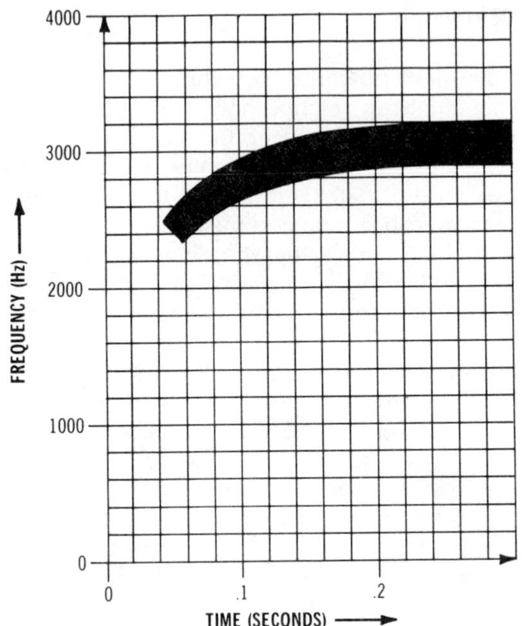

(A) Portion of a spectrogram.

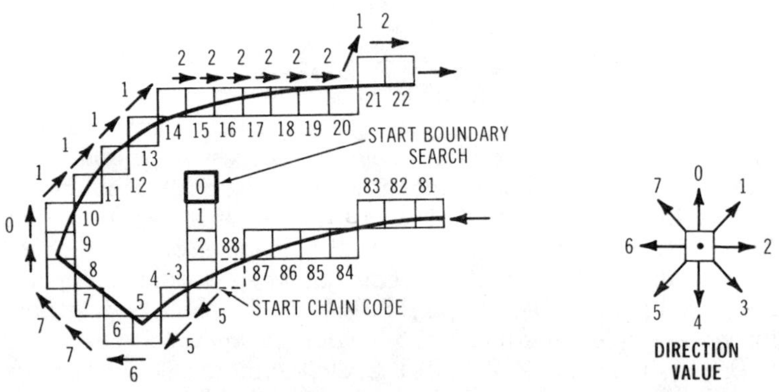

(B) Chain code generation.   (C) Chain code legend.

Figure 6-5.
The chain code generation process.

that chain would be (5, 1). The more compact chain code description
of the example in Fig. 6-5 would take the form: (2, 5) (1, 6) (2, 7)
(2, 0) (4, 1) (6, 2) (1, 1) (etc.). This shows that the previous chain code
sequence has been shortened considerably in length by simply encod-

ing the chain code pattern as the number of unit lengths and direction of each equidirectional grouping.

The process that has been described is that of pattern boundary measurement. Rather than store the entire spectrogram for later comparison with other spectrograms, only the major pattern features of the spectrogram boundaries have been stored. These can be matched against other words more quickly than matching the entire X by Y pixel matrix of a speech spectrogram.

Since the illustration given above yields a chain code for only one formant frequency track, the remaining two or three formants must also be chain coded for each stored word. The process of coding these spectrographic features is identical to that given above. What will result from the coding process of each spectrogram will be three or four sets of chain codes which may be used to compare incoming word boundaries. Although the computation seems more complex by searching for value regions in spectrographic information, the computer time utilized is much more efficient than simply performing an X by Y scan comparison of one spectrogram against another. The time saved will be considerable with very little loss in accuracy or recognition resolution. An important characteristic of this process to notice is that we have, by chain code generation, extracted features (the chain code) from an incoming speech waveform which are not directly relatable to the speech signal itself. This is why feature-based speech recognition and pattern template matching recognition exist with considerable crossover between the two methods. As previously mentioned, feature-based recognition uses speech features like pitch, formant frequencies, envelope contours, noise levels, etc., rather than chain codes. These are then template matched against other stored vocabulary words. The template matching process described here also extracts some features (to be more efficient) but these are features of boundary values and shapes, not directly correlatable with speech characteristics. Thus, there are intertwined feature and template matching processes in either of these two classes of recognition.

Alternative Algorithms

The general flow of the speech-recognition process formulated during the first part of this chapter resembles the flow diagram in Fig. 6-6. Although the functions of this flowchart attempt to make no inferences about the semantic or contextual content of a message, they do identify words, phrases, and sentences for subsequent parsing and interpretation.

Each of the blocks within the flow has, off to the side, the generalized results from the specific process. In certain types of speech recognition, some of these processes are omitted, producing a shortened recognition diagram. There are also other means of recognizing speech which differ

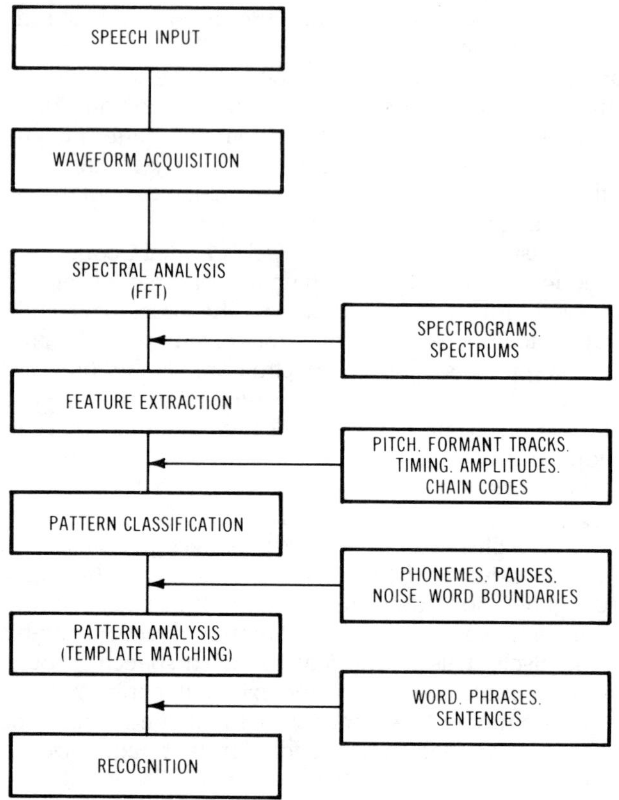

Figure 6-6.
A general speech recognition flow diagram.

markedly from the general flow by utilizing more unorthodox procedures for pattern matching and speech phrase identification.

One of these algorithms which departs from the previous flow diagram is shown in Fig. 6-7. The recognition procedure illustrated here is based upon LPC (linear predictive coding) filtering of incoming speech. This process (utilized primarily by Texas Instruments), mathematically filters an incoming speech signal into 20-millisecond segments to provide a time series of ten-LPC-coefficient frames. The output of the LPC filter yields ten filter values for each 20 milliseconds of speech (500 values per second). Then, the values are compared against the sequentially stored LPC coefficients of the vocabulary words in an inverse filtering operation to determine the closest match. TI has found that a match between every other sample is sufficient for speech recognition so there are only 250 matches per second of speech required. This must, of course, be done for each vocabulary word, so as the vocabulary increases, so does the recognition time.

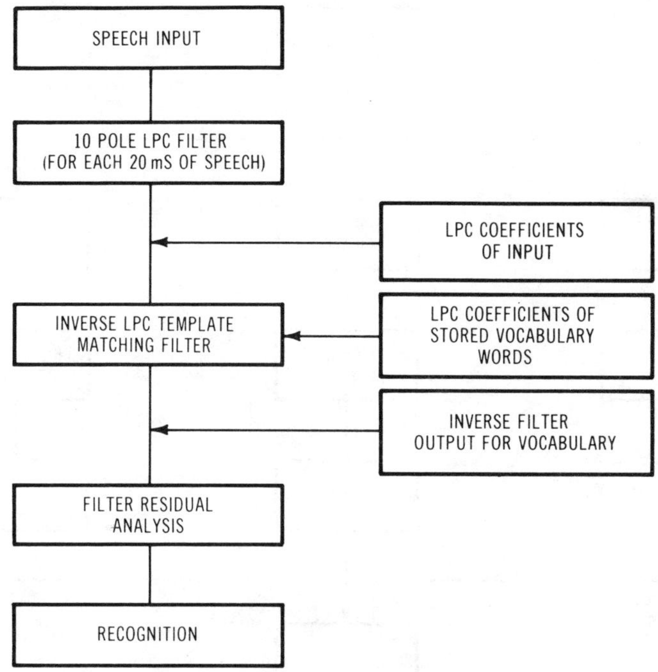

Figure 6-7.
LPC-based speech recognition.

The output of the template-matching inverse LPC filter is analyzed for least signal activity—or the most number of inverse matches—which indicates the closest vocabulary match. Thus, the phrase or word is recognized in a process similar to feature extraction and template matching with the features being LPC codes of speech.

Another method of speech recognition which is more hardware dependent but simpler in terms of computer operations is the zero crossing speech recognition process shown in Fig. 6-8. It is very similar to the spectral analysis method presented in Fig. 6-6; however, the filtering of three major passbands attempts to separate each formant frequency from the speech signal. The output of each bandpass filter is then compared for zero crossing (when the signal goes through a dc zero value) and the number of these crossings is then counted for preset periods of time. The system effectively becomes three frequency counters which attempt to measure the frequency of each formant track over time. The template matching process which follows the three counters has to match only three values for each selected speech frame. Notice that there is no speech digitization or spectral analysis algorithm needed here. The process is fast and can perform real-time speech recognition at extremely low cost.

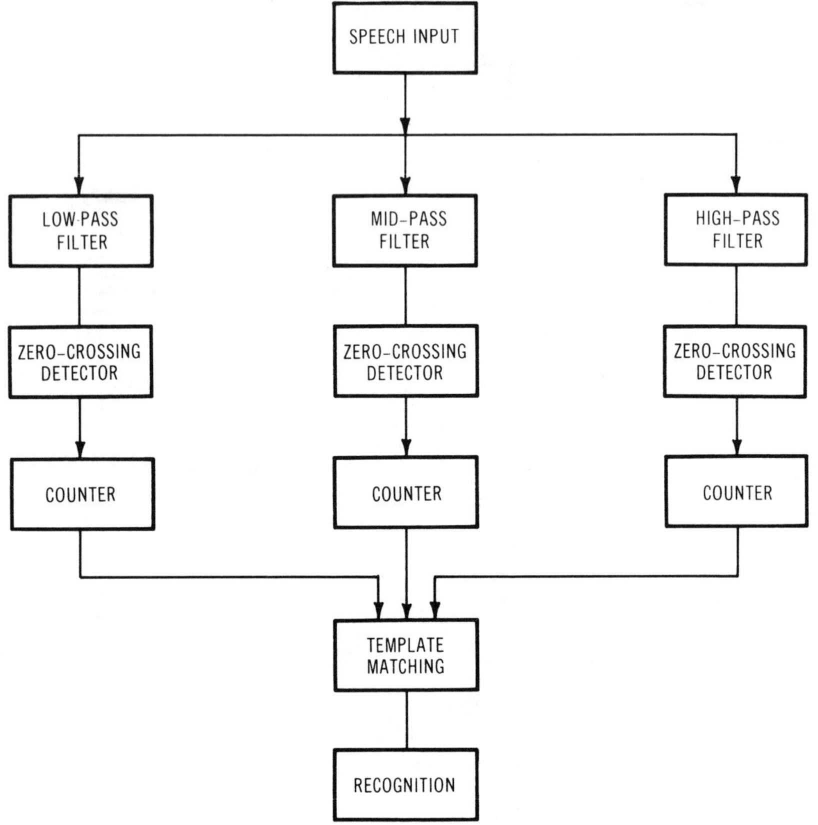

Figure 6-8.
Zero-crossing speech recognition.

There are more speech-recognition algorithms in use than those presented here. However, these are usually some form of the previous methods. The exact choice of how the recognition is performed should be based upon the desired system cost and performance accuracy needed.

Now that we have seen how to identify words and phrases, we must move our examination to determine, during the recognition process, what to do with these words and phrases. This is where the computer must really begin to think. The computer activity termed "transaction interpretation" or "speech interpretation" must analyze what we mean, by what we say. Although not so important in isolated word recognition, the interpretation process becomes a matter of necessity when we begin to evaluate and recognize connected speech. We also begin to get our first glimpse into the world of artificial intelligence in computers.

CHAPTER 7

From Words to Actions (Interpreting Commands)

We reside in an age of wonder. The generations of people alive on this earth today have seen more technological achievements in ten years than each of the preceding generations has seen in a lifetime. And, with the conquest of each new challenge, our expectations increase. Many of you reading this book experienced the introduction of the electronic hand-held calculator. Remember the first time you held one in your hand and glanced over at the nearby slide rule? Well, that was in the mid-1960s. Ten years later the microprocessor was undergoing integration into our society. Within five years from that time, personal computers with computing capabilities greater than the first vacuum tube monstrosities were on sale at almost every street corner throughout the country. We are now approaching the next five-year period. What will it bring?

One of the major drives in technological research during the current period is that of implementing a form of reasoning and intelligent behavior in computing machinery. Although research has been going on some 26 years, for many of those years it was cloaked under the secrecy of government research. Just recently, in April 1982, the Japanese Ministry of International Trade and Industry (MITI) announced the creation of the Fifth Generation Computer Systems Project. The ultimate goals for this supercomputer will be natural speech conversation—probably Japanese—a voice-activated typewriter with speaker independence and a vocabulary near 10,000 words, a Japanese translating computer which can translate up to 100,000 words into the other major world languages, and finally an optical character reader system which can read written Japanese pictographic characters.

Among the general plans for the Fifth Generation project, the Japanese hope to create within the machine, in addition to the visual and auditory senses, a sense of inferential reasoning. This is one of the major hues in the artificial intelligence rainbow. At the rainbow's end lies a network of Fifth Generation computers, all talking to each other faster than we can comprehend, with ideas passing among them above our level of understanding. (Remember the computer interchange in the movie *The Forbin Project?*)

The proclamation by the Japanese government has set off a veritable avalanche in computer intelligence research. In response to the Japanese "challenge," a number of U.S. firms have voluntarily formed, through the auspices of the sponsoring corporations, an intensive research project in Austin, Texas to be known as MCC (the Microelectronics and Computer Technology Corporation), a rather unassuming name. The goal of this organization, which will employ among its permanent staff some of the world's leading experts in computer technology and artificial intelligence, is to build an equivalent U.S. supercomputer. Their positions at MCC are temporary, however. The major electronic corporations involved in this endeavor have agreed to donate experts for certain periods of time to interact with others present during the interim. The outcome of the potpourri of expert knowledge should be interesting to say the least.

As I read the reports on the Fifth Generation project and sit in wonderment about the fate of the human race as a secondary intelligence, I also secretly ponder those previous four generations of computers which teamed together to spawn this upcoming pedagogue. For the record, computer genealogy lists the predecessors in the following order. The first generation computers used vacuum tubes to fill their rooms with computing power. In the 1940s, the ENIAC computer was developed at the Moore School of the University of Pennsylvania for the purpose of calculating bombing tables for the military. The Rand UNIVAC computer was also very prevalent during this generation.

The second generation computers came soon after the invention of the transistor and filled the same computing space with transistors, thus giving a much larger computational force. IBM was around at this time and had many of the first transistor computers in the second tier of the family tree.

The third generation of computers was based upon the integrated circuit and, to a considerable extent, still exists in today's computing palaces. Almost every major computer manufacturer can be listed as a third generation manufacturer.

The fourth generation of computing machinery is the supercomputer. It will most likely spend the next ten years maturing. Its reliance on very large-scale integrated circuits (VLSI) and extremely compact circuit spacing (the speed of light through an inch of wire will slow these computers) dictates that they must be designed by other computers.

Manufacturing contenders in this area appear to be CRAY, Control Data Corporation (CDC) with the Cyber line of computers, and possibly IBM.

The fifth generation will take the technology from the fourth and through very complex networking produce parallel processors with array sizes in the range of 16K and up. Remember, these are CPU arrays and not memory arrays! A typical goal is to reach 1 *billion* instructions per second!

With all of the interest in computing hardware, there is also a very strong software drive. The two fields have a symbiosis. The software predecessors leading to inferential reasoning in the fifth generation computers have had a rather interesting background. It has not always been popular to consider the field of reasoning computers a realistic challenge.

Old McCarthy Had a Forum, AI? AI. Oh!

The relationship between computer speech recognition and artificial intelligence lies in the natural language processing involved in the interpretation of connected speech. As we work with the technical terminology which rolls rather smoothly from our tongues, there is considerable human interest behind the creation of the field of artificial intelligence. It is really quite hard to say whether the Dartmouth Conference was the beginning or the end of an age. What really happened during the summer of 1956 on the peaceful campus at Dartmouth College in Hanover, New Hampshire, was the awakening of a sleeping giant.

The meeting had come about through a proposal for a two-month, ten-man study of machine intelligence by a group of four expert scientists to the Rockefeller Foundation. The main organizer, John McCarthy, envisioned a retreat atmosphere with total devotion to the subject. His influence on the college as an assistant professor of mathematics provided the location. The other three equally important members on the chartering committee included Marvin Minsky at Harvard with interests in mathematics and neurology, Nathaniel Rochester, working at the IBM research center on information research, and Claude Shannon, a Bell Telephone Laboratories mathematician.

The Rockefeller Foundation did in fact fund the seminar with an endowment of around $8,000. Other participants in the meeting were Herbert A. Simon, Allen Newell, Arthur Samuel, Oliver Selfridge, Trenchard More, Ray Solomonoff, Alex Bernstein, and a few other prestigious visitors.

The proceedings of the forum were not quite as organized as the creators had envisioned. Reluctance to expose previous research and experimental endeavors continuously slowed the exchange of information between the scientists. However, the conference did perform the venerable task of naming the field of study in germination (artificial intelligence). It came about through the original conference name: The Dartmouth Summer Research Project in Artificial Intelligence. The name was not unanimously received. Some scientists at the conference felt that the term "artificial" was derogatory and continued searching for other more respectable names. Nevertheless, the original title created by McCarthy stuck. We now have a field of computer science concentrating on computational reasoning called artificial intelligence.

It should be noted that none of the participants in the original forum were novices in the field of machine intelligence. Most of them had been working or interested in the field for many years prior to that time. In fact, they were chosen for this meeting with their prior knowledge to form the nucleus of forthcoming research in machine intelligence. As evidence, Allen Newell, J. C. Shaw, and Herbert Simon were the primary creators of a computer language for machine intelligence in 1956 known as IPL (**I**nformation **P**rocessing **L**anguage). Shortly thereafter, a second language was created primarily by John McCarthy called LISP (**Lis**t **P**rocessing). McCarthy created a language which has often been quoted as being one of two classes of programming languages: LISP and all the other programming languages. LISP provides us with a tool for processing spoken English which is still contemporary with its peer languages. The principles of LISP are used not only to evaluate the semantics and syntax of spoken messages, but also in the complex process of pattern recognition and feature extraction described in the previous chapter.

It was a good year, 1956. The world of computing has changed in evolutionary cycles since then. The vintage bottling of artificial intelligence will be truly ready for testing in the mid-1990s. Then its time will be right.

Transaction Interpretation

In Chapter 3, we learned about semantic and syntactic interpretation of phrases. The intent of that chapter was to explain the complexities of evaluating the English language during interpretation. As we couple the interpretation process with the next logical "words to actions" process, we have a speech-recognition function which is referred to as speech transaction interpretation. A speech transaction with the computer may be visualized by referring to Fig. 7-1. This rather simple diagram illustrates the connection of the speech-recognition system with an interpretation computer—which may be the same computer—to convert spoken messages or commands into the desired actions.

In the most elementary terms, the transaction process consists of the handshaking interaction which must occur between the human and the computer during the desired speech input transaction. Exactly how this

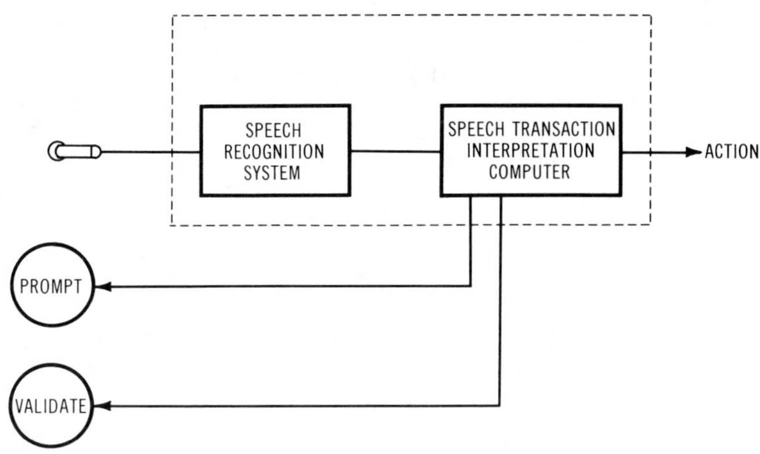

Figure 7-1.
A transaction interpretation process.

is accomplished is ultimately left up to the user; however, a few guidelines are helpful as a baseline starting point. First of all, the operator must be told when the computer is expecting a speech message. This is usually performed with some form of prompting message from the computer. It may be visual as in a lighted indicator or crt message, or acoustic through a voice-response system. If the operator is visually *unable* to observe a prompting message, then the speech-response system provides an ideal human interaction method. A typical prompting message could be something as simple as "please input speech command" or "ready." This provides the speech transaction operator with the cue to begin speaking. If we assume that the computer has already been vocabulary trained (this is a speech transaction process in itself), then upon hearing the operator's command, the computer must interpret the message according to internally programmed rules. It should then return to the operator for message verification or validation. In this case, as in the previously mentioned transaction step, feedback to the operator concerning the computer's interpretation of the command is highly desirable before the action is started. If the vocabulary words are stored within a template memory for recognition, then it is a relatively simple matter to also store the voice response equivalents for the same words. In this manner, the computer may aurally query the operator with an echoed message command so that the final speech-based decision (on whether to proceed or not) is based on a simple *yes* or *no*. Since the difficulty in separating these two commands is relatively trivial, there is a high probability of correct message interpretation. As a consequence of the handshaking between the computer and human operator, the transaction time is approximately doubled; but, if the transaction is not time critical, this is the best way to go.

If the speech system operator has at his command a crt and key-board, then the interpreted speech can be fed back through a printed message on the screen requiring either a Y or N typed response. But in a more practical situation, the speech transaction should be kept in an aural mode so that the total operator interfaces are a microphone and headset or loudspeaker. Suppose, for example, that an automobile rental agency at the local airport has replaced the normal rental counter with a speech-activated panel for ordering the rent cars. As you approach the stainless steel wall panel, you insert a credit card that provides the computer with your identity and an indication of your presence. The hypothetical speech transaction that would follow might be something like this.

Computer   Welcome to the Hertz automatic car rental system. We currently have Chevrolets, Pontiacs, Oldsmobiles, and Chryslers available for rental at this location. Which one would you like?

You   Pontiac.

Computer   Is Pontiac correct?

You   Yes.

Computer   Would you like a compact, mid-, or full-size Pontiac?

You   Mid-sized.

Computer   Will a Pontiac Firebird be satisfactory?

You   Yes.

Computer   We have Firebirds in black, grey, and red. Do you have a preference for color?

You   Black.

Computer   Thank you. Your black Pontiac Firebird is parked on Row 3 in Slot 31 in the Hertz lot. How many days do you wish to rent the car?

You   . . .

The preceding hypothetical speech transaction accomplished in a few short words the desired outcome. Each step of the transaction was verified through operator interaction to be correct according to his desires. There are, of course, alternative transactions which would also involve speech. For instance, the complete inventory of cars available on the lot might be shown numbered on a crt screen and the renter asked to state the number of the car he desires. This would, in one spoken utterance, classify the make of the car, its size, and color. For instance, as the renter scans a crt screen, he might see the following:

12   Blue Oldsmobile Cutlass
13   Grey Pontiac Firebird
14   Red Pontiac Firebird

15   Black Pontiac Firebird
16   Green Chrysler Cordoba

In this type of speech operating system, to rent the same car as above, you would simply say "fifteen." But now the system has grown so much in complexity that included in the rental electronics is a crt which must be serviced and maintained. Initial cost and maintenance trade-offs between the systems will ultimately determine which method will be used. Obviously the speech-related software costs for the first system will be much higher than for those of the second.

The major idea behind this section on transaction interpretation is the necessity of a continual feedback to the operator for verification of correct entry. This process will not seem unusual to the human user because we are accustomed to the same type of feedback from other humans. In the case of transactions such as those mentioned above, feedback becomes even more important to ensure that the user is satisfied with the ultimate transaction.

Speech Input Operating Systems

During complex speech interactions like those presented in the previous section, the computer must have a transaction capability in software to recognize spoken commands and phrases. The software that operates these computers is normally in the form of an operating system which relies on natural language for its fundamental data transfer. Considerable work has been done in this area through research in artificial intelligence. The foundation behind all of the AI natural language systems is a software "subroutine" referred to as an augmented transition network (ATN). The concept of an ATN is straightforward, based upon sentence parsing through recursion. The term "recurse" as applied to software means a software system which calls itself repeatedly until finished. The variable storage which must somehow be organized through multiple self-calls relies upon stack-type operations which are called "stack pushes" and "stack pops." The mechanism behind the ATN is probably more easily understood by viewing the simplified software flowchart in Fig. 7-2. The trace simulation shows how the augmented transition network accepts the sentence "The computer has a voice," and by scanning from left to right accepts noun phrases and verbs based upon preprogrammed algorithms.

The augmented transition network is an almost universal method of parsing natural language phrases and sentences, and is typically written in the computer language of LISP. Programs have been written in LISP that attempt to understand keyboard-entry natural language and provide some semantic interpretation from the messages. A program written in 1972 at the Massachusetts Institute of Technology (MIT) has

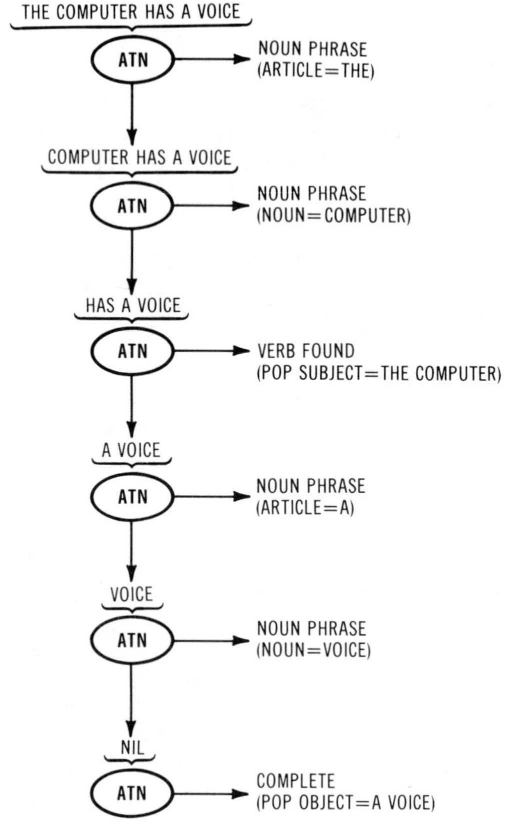

Figure 7-2.
An augmented transition network trace simulation.

become rather famous for its manipulation of geometrical shapes based upon natural language input commands. The natural language processing system SHRDLU was written in LISP by Terry Winograd as a doctoral research dissertation subject. Based upon statements like "move the blue block which is on the red block into the cube," the computer graphically picks up the identified blue block and, through animated computer graphics simulating a small crane from the top of the screen, places the block within the commanded cube. The program also allows statements that provide comparative references such as moving the tallest or largest cube or even deciding which objects lie behind, in front of, or on top of other objects. The software system is quite sophisticated and impressive to observe in action. And, although it does not rely on spoken inputs, it does accept natural language keyboard statements and even learns new commands and words during an instruction session.

Listing 7-1.
A Parsing Program for English That Learns.

```
1 REM LISTING 7-1 -- A PARSING PROGRAM FOR ENGLISH
2 DIM PROP$(20,30),AR(30)
3 DIM VOC$(30),MP(30),NP(30),PP(30),VP(30),AP(30),JP(30),IP(30)
  ,VT(30),W$(20)
5 VOC$(0)="NIL"
6 VOC$(1)="NOT":VC=1
7 AP(1)=1
9 GOTO995
10 PRINT:PRINT:PRINT"PLEASE HELP ME LEARN A NEW WORD"
20 Q$="NEW WORD= ":GOSUB 2005
25 VC=VC+1
30 GOSUB 1000
35 IF FOUND=1 THENPRINT"I KNOW THAT WORD ALREADY..NEXT PLEASE":
   GOTO20
38 IF FOUND=0 THEN VOC$(VC)=ANS$
40 REM NOW LEARN THE WORD
50 Q$=" A NOUN":GOSUB 2000
55 NP(VC)=R:IF R=1 GOTO200
60 Q$=" A PRONOUN":GOSUB 2000
65 PP(VC)=R:IF R=1 GOTO 200
80 Q$=" A VERB":GOSUB 2000
90 VP(VC)=R:IF R=1 GOTO 200
100 Q$=" AN MODIFIER":GOSUB 2000
110 AP(VC)=R:IF R=1 GOTO 200
120 Q$=" A PREPOSITION OR CONJUNCTION":GOSUB 2000
125 JP(VC)=R:IF R=1 GOTO 200
130 Q$=" AN INTERJECTION":GOSUB 2000
135 IP(VC)=R:IF R=1 GOTO 200
140 Q$=" AN ARTICLE":GOSUB 2000
145 AR(VC)=R:IF R=1 GOTO 200
200 REM NOW FIND OUT MORE
210 IF NP(VC)=0 THEN 220
211 Q$="(1)COMMON (2)PROPER (3)COLLECTIVE (4)ABSTRACT":GOSUB 20
    00
212 NP(VC)=VAL(ANS$)
220 IF PP(VC)=0 THEN 230
221 Q$="(1)PERSONAL (2)POSSESSIVE (3)DEMONSTRATIVE (4)INTERROGA
    TIVE (5)RELATIVE (6)INDEFINITE":GOSUB 2000
222 PP(VC)=VAL(ANS$)
230 IFVP(VC)=0 THEN 240
231 Q$="(1)ACTION VERB (2)BEING VERB (3)HELPING VERB":GOSUB 200
    0
232 VP(VC)=VAL(ANS$)
233 Q$="(1)PRESENT (2)PAST (3)FUTURE  TENSE":GOSUB 2000
234 VT(VC)=VAL(ANS$)
260 RETURN
990 Q$="WANT TO ADD MORE":GOSUB 2005:RETURN
993 IF R=0 THEN 996
995 GOSUB 10:GOSUB 500:IF R=1 THEN 995
996 GOSUB 3000
998 GOTO 3050
999 REM
1000 REM WORD FINDER SUBROUTINE
1001 TMP$=ANS$
1002 RC=0:RMD$=""
```

Listing 7-1—Continued
A Parsing Program for English That Learns.

```
1003 IF LEN(ANS$)<=2 THEN RC=2
1005 FOUND=0
1010 FOR WC=0 TO VC
1015 IF FOUND=1 THEN 1030
1020 IF VOC$(WC)=ANS$THEN FOUND=1:VP=WC
1030 NEXT WC
1040 IF FOUND=0 AND RC<2 THEN RMD$=RMD$+RIGHT$(ANS$,1): ANS$=LE
     FT$(ANS$,LEN(ANS$)-1):RC=RC+1:GOTO 1005
1042 IF RMD$=""THEN 1045
1043 IFRMD$<>"SE"AND  RMD$<>"S"AND RMD$<>"D"AND RMD$<>"DE"AND R
     MD$<>"S'" THEN FOUND=0
1045 IF FOUND=0 THEN ANS$=TMP$
1050 RETURN
2000 PRINT"IS IT";
2005 PRINTQ$;:INPUT ANS$
2010 IF ANS$="N"OR ANS$="NO" THEN R=0ELSER=1
2020 RETURN
3000 PRINT"-----------------------------------------------":Q$="OK TRY
     A SENTENCE":GOSUB 2005:QM=0
3001 IF RIGHT$(ANS$,1)="?"THEN ANS$=LEFT$(ANS$,LEN(ANS$)-1):QM=
     1
3003 PC=0
3004 FORX=0 TO 10:W$(X)="":NEXT X
3005 FOR SL=1 TO LEN(ANS$)
3007 PS$=MID$(ANS$,SL,1)
3010 IF PS$<>" " THEN W$(PC)=W$(PC)+PS$
3020 IF PS$=" " THEN PC=PC+1
3030 NEXT SL:RETURN
3050 FOR I=0 TO PC
3044 ANS$=W$(I):GOSUB 1000
3070 IF FOUND=0 THEN PRINT"I DON'T KNOW THE WORD:";W$(I):WP(I)=
     0:ELSE 3075
3072 Q$="WOULD YOU LIKE TO ADD IT":GOSUB 2005:IF R=0 THEN 3075
3073 NF=1:PRINT:ANS$=W$(I):PRINT"FOR WORD ";W$(I);":":PRINT:GOS
     UB 25:GOSUB500:IFR=1THEN 995
3074 ANS$=W$(I):GOSUB 1000:NF=0
3075 IF FOUND=1 THEN WP(I)=VP
3080 NEXT I:IFI=1AND FOUND=0THEN 996
3085 GOTO 3160
3090 FOR I= 0 TO PC
3095 IF VOC$(WP(I))="NIL"THEN3150
3097 IF MP(WP(I))=0 THEN 3150
3100 PRINT"PROPERTIES OF ";VOC$(WP(I));" ARE:"
3110 FOR IX=0 TO MP(WP(I))
3120 PRINTPROP$(IX,WP(I))
3130 NEXT IX
3150 NEXT I
3160 NT=0
3200 IF QM=0 THENPRINT"********** SENTENCE DIAGRAM **********":
     PRINT:PRINT
3210 FOR I=0 TO PC
3220 GOSUB 6000
3230 IF QM=0 THEN PRINTWD$;
3235 NEXT I
3240 PRINT
3300 IF QM=0 THEN PRINT"*********************************************"
```

Listing 7-1—Continued
A Parsing Program for English That Learns.

```
3305 AQ=0:SUB$="":OBJ$="":VERB$="":SUB=1:SI=0:OI=0:VI=0
3310 FOR I=0 TO PC
3340 IF SP(I)=2 AND QM=1 THEN AQ=1:VERB$=VOC$(WP(I)):SUB=0:VI=W
     P(I):VW=I
3350 IF SP(I)=2 AND QM=0 THEN SUB=0:VERB$=VOC$(WP(I)):VI=WP(I):
     VW=I
3360 IF SUB=1 AND(SP(I)=1OR SP(I)=4  OR SP(I)=3 )THEN SUB$=VOC$
     (WP(I)):SI=WP(I):SW=I
3365 IF WP(I)=1 THEN NT=1
3370 IF SUB=0 AND(SP(I)=1 OR SP(I)=4  OR SP(I)=3 )THEN OBJ$=VOC
     $(WP(I)):OI=WP(I):OW=I
3372 IF QM=0 THEN PRINTVOC$(WP(I))+" ";
3375 NEXT I
3378 IF QM=0 THEN PRINT:PRINT:PRINT".......... SENTENCE PARSE .
     ........."
3380 IF QM=0 THEN PRINT "SUB=";SUB$,"OBJ=";OBJ$,"VERB=";VERB$
3385 IFAQ=1 THEN GOSUB 7000:GOTO996
3400 PL=MP(SI):T1=0
3401 IF OBJ$="" THEN 3500
3405 CHK$=OBJ$
3409 ZZ=SI:GOSUB8000
3410 IF AQ=0 AND PF=0 THEN PROP$(PL,SI)=OBJ$+"."ELSE 3425
3415 IF NT=1 THEN PROP$(PL,SI)=PROP$(PL,SI)+"-."
3420 PL=PL+1
3424 MP(SI)=PL
3425 T1=1
3430 IF SP(OW-1)=1 OR SP(OW-1)=3 OR SP(OW-1)=4 THEN 3431 ELSE 3
     485
3431 IF W$(OW-1)="NOT"THEN 3485ELSEPL=MP(SI):CHK$=W$(OW-1):ZZ=S
     I:GOSUB 8000
3432 IF PF=0 THEN PROP$(PL,SI)=W$(OW-1)+"."ELSE 3485
3433 IF NT=1 THEN PROP$(PL,SI)=PROP$(PL,SI)+"-."
3440 PL=PL+1
3485 PRINT"=================================":IF PF=1 AND T
     1=1 THEN PRINT"TRUE!    ";
3490 PRINT" O.K. "
3500 MP(SI)=PL
4999 PRINT:PRINT:GOTO 996
6000 IF NP(WP(I))>0 THEN WD$="(NOUN)":SP(I)=1
6010 IF VP(WP(I))>0 THEN WD$="(VERB)":SP(I)=2
6020 IF PP(WP(I))>0 THEN WD$="(PRONOUN)":SP(I)=3
6030 IF AP(WP(I))>0 THEN WD$="(MODIFIER)":SP(I)=4
6040 IF JP(WP(I))>0 THEN WD$="(PREPOSITION)":SP(I)=5
6050 IF IP(WP(I))>0 THEN WD$="(INTERJECTION)":SP(I)=6
6053 IF AR(WP(I))>0 THEN WD$="(ARTICLE)":SP(I)=7
6055 IF VOC$(WP(I))="NIL" THEN WD$="(     )":SP(I)=0
6060 RETURN
7000 PRINT"================================="
7002 PRINT:PRINT:PRINT
7200 IF SUB$="" THEN ANS$=W$(1):GOSUB 1000 ELSE 7300
7220 IF FOUND=1 THEN PL=MP(VP):ZZ=VP:CHK$=OBJ$:GOSUB 8000
7225 T1$=RST$:GOSUB 9000:IF NT=0 AND CAR$="-"THEN PRINT"NO.":GO
     TO7900
7228 IF NT=1 AND CAR$="-"THEN PRINT"YES.":GOTO7900
7230 IF NT=0 AND PF=1 THEN PRINT" YES .": GOTO 7900
7235 IF NT=1 AND PF=1 THEN PRINT"NO.":GOTO 7900
```

Listing 7-1—Continued
A Parsing Program for English That Learns.

```
7240 PRINT" I DON'T KNOW . I HAVE NOT LEARNED THAT YET."
7900 PRINT"------------------------------------------"
7920 PRINT:PRINT:
7999 RETURN
8000 RST$="":PF=0:FOR I=0 TO PL
8002 T1$=PROP$(I,ZZ):GOSUB9000
8005 IF CAR$=CHK$ THEN PF=1:RST$=CDR$
8010 NEXT I
8020 RETURN
9000 Q=1
9005 IF T1$="" OR T1$="NIL"THEN CAR$="NIL":CDR$="NIL":GOTO 9025
9010 IF MID$(T1$,Q,1)="."THEN CAR$=LEFT$(T1$,Q-1):CDR$=RIGHT$(T
     1$,LEN(T1$)-Q):GOTO9020
9015 IF Q=LEN(T1$) THEN 9025
9018 Q=Q+1:GOTO9010
9020 IF CAR$=""THENCAR$="NIL"
9022 IF CDR$=""THEN CDR$="NIL"
9030 RETURN
```

More recently, the same task of understanding natural language has been extended into the speech-recognition field. Much of the research has been funded by the Advanced Research Projects Agency of the U. S. Government (ARPA) with the major contractors being SRI International, Carnegie-Mellon University, and Bolt Beranek, and Newman, Inc. The programs, most written in LISP, were given such names as HARPY, HEARSAY, HWIM (Hear What I Mean), and also DRAGON and SPEECHLIS. Although each of these programs was written with the ultimate task of understanding human speech, their applications were directed toward different problems. HARPY and HEARSAY II, for instance, used speech input to control a document retrieval system. An earlier version of HEARSAY (HEARSAY I) was designed to play voice chess. The programs from SRI International and HWIM provided the operator with answers to data base questions from direct speech input.

Most of the ARPA funded speech input research occurred in the early to mid-1970s. More recent work has been done, and is on-going by such research innovators as IBM, Bell Laboratories, Lincoln Laboratories, and, of course, most of those manufacturers now involved in speech recognition products.

The overall goals in the speech research programs have included parameters such as fully connected speech recognition, greater than 1000 word vocabularies, and accepting speech with real-time response.

Not meaning to detract from the glamour of these highly sophisticated and intelligent software systems, crude but illustrative parsing programs may be written in languages such as BASIC which are clumsy in comparison to the LISP equivalents. A little demonstration program is given in Listing 7-1 that, when typed into a BASIC computer, attempts to understand and parse English language sentences. There is

```
    RUN "PARSE"

    PLEASE HELP ME LEARN A NEW WORD
    NEW WORD= ? A
    IS IT A NOUN? N
    IS IT A PRONOUN? N
    IS IT A VERB? N
    IS IT AN MODIFIER? N
    IS IT A PREPOSITION OR CONJUNCTION? N
    IS IT AN INTERJECTION? N
    IS IT AN ARTICLE? Y
    WANT TO ADD MORE? Y


    PLEASE HELP ME LEARN A NEW WORD
    NEW WORD= ? THE
    IS IT A NOUN? N
    IS IT A PRONOUN? N
    IS IT A VERB? N
    IS IT AN MODIFIER? N
    IS IT A PREPOSITION OR CONJUNCTION? N
    IS IT AN INTERJECTION? N
    IS IT AN ARTICLE? Y
    WANT TO ADD MORE? Y


    PLEASE HELP ME LEARN A NEW WORD
    NEW WORD= ? COMPUTER
    IS IT A NOUN? Y
    IS IT(1)COMMON (2)PROPER (3)COLLECTIVE (4)ABSTRACT? 1
    WANT TO ADD MORE? Y


    PLEASE HELP ME LEARN A NEW WORD
    NEW WORD= ? IS
    IS IT A NOUN? N
    IS IT A PRONOUN? N
    IS IT A VERB? Y
    IS IT(1)ACTION VERB (2)BEING VERB (3)HELPING VERB? 2
    IS IT(1)PRESENT (2)PAST (3)FUTURE   TENSE? 1
    WANT TO ADD MORE? Y


    PLEASE HELP ME LEARN A NEW WORD
    NEW WORD= ? ARE
    IS IT A NOUN? N
    IS IT A PRONOUN? N
    IS IT A VERB? Y
    IS IT(1)ACTION VERB (2)BEING VERB (3)HELPING VERB? 2
    IS IT(1)PRESENT (2)PAST (3)FUTURE   TENSE? 1
    WANT TO ADD MORE? Y


    PLEASE HELP ME LEARN A NEW WORD
    NEW WORD= ? YOU
```

Figure 7-3.
Run "parse."

```
IS IT A NOUN? N
IS IT A PRONOUN? Y
IS IT(1)PERSONAL (2)POSSESSIVE (3)DEMONSTRATIVE (4)INTERROGATIVE
 (5)RELATIVE (6)INDEFINITE? 1
WANT TO ADD MORE? Y

PLEASE HELP ME LEARN A NEW WORD
NEW WORD= ? SMART
IS IT A NOUN? N
IS IT A PRONOUN? N
IS IT A VERB? N
IS IT AN MODIFIER? Y
WANT TO ADD MORE? Y


PLEASE HELP ME LEARN A NEW WORD
NEW WORD= ? DUMB
IS IT A NOUN? N
IS IT A PRONOUN? N
IS IT A VERB? N
IS IT AN MODIFIER? Y
WANT TO ADD MORE? Y


PLEASE HELP ME LEARN A NEW WORD
NEW WORD= ?BIG
IS IT A NOUN? N
IS IT A PRONOUN? N
IS IT A VERB? N
IS IT AN MODIFIER? Y
WANT TO ADD MORE? Y


PLEASE HELP ME LEARN A NEW WORD
NEW WORD= ? SMALL
IS IT A NOUN? N
IS IT A PRONOUN? N
IS IT A VERB? N
IS IT AN MODIFIER? Y
WANT TO ADD MORE? Y


PLEASE HELP ME LEARN A NEW WORD
NEW WORD= ? HUMAN
IS IT A NOUN? Y
IS IT(1)COMMON (2)PROPER (3)COLLECTIVE (4)ABSTRACT? 1
WANT TO ADD MORE? Y


PLEASE HELP ME LEARN A NEW WORD
NEW WORD= ? FAST
IS IT A NOUN? N
IS IT A PRONOUN? N
IS IT A VERB? N
IS IT AN MODIFIER? Y
WANT TO ADD MORE? Y
```

Figure 7-3—Continued
Run "parse."

```
PLEASE HELP ME LEARN A NEW WORD
NEW WORD= ? SLOW
IS IT A NOUN? N
IS IT A PRONOUN? N
IS IT A VERB? N
IS IT AN MODIFIER? Y
WANT TO ADD MORE? N
```

Figure 7-3—Continued
Run "parse."

no attempt to implement the augmented transition network (ATN) because BASIC does not easily handle stack variables. Instead, the system attempts to learn properties about English words and connect meanings between them. Although the program does not have a particular application, the English parsing function may be extended into a useful operating system. Obviously, adding speech input to the operating characteristics will complicate matters even further. It is, however, a starting point which can provide an insight into the complexity of the English language interpretation, and grammatical and syntactical analysis.

When operated, the program learns new words from the user by asking questions about them. This is where you have to supply information which might require delving into dictionaries or grammar books from the past. However, once the computer has been trained with a basic vocabulary, it can perform quite well in a limited sentence structure domain. Fig. 7-3 illustrates a typical operator/computer interaction during the learning process. Then following the initial training session, the computer provides sentence analysis and interpretation in a manner illustrated in Fig. 7-4 and Fig. 7-5.

The BASIC language used for this program is a standard Microsoft BASIC so it should be usable on most computers directly without translation difficulties. It is *not* guaranteed to be bug-free since English language interpretation is so intricate. Try it and see how a computer can begin to understand the way we talk and think.

Recognition Accuracy Problems

As we discuss the results of speech transactions from voice control, we cannot forget the possibility of that inevitable error which may creep into system operation. Probably one of the most important factors in creating a speech recognition system is including a type of fail-safe programming to ensure that if errors do occur, their effects are minimized.

A speech-recognition system has four possible modes of error creation during a speech transaction. The first mode will be called the

```
-------------------------------------------
OK TRY A SENTENCE? YOU ARE A FAST COMPUTER
********** SENTENCE DIAGRAM **********


(PRONOUN)(VERB)(ARTICLE)(MODIFIER)(NOUN)
*************************************
YOU ARE A FAST COMPUTER

.......... SENTENCE PARSE ..........
SUB=YOU        OBJ=COMPUTER   VERB=ARE
======================================
   O.K.


-------------------------------------------
OK TRY A SENTENCE? YOU ARE NOT SLOW
********** SENTENCE DIAGRAM **********


(PRONOUN)(VERB)(MODIFIER)(MODIFIER)
***********************************
YOU ARE NOT SLOW

.......... SENTENCE PARSE ..........
SUB=YOU        OBJ=SLOW       VERB=ARE
======================================
   O.K.


-------------------------------------------
OK TRY A SENTENCE? YOU ARE NOT BIG
********** SENTENCE DIAGRAM **********


(PRONOUN)(VERB)(MODIFIER)(MODIFIER)
***********************************
YOU ARE NOT BIG

.......... SENTENCE PARSE ..........
SUB=YOU        OBJ=BIG        VERB=ARE
======================================
   O.K.


-------------------------------------------
OK TRY A SENTENCE? YOU ARE A SMALL COMPUTER
********** SENTENCE DIAGRAM **********


(PRONOUN)(VERB)(ARTICLE)(MODIFIER)(NOUN)
*************************************
YOU ARE A SMALL COMPUTER

.......... SENTENCE PARSE ..........
SUB=YOU        OBJ=COMPUTER   VERB=ARE
======================================
   O.K.
```

Figure 7-4.
Training the parsing program with ideas.

```
------------------------------------------
OK TRY A SENTENCE? ARE YOU A COMPUTER?

==========================================


YES .
------------------------------------------


------------------------------------------
OK TRY A SENTENCE? ARE YOU SLOW?

==========================================


NO.
------------------------------------------


------------------------------------------
OK TRY A SENTENCE? ARE YOU FAST?

==========================================


YES .
------------------------------------------


------------------------------------------
OK TRY A SENTENCE? ARE YOU SMALL?

==========================================


YES .
------------------------------------------


------------------------------------------
OK TRY A SENTENCE? ARE YOU A HUMAN?

==========================================


I DON'T KNOW . I HAVE NOT LEARNED THAT YET.
------------------------------------------
```

Figure 7-5.
Testing the parser with questions.

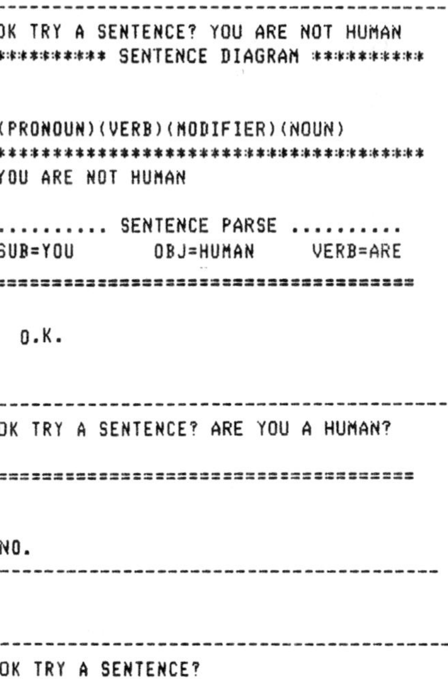

Figure 7-5—Continued
Testing the parser with questions.

"Daydreaming Error." The incident is most like talking to a person who is daydreaming in that you receive no response at all from your spoken message. To correct the error, as with a person, you simply speak the same phrase over in a louder voice. The effect of the error on system operation is minimal in that no action is taken because no input message was registered.

A second error which may occur will be called a "preoccupied error." The response you get from the system after a spoken input would be equivalent to that from a person that was preoccupied: "What?" A more likely computer response would be: "Please repeat." No matter what the reprompting message is, it signifies to the operator that the system received a word but did not understand it. Since the rejection of the message created *no match* within the vocabulary, there was no action taken and thus no harm was done.

A third error which may occur that will possibly cause serious consequences is that of a "substitution" error. A substitution error occurs when the speech-recognition system misunderstands the incoming word and improperly matches it to another word within the vocabulary. For instance, if the computer says, "Do you want to go?" and you respond with, "No," there are two possibilities for matching the input word "no." If the computer picks *no,* then you are safe. However, if the incorrect match to the word *go* is made, then you may have a serious problem. This is one reason why operator verification of the input message is so important.

The fourth type of error which can also have serious consequences is the "false alarm" input error. It will most likely occur in noisy environments where speech recognition systems are more prone to incorrectly interpret a noise burst or extraneous sound as the desired input signal. If a match is made within the vocabulary to the ambient sound, then a system without operator verification will autonomously go into action. Since this event can occur without an operator present, its consequences can be most disastrous. Not only does this type of error emphasize the necessity for operator validation, it also illustrates the need for an operator advisory before the action is taken.

The major effects upon system operation created by errors can be of varying severity, depending upon the application. Because of this, the amount of safeguards which are placed upon system operation should also be dependent upon the costs of an error. If a user is speech controlling a word processor with an annoying number of error prevention controls, then he will quickly become frustrated. On the other hand, the operator of a 10,000-ton metal punch in a machine shop will probably regard the same error precautions with high esteem. In any case, if the error rate is above 2% to 3% of all transactions, the operator will become disenchanted with the speech operated system and the system's usefulness will quickly avalanche into chaos.

In an overall evaluation of error performance, the successful system will be one that the operator perceives as having the most error potential free operation with the simplest operator interactions for error correction. With those admonitions in mind, let's review some applications for speech-recognition systems.

CHAPTER 8

Applications of Listening Computers

Throughout this book we have touched on a number of uses for speech recognition systems. In this chapter, we will look in more detail at the considerations and consequences in the application of speech recognition systems. Obviously, there are many more potential areas where these systems may be applied than those that can be listed. However, the uses which *are* mentioned in this chapter may spark the imagination or start you searching into some uncharted waters of speech recognition uses.

First of all, how do you identify the areas in which speech recognition might be advantageous? There are a few distinct characteristics of potential applications which definitely indicate positive use values. For instance, in tasks that involve close hand-eye coordination, the operator has very little time for the distraction of operating a computer keyboard. Speech recognition applied here will probably work. Another potential indicator to watch for occurs in operator controlled computer systems in which the operator must be mobile. Inventory tasks of large warehouses are a prime example of where the operator may verbally assess the stocking levels with speech recognition through a wireless radio link. Another distinct indicator for the use of speech recognition is when data entry reliability must be high for unskilled computer operators *and* people that do not know how to type.

In general, if any one or more of the previous conditions are met, then the application of a speech recognition system should be considered. However, if such an application causes the operator more work than before its use, then it probably will not be successful. In other words, it must make the operator's *current* task simpler. If you expect one man and a speech recognition system to replace two or three men on the same task, experience shows that the additional work load and peer pressure on the lone worker will create problems.

An extremely important consideration when selecting speech recognition for an application involves the commitment applied to its use. If a computer hobbyist is planning to implement speech recognition in a home-based system, then the commitment is based on curiosity and need. The learning process involved in its implementation is certainly a powerful motivational force to the hobbyist. On the other hand, if a corporation is planning to supplement a production process with speech recognition, there could be significant delays and disturbances created by the substitution process. It's not really going to happen overnight. The company should ensure that sufficient motivation *and* capitalization are present before engaging in the integration of a speech-recognition system into the corporate process. If either of these elements is not available in almost unlimited quantities, then there is a strong possibility that the corporate position following the implementation will be negative, and the system will be rejected.

This observation brings out a feature of speech-recognition systems that is rather obscure in the specifications of these devices. While you or I, or any corporate executive, can buy a very sophisticated speech recognizer costing from $500 to $20,000, we have not purchased a true turnkey system. For any computer peripheral to be effectively integrated into a system, the application software in the main computer must also exist. This is where the costs arise. Typical estimates and experience show that the manpower required to adequately integrate a speech recognizer into a production or office environment is somewhere between six and twelve months of programming time. Not only is this costly in terms of man-hours, it will also disturb the process being replaced to a considerable extent. Thus, the *a priori* commitment determines its success or failure.

Lastly, the noise environment in which the speech recognizer will function must be considered. If the ambient noise (whether continuous or transient) in the proposed location of the speech recognizer exceeds 85 to 95 dB, then the likelihood of success is minimal. To get a feel for those numbers, 0 dB is the threshold of hearing in children (whose hearing has not deteriorated through age). The ambient noise level within a private business office or average residence runs around 50 to 55 dB. Noise levels between 80 and 100 dB are equivalent to those found in construction sites with pneumatic drills, boiler rooms, printing press plants, and subway stations. In fact, the 85-dB figure seems to be a threshold number where sustained proximity will begin to cause ear damage. (The Surgeon General has determined that 85 dB is dangerous . . . .)

With these rules-of-thumb in mind for speech recognition application, let's look at a few typical areas for further consideration.

Speech-Controlled Systems

In our definition of speech-controlled systems, we will assume that the operator is commanding a computer to accomplish some task through voice command. In an ideal case, the speech recognizer will include this function with other modes of speech recognition, but we will assume that the system we are speaking of here is required to do nothing more than follow verbal commands.

One of the most obvious and humanitarian uses for speech recognition that comes to mind is an aid for disabled people. The physically handicapped can, through speech recognition, control devices with their voice which would not be possible otherwise. One system of this type was reported by *Time* magazine in the 13 December 1982 issue. The home-based system was developed for an unfortunate youngster who lost the use of his limbs in a severe car accident at the age of 17. However, he was left with his voice intact, so that recently the application of speech recognition has begun to open new worlds for him. His friends have pieced together a system using an Apple® II computer combined with the Scott Instruments Shadow/Vet® voice entry terminal to control the positioning system on a home satellite dish.

The system works like this. Based upon an initial command that keys the computer for satellite positioning "Satellite Search," the computer responds vocally with a question "Which satellite do you want?" At this point, the computer is listening to the next verbal command which contains the information for one of the many satellites in the sky. The response "Sat Com F3R" starts the parabolic dish searching the sky for the proper coordinates for that satellite. Once correct positioning has occurred, the computer says, "Which transponder do you want?" A human response such as "New York" produces a flash on the tv screen and suddenly tv station WOR from New York appears.

The technology of speech recognition is certainly going to be a friend for the nearly 500,000 Americans suffering physical disabilities. As this technology becomes integrated with the technology of robotics, additional new worlds will open for the physically handicapped. If you are looking for an application to evaluate using a newly acquired speech recognizer, then this is an admirable place to begin experimenting. There is probably no application where speech recognition will be more appreciated. And, if you now have the full function of your limbs, do not think you are immune. For, if the finger of fate points at you tomorrow on the way to work or school and you are placed in that 500,000 number, then you would *certainly* appreciate your own efforts.

While we are on the subject of satellites and space, it may be of interest to note that NASA is heavily involved in speech-recognition research. The applications here relate to the control of aircraft and spacecraft through voice commands (Fig. 8-1). There is probably no place where physical and mental coordination is more important than

Figure 8-1.
Voice commands could be valuable in controlling aircraft and spacecraft operations.

in docking or landing a space vehicle. With the multitude of cockpit instruments and control levers needed to accurately position a space vehicle in three-dimensional space, the capability of speech control is most definitely an advantage.

One of the outcomes of the NASA research in this area tells us something about the relationship of ambient noise levels to speech-recognition accuracy. The problem which exists in this application (and in many others) relates to the training of speech recognizers in a noise environment which is changing. For example, if the recognizer is to be trained for use during the firing of retro rockets upon landing, how is it trained in the relation to the noise environment? Should it be trained at a high noise level or trained in quietness? Prior to the NASA research, it was generally thought that of the four possible combinations of training and use:

1. Quiet training and quiet recognition
2. Quiet training and noisy recognition

3. Noisy training and quiet recognition
4. Noisy training and noisy recognition

the best condition, of course, was number 1. The next best condition for speech recognition accuracy occurred in number 4 when both training and recognition took place in the noisy environment. Number 3 was placed next in the order with training in noise and recognition in quiet, while number 2 was least desirable with training in quiet and recognition in noise. Although the performance was degraded to varying degrees during previous tests, the total recognition accuracy difference from the best to the worst case was only on the order of 18%.

Recent NASA testing with speech recognizers in the four differing noise environments concluded that very little difference was found in the four combinations. These results have been encouraging for the future of speech recognition in the space program. Its use in future spacecraft is fairly certain.

If the technology is acceptable to NASA for use within critical applications such as spacecraft control, then eventually it will surely creep into our daily lives through control of automobiles. While it is unlikely that it will replace the actual control mechanisms of a car—the steering wheel and brakes—speech recognition may certainly be applied to control the internal functions in the cabin of the car. For example, assume that a car with an internal computer capable of speech recognition is programmed with a mileage-logging function. The driver might say "Please respond in 10.5 miles." If he is following a map with a turnoff point 10.5 miles ahead, then at that point the computer would speak "10.5 miles reached." There might even be panic voice controls for pending emergencies that would activate skidless braking systems and thereby eliminate the 0.2- to 0.5-second reaction time involved in moving the foot to the brake pedal. We should call these "Backseat Driver Controls." Other commands could certainly be implemented with less hazardous consequences such as the control of lights, door locks, and even power windows. It would really be convenient to eliminate that elusive lever (which no one can seem to find) that controls the seat position. A useful voice command would be one to control the hazard lights, which might be something as simple as "hazard on" and "hazard off." The main problem with this type of recognition system is that it must be speaker independent. Once the technological barriers of speaker dependence have been hurdled, then speech recognition within automobiles will be practical.

Other applications of voice control include elevators (simply speak the floor number), hospital rooms where patients may request allowed medicines and can control bed positioning, and even voice-identification door locks for homes and businesses.

Speech-recognition systems are already beginning to appear in such everyday devices as watches (yes, that's right!). They can listen to the owner for setting the alarm or time and also speak the same messages from the owner's wrist (Fig. 8-2). Seiko Time Corporation has announced such a watch, which should be available for around $200. A Swiss research lab, ASULAB,AG recently demonstrated a watch having a speech-recognition capability of 15 words. No price has been announced for this product.

Yet another application for speech recognition is found in the Scratch Pad Software from Super Soft with Voice Drive. This spreadsheet software package for the IBM PC, in combination with a hardware plug-in board from Tecmar, allows the user a 97-word vocabulary for controlling the spreadsheet with speech. With the software and hardware package installed in an IBM PC, the user may verbally command such instructions as "delete line" or "load file." The user must repeat each of the 97 commands, three times to train the speech recognizer. Voice-identification files are kept separately by the software package to allow multiple users. The software package is expected to sell for around $500. The combined software and hardware system will retail for somewhere in the range of $1000.

Vocal Data Entry Systems

The current technology for data entry speech recognition is improving daily. The major hurdles which must be overcome before being com-

Figure 8-2.
Soon, watches will verbally announce the time.

pletely acceptable are those of speaker dependence and connected speech limitations. However, since voice technology is acclaimed as being the most natural way of inputting information into a machine, you can be assured that these obstacles will eventually be overcome.

The automated office is beginning to see a technology shift toward voice processing. Although there are few, if any, speech-recognition products currently available for office use, the applications are many. Consider the accountant who must balance large ledger books while simultaneously viewing columns of figures from many sources. If he could simply read the figures from the columns into a computer for verification and balancing, the potential for keyboard-induced errors would be eliminated.

An area where speech recognition is being used today, to improve productivity and accuracy, is in the production of machine tool programming tapes. Past procedures dictated that an operator skilled in reading blueprints transfer dimensions manually from blueprints to written dimensions. The handwritten dimensions were then manually typed into a tape punch for generation of the controlling tape. The process now consists of the same skilled draftsman visually reviewing the blueprint while aurally reciting dimensions into the computer. The tape is produced directly from the recognized speech following verification by the operator. The elimination of the intervening steps in the production of the numerically controlled tape has dropped production time by 80% to 90%. The overall costs, including the speech-recognition system, are approximately one-half of those required for original tape production.

A potential use for speech recognition exists in the production assembly line where a quality control inspector must visually examine products for defects, while recording quality control data about the products. Operators fitted with boom-microphone headsets are given the freedom to use their hands to manually inspect a part while verbally describing defects or rejection routing instructions. One similar operation in a canning company allows the quality control inspector of pull-top can lids to verbally communicate with the computer about the quality of individual production runs. Productivity has been said to increase by 40% through the use of speech recognition in this instance.

More applications for speech recognition can be found in the jobs of inventory clerks who must wander through warehouses while counting and reporting stocking levels to a computer. With wireless radio-linked headsets and microphones, the inventory personnel may verbally communicate with the corporate computer for virtually error-free inventory reporting.

Uses of speech recognition in the home include verbal systems for balancing a checkbook (if you have ever done this, you know that you really need your hands), inventory of household goods for insurance purposes, and even inventory of the kitchen pantry for generation of a shopping list. Another item which almost everyone would find to be invaluable is the voice-activated transcription system.

Voice-Activated Typewriters

I would like to state in this section that three major electronics companies have successfully designed and developed voice-activated typewriters and are currently readying them for the market place, but alas, that news may have to wait for the next decade or even century. At the present time, the technology for implementing this type of speech-activated system is just too immature. Needless to say, the voice-activated typewriter is "the Holy Grail" of products for the office and business environment (and even book authors), so we all know that there are qualified teams of researchers moving in this direction. We must all wait and see.

If the world's experts in speech recognition and artificial intelligence have their wishes, then we should see the first development in this area in the early 1990s. Japan's Fifth Generation Computer project has as its goal, among other things, a speech-activated typewriter with a vocabulary of at least 10,000 words and the capacity to handle the voice patterns and frequencies of hundreds of speakers without retraining. When this research is successful as part of the ten-year plan, *then* the voice activated typewriter will exist. Of course, to use it, you will have to speak Japanese! But be assured that if it happens over there, then it will certainly happen here, too.

In the meantime, however, we may have to be satisfied with a stop-gap measure like the "typing talkwriter" described in Chapter 3. While a speech-to-phoneme transcription device would have limited usefulness, it should be at least as accurate and useful as the stenographic machine used by court stenographers throughout the world. If the machine relies on a phonetic language transcription such as Unifon, then there will surely be Unifon readers available for the reduction of the pictograms to English text.

Futuristic Systems

In some marvelous way, Japan has issued an edict that the world is years behind in computer development. All of a sudden, *everyone* is scrambling to catch up with someone else in computer technology. The scene is much like the race for space when we landed the first man on the moon. Although the eventual outcome may not be quite as exciting as watching man put the first footprint on lunar soil, the effect upon our society may be more startling. Since the technology for speech recognition is incorporated within this research drive, it is of primary concern to the topic of speech recognition applications.

The voice-recognition system of the future will be much like that of today. Connected speech recognition will be found in applications ranging from bank tellers to telephone answering systems. More than likely, our automobiles will incorporate some means of voice recognition for control over vehicle operation. While the cost of incorporating a voice-recognition system in today's automobile might typically double the cost of the car for some systems, when the production costs drop to around $1000 or less, then these will be offered as options like the expensive stereo systems of today. Then, if they are successful in their application, you can be sure that government regulations will force their mandatory use in *all* automobiles. Think of that market!

There are several ways of staying knowledgeable about applications and potential applications for speech-recognition systems. Periodicals and trade magazines have occasional articles concerning new applications for these systems. There are two publications specifically aimed at the speech input/output community. These provide considerable in-depth information for potential users of speech recognition systems. *VoiceNews* is a newsletter published ten times per year which provides valuable information about products and applications. The cost of the subscription within the U. S. is $95.00 per year. Subscriptions are available from:

> VoiceNews
> Stoneridge Technical Services
> P. O. Box 1891
> Rockville, MD 20850

The publisher of *VoiceNews*, Mr. Bill Creitz, includes within his newsletter important information about current and future directions of voice technology. While the cost of the publication may be rather expensive for the home experimenter, the corporation interested in voice recognition will find this a very effective way of keeping abreast of research trends in the field.

Another publication pertinent to this topic is *Speech Technology*. This quarterly magazine, which began publishing in mid-1982, carries information about all facets of speech input and output for computers. The cost of an annual subscription is $50.00. Potential subscribers should contact:

> Speech Technology
> 525 East 82nd Street
> New York, NY 10028
> Telephone Number (212) 680-6451

As a final indicator of the importance of speech technology in computer applications, it may be of interest to learn that in 1982 an industrial society was chartered for speech input/output users and technologists. This working group, named the American Voice Input/ Output Society (AVIOS), has as one of its main goals the continual awareness of its members in the field of speech-recognition technology.

Applications for speech-recognition devices are practically innumerable. If you look around you, you will see areas where the technology will eventually be applied. Sometimes it will be successful; other times it will fail. Much of the success of speech-recognition integration into today's society depends upon the human factors considered during the implementation. Who will be the innovators who do this? Many of them will probably be today's leaders in speech recognition technology. They may be found in the next chapter on currently available voice recognizers.

CHAPTER 9

A Review of Available Voice-Recognition Systems

Although the inclusion of an available products chapter is considered mandatory by the author in a technical book, it is always added with a small amount of reluctance. A remote but rather accurate analogy may be made by trying to write a chapter on the exact position of the planets within the solar system. For, the writer knows that even as he writes, the positions that he is describing are changing dynamically and thus, by the end of the chapter, will have changed from those described within it. Even though it adds a planned obsolescence factor into the contents of a book, it also gives you, the reader, considerable insight into what is currently available on the market at a snapshot in time during the writing of the book. The most obvious change to this chapter will be additions to the list of available products. Unfortunately, there will also be some deletions from those companies with high ambitions and low funding. The particular corporate failure rate being described is due to a phenomenon known as market lag. And, in a dynamically changing science like speech recognition, there is even a greater market lag than in an accepted, proven, field.

Although the exact failure mechanism is somewhat nebulous, the general concept is that as companies bring their products to market, there is a considerable waiting time before the product becomes publicly accepted and financially successful. If the field of market is fm stereo radios, then we all know that the concept behind stereo fm works and is a low risk investment. On the other hand, in a dynamic field like speech recognition, the algorithms for recognition are being improved daily so that each speech recognizer brought to the market probably has some advantages over the previously introduced ones. So, being normal and efficient purchasers, we all wait around for the best product to become available. As we do this, companies will drop off or merge with other companies on the list of products in this chapter.

Nevertheless, the snapshot of products *will* be presented if for nothing more than historical records in the future. It is given in Table 9-1. The columns in the table identify the company of each product, the associated model numbers for the speech-recognition products, and the approximate prices of the items as of press time. Also included are some characteristics of the recognizers like the type of speech accepted and the numbers of speakers with the vocabulary size allowed. Other columns describe the products, their recognition accuracy and the particular computer interface that is employed to communicate wth the host computer. Finally, recognition time is given which tells you how long you will have to wait for your last spoken word to be acted upon.

The products are listed in alphabetical order based upon manufacturer. The addresses of these manufacturers are given in Appendix C so that you may contact them directly for more information. A few of these devices are also available at your local computer stores. Don't expect to find much of anything below $1,000. That number seems to be the established price for a usable personal computer speech-recognition interface. Of course, in time these prices will drop, but the complexity in hardware and software will tend to keep the average price of the speech recognition system considerably above the speech synthesis peripheral.

Now that you have had a look at the available products grouped together for comparison, the remainder of this chapter will isolate each manufacturer's products and attempt to describe them in specific terms with a relatively brief theory of operation discussion on how each product operates (if the manufacturer released this information). These isolated discussions should really give you a better insight into what's happening in the real, competitive world of speech-recognition products.

INTEL Corporation

The speech-recognition products offered by INTEL Corporation to date have consisted primarily of speech-recognition development systems. These are designed to let you evaluate and experiment with the application of speech recognition in your systems. The development system family offered by INTEL consists primarily of upgradable hardware with similar software to allow the user to work with speech recognition experimentally before integrating the technology into products. INTEL's reasoning behind this is based on our conceptual model for crt/keyboard interaction from our experience with typewriters which have

Table 9-1.
Available Voice-Recognition Products

Company	Model Number	Type Speech	Speaker Related	Vocabulary Size (Words)
Intel Corp.	iSBC® 570	ISOLATED	Dependent	200
	iSBC 576	ISOLATED	Dependent	200
	iSBC 577	ISOLATED	Dependent	200
Interstate Electronics	VRT 101	ISO.	Dep.	100
	SYS 300	ISO.	Dep.	100
	VRT 300	ISO.	Dep.	100
	VRT 200	ISO.	Dep.	100
	VRQ 400	ISO.	Dep.	100
	VRM 102	ISO.	Dep.	100
	VRC 100-2	ISO.	Dep.	200
	VRC 008	ISO.	Indep.	16
NEC Corp. (Nippon Electric Company)	DP-200	Connected	Dep.	50
	SR-100	ISO.	Dep.	120
	μPD7761D	ISO.	Dep.	128
Scott Instruments	VET-2	ISO.	Dep.	40
	SHADOW/VET	ISO.	Dep.	40
	VBLS™	ISO.	Dep.	
Super Soft-Techmar	Voice Drive-Scratchpad	ISO.	Dep.	97
Threshold Technology, Inc.	T-500/580	ISO.	Dep.	60
	T-600/680	ISO.	Dep.	50
	T-950	ISO.	Dep.	80
	Auricle-1	ISO.	Dep.	80
	Auricle-HP	ISO.	Dep.	120
	Aur-1/RM	ISO.	Dep.	80
Texas Instruments, Inc.	TI Speech Board	ISO.	Dep.	40
Verbex	Verbex 3000	Connect.	Dep.	360
Voice Machine Communications, Inc.	VIM-1	ISO.	Dep.	80
	VIM-le	ISO.	Dep.	80
	VOCS	ISO.	Dep.	?
Votan	V1000	ISO.	Dep.	
	V2000	ISO.	Verify	
	V4000	ISO.	Dep.	
	V5000	ISO.	Dep.	256
	V6040	ISO.	Indep.	
	V7000	ISO.	Verify	
	V8000	ISO.	Dep.	256
Weitek Corp.	WTV008	ISO.	Indep.	16
	WTV108	ISO.	Indep.	16

been around many, many years. And we *do* expect certain features and actions from the crt/keyboard combination from our experience with the conventional typewriter mechanism. As we enter a new field of computer interaction such as speech recognition, we tend to base our expectations on the previous experience through human listeners. Because of this ideological fallacy, users of speech recognizers are often disappointed with the interactive results upon their first encounter with

Description	% Accuracy	Computer Interface	Maximum Response Time (ms)	Approx. Cost $
Development Set	99 +	Intel Multibus®	500	4,900.
Transaction Board	99 +	Intel Multibus®	500	2,900.
8-chip Set	99 +	Intel Multibus®	500	600.
Full System with CRT	99 +	RS-232C	125	5,300.
Speech System	99 +	RS-232C	150	2000.
DEC VT100 Module	99 +	DEC VT100 Board	150	1300.
ADM3A, ADM5 Module	99 +	Single Board	125	2000.
Q-Bus® Module	99 +	Plug-in Board	125	2000.
Multibus® Module	99 +	Plug-in Board	125	2000.
2-chip Set	99 +	MC68B03μP	150	385.
28 pin Chip	90	TTL I/O	200	19. @ 1000/ea.
Speech Recognizer	?	RS-232C; GP1B	300	12000.
Voice In Terminal	99 +	RS-232C	300	
3-chip Set	98 +	TTL I/O	500	
Voice Entry Unit	98	Apple II	?	795.
Voice Entry Unit	98	Apple II, II +	?	995.
Learning Software		Apple/VET	?	895.
Hard/Software Pkg. (Spreadsheet)	?	IBM PC	?	995.
Voice Entry Terminal	99	RS-232C	?	12000.
Voice Entry Terminal	99	RS-232C	?	14000.
TeleVideo Board	99	TeleVideo 950	?	1300.
Voice Input Unit	99	RS-232C; GP1B	300	1500.
Voice Input Unit	99	HP Series 80 Computers	300	1500.
Voice PC Board	99	RS-232C	430	1500.
TMS320 Recognition Board	99	T.I.P.C., IBM P.C.	300	2600.
Voice Entry Terminal	99 +	RS-232C	300	17,900.
Voice Input Module	98 +	Apple II, II +	150	850.
Voice Input Module	98 +	Apple IIe	150	920.
Voice Medical System	98 +	Contained		19,500.
	99 +			
Voice Identifier	99 +			
	99 +			4,200.
Development System	99 +			5,000.
	99 +			8,500.
	99 +			
Voice System/Computer	99 +	IBM PC		10,000.
Demo Kit	90 +	TTL I/O	?	450.
1-chip Recognizer	90 +	TTL I/O	?	195.

them. The use of the speech transaction development systems produced by INTEL allows the potential user of speech recognition to evaluate and understand the human-to-computer interface before the technology is integrated. It also allows him to most properly adapt the recognition operation to his particular product.

The first INTEL development system listed in Table 9-1 is the iSBC® 570. This hardware combination is a complete development support set for the INTEL speech product family. It includes as its hardware, the iSBC® 575 Operator Control Unit, the iSBC® 576 Speech Transaction Board to be described shortly, and a head-mounted microphone. Also included is a software package for the Intellec® microcomputer development system consisting of a demonstration program and the Speech Transaction Generator program. Of course, a thorough design manual for speech transactions is also supplied as system documentation. The components of the iSBC® 570 are shown to the right of Fig. 9-1. Also shown in this figure is the Intellec® microcomputer development system with which the speech transaction development set is to be used. The development set in combination with the microcomputer development system allows you to evaluate speech technology and experience the major attributes of a speech input/output system. It also provides you with a software package for designing and testing speech transaction scenarios for product implementation. The somewhat high cost of this unit, especially when combined with the Intellec® microcomputer development system, targets its use for corporate research. But like many of the other products listed in this chapter, the rather high cost is still much lower than what might be expected in evaluating and applying the technology of speech recognition.

The second product listed by INTEL is the iSBC® 576 Speech Transaction Board. Since it is included within the previously described devel-

Figure 9-1.
The iSBC® 570 Speech Transaction Development Set
(Courtesy Intel Corp.).

opment set, many of comments on this unit also apply to the previous description. As stated by INTEL, the iSBC® 576 Speech Transaction Board is the heart of a speech i/o system. Included on the board shown in Fig. 9-2 is a speech recognizer which provides complete automatic speech recognition capabilities and a ROM-resident Speech Transaction Manager in firmware on a Multibus® compatible printed circuit board. Contained on the board is an 8086 microprocessor and two 2920/21 digital signal processors. An 8-bit single-chip 8048 microcomputer is also included as a parallel processor for the 8086 processor. The single board computer will fit into any Multibus® compatible computer and communicate over an RS-232 serial host interface. The input to the board is a 500-ohm microphone connection accepting up to 50 milli-volts peak-to-peak speech input. The recognition vocabulary allowed numbers 200 words or phrases. The duration of each of these can range from 100 milliseconds to slightly under 2 seconds. The response time is relatively fast, being somewhere around one-half second for the full 200-word vocabulary. As an option, the speech transaction board will also generate electronic speech synthesis to provide audio feedback and verification of input.

The next listed product by INTEL in Table 9-1 is an 8-chip set shown in Fig. 9-3. This group of integrated circuits is sold by INTEL as the

Figure 9-2.
The iSBC® 576 Speech Transaction Board
(Courtesy Intel Corp.).

Figure 9-3.
The iSBC® 577 Speech Transaction Recognition Chip Set
(Courtesy Intel Corp.).

iSBC® 577 Speech Transaction Recognition Chip Set. It is downward compatible with all of the previously listed INTEL products, and software generated with the previous development systems is fully compatible with these INTEL components. The obvious use for the chip set is in a low-cost high volume product as an integrated speech recognizer. Included within the collection of integrated circuits are the digital front end processors, a preprogrammed 8048 interface processor, the 8086 speech recognition processor, and four 27128 EPROMs that contain the Speech Transaction Manager firmware for the chip set. The use of this chip set in a product allows the integration of speech recognition into smaller systems which have been evaluated and tested using the speech development system.

Since these chips are used in all of the previously listed products, the operating specifications from them also applies here. To get a better idea of how all of the INTEL components fit together, Fig. 9-4 shows how the three previously listed products are integrated together into the family of INTEL speech products.

More recent INTEL products include stand-alone speech recognition systems which have been designed with adaptive training for speech enrollment. The process includes confirmation and feedback during

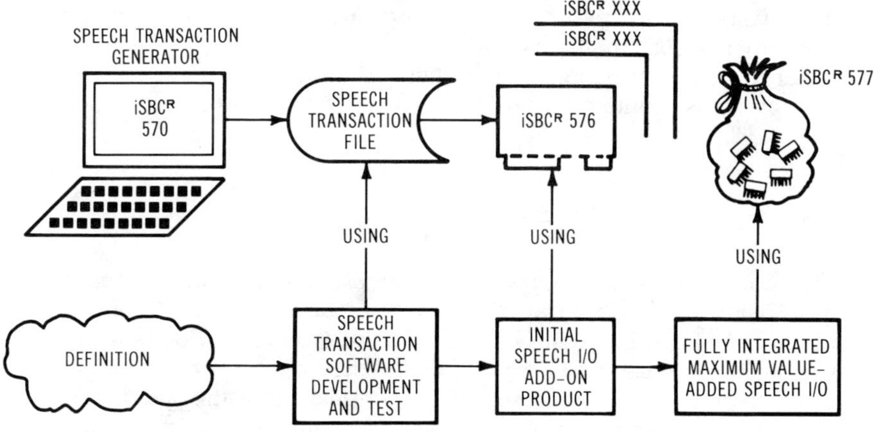

Figure 9-4.
The integration of the Intel family
(Courtesy Intel Corp.).

enrollment with the capability of modifying the reference templates for gradual speech changes. The INTEL product line will certainly be a powerful force in the speech recognition field for quite some time to come.

Interstate Electronics Corporation

The family of products from Interstate Electronics Corporation is seen to be rather large upon examination of Table 9-1. However, because the release of publishable information from them was restricted, the information given here will necessarily be rather sketchy.

The large portion of the Interstate Electronics speech recognizers has identical operating characteristics. Accordingly, the technology used in each product is probably the same. With the exception of the last two listed items which are integrated circuit chips, most of the items offered by Interstate Electronics are single board interface modules designed to be plugged into existing standardized bus systems. Although the first two listed items, the VRT101 and SYS300, are stand-alone speech recognition systems, the remainder of the items are designed to be used with existing computer systems. All units are user programmable in terms of speech vocabulary and have a vocabulary size of up to 100 words. The most interesting of the items listed under the Interstate Electronics family are the chip sets, the VRC100-2 and the single chip recognizer, the VRC008. The single chip speech recognizer accepts up to a 16-word vocabulary and provides *speaker independent* recognition. Accuracy for the general population is claimed to be 90% or better.

It is available with the evaluation hardware as a speech recognition experimental system: the EVL008.

For further information on the Interstate Electronics speech recognition products, contact them directly. Their address may be found in Appendix C.

NEC Corporation

This company seems to be the only real contender in the speech-recognition market from another country, namely Japan. If you have not heard of them, the NEC stands for Nippon Electric Company, Ltd. whose home base is in Tokyo, Japan. They offer a limited range of products from stand-alone speech recognizers (from the systems division) to speech-recognition chip sets (from the NEC microcomputer division). According to NEC, they have created a breakthrough in man-machine interfaces. With their speech recognizers, specifically the DP-200, the process of inputting data or controlling machines is as simple as conversing with another person. The reason for this claim is that the DP-200 allows recognition of *fully* connected speech without the associated pauses from discrete word recognizers.

The DP-200 Connected Speech Recognizer although somewhat expensive at around $12,000, provides a corporate capability for fully connected speech recognition. The hardware system is shown in Fig. 9-5. Included in the DP-200 package are the speech-recognition terminal, the remote control terminal with visual display, a remote switch and microphone assembly, and cabling for system connection. A typical system configuration for the DP-200 is shown in Fig. 9-6. The connection of each of the pieces of hardware is relatively foolproof with the various interfaces to the computer and machine-controlled equipment provided through a number of control interface lines. These standard

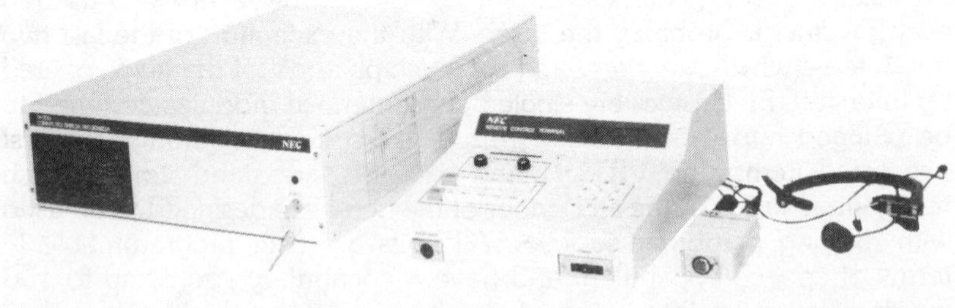

Figure 9-5.
The NEC DP-200 Connected Speech Recognizer System
(Courtesy NEC Corp.).

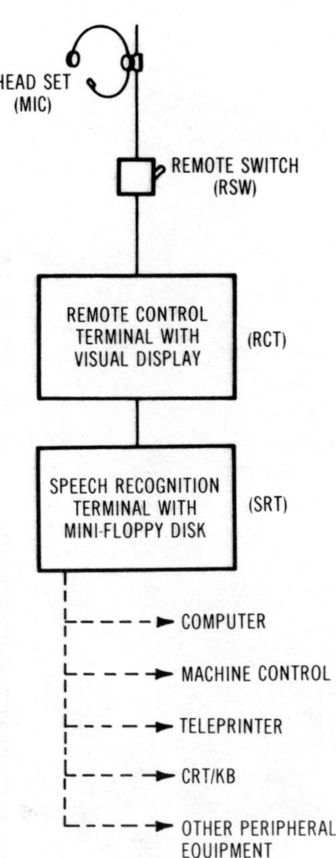

**Figure 9-6.
The NEC DP-200
system configuration
(Courtesy NEC Corp.).**

interfaces consist of RS-232C, RS-422, 20 mA loop for teletypes, and the IEEE-488 general purpose interface bus (GPIB).

The DP-200 will accept a vocabulary size of 50 words and recognize them in connected speech of 25 words per sentence. The recognition time at the end of the spoken sentence is 300 milliseconds. An interesting feature of the DP-200 is that it requires only a single training (enrollment) entry for each word. The complexity behind the connected speech-recognition capability is shown in the DP-200 block diagram in Fig. 9-7. Like most voice recognizers, the system utilizes spectrum analysis of speech input, but the dynamic programming processor provides the capability for connected speech recognition. The multiple processors within the system allow high speed matching of sentences and words while communicating in near real time with the outside world of machines and computers.

Although the DP-200 has a standard vocabulary of 50 words, there is an optional expandable hardware package that allows up to 500

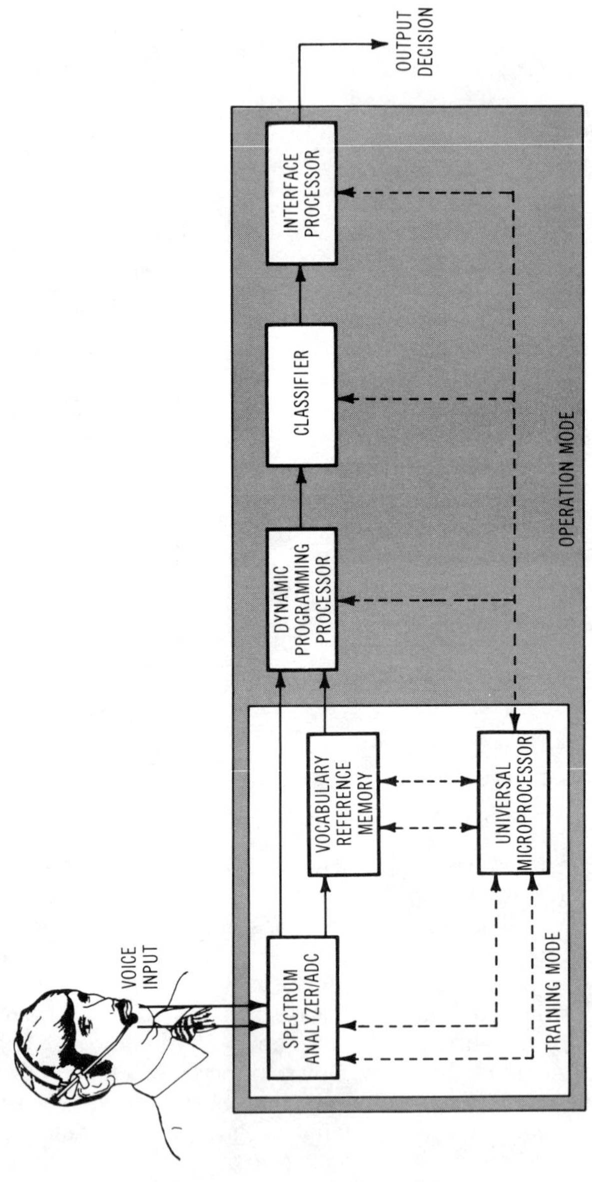

Figure 9-7.
The NEC DP-200 block diagram
(Courtesy NEC Corp.).

words for discrete word recognition. The DP-200 also provides excellent recognition performance in factory noise levels up to 85 dB(A).

The second stand-alone speech recognizer offered by NEC is the SR-100 Voice Input Terminal. The voice-recognizer hardware shown in Fig. 9-8 uses the same microphone as the DP-200 in the previous figure. Since this unit is not designed to be a connected-speech recognizer, its cost is lower but it still provides excellent performance with a recognition vocabulary of up to 120 words. Training the SR-100, as in the DP-200, requires only a single pass for discrete word recognition. The system interface to other computers is half-duplex RS-232C at 19.2K baud. Since the capability exists within the SR-100 to upload and download template patterns from the entire vocabulary; once trained, the system may be reloaded from the voice files stored within a main host computer.

The last product listed from NEC in Table 9-1 is the microcomputer-controlled Voice-Recognition Chip Set, the μPD 7761D. While the previous systems listed by NEC have come from the Systems division, this particular chip set is offered by the NEC Microcomputer division. Although the parent company for each division is the same, they are physically separated by several hundred miles (one is in New York, the other in Massachusetts).

The three-chip set offered by NEC includes three integrated circuits: the μPD 7761D, μPD 7762G, and the MC-4760. The concept behind the marketing of this chip set is to allow the user to produce a low-cost, low total chip count speech recognizer. A typical connection of the voice-recognition circuit as suggested by NEC is shown in Fig. 9-9. Although in the final system connection there are really more than three chips, the extra chips are primarily memory for storage of vocabulary information, and the serial input/output and parallel input/output port chips. As shown in the block diagram, the MC4760 contains the analog input for connection to the microphone or voice grade tape system. Of

Figure 9-8.
The SR-100 Voice Input Terminal, less microphone
(Courtesy NEC Corp.).

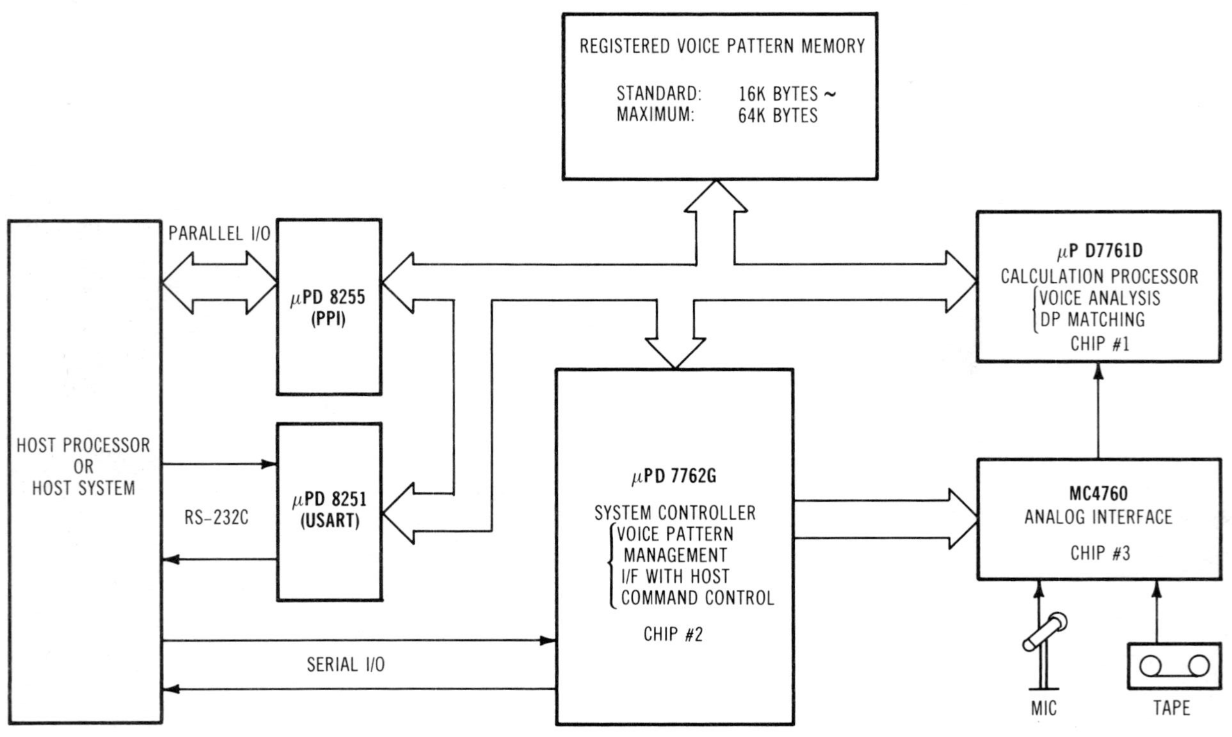

Figure 9-9.
NEC's three-chip Speech-Recognition System
(Courtesy NEC Corp.).

the remaining chips, the μPD7761D provides voice recognition capabilities and dynamic programming pattern matching while the μPD7762G controls the storage of patterns in memory and communicates with the host computer system.

The interaction may be more easily seen in the functional block diagram of Fig. 9-10. This figure shows the chip set combined with the 64K bytes of random access memory (RAM) needed for vocabulary storage. The system is still relatively low in chip count while providing full recognition features.

The characteristics of the three-chip recognizer when integrated into a system include a 128 word vocabulary with registration for up to 512 words, a one-half second recognition time and a recognition accuracy greater than 98%. The combination of recognizer chips also provides three types of communication with a host computer: parallel, synchron-

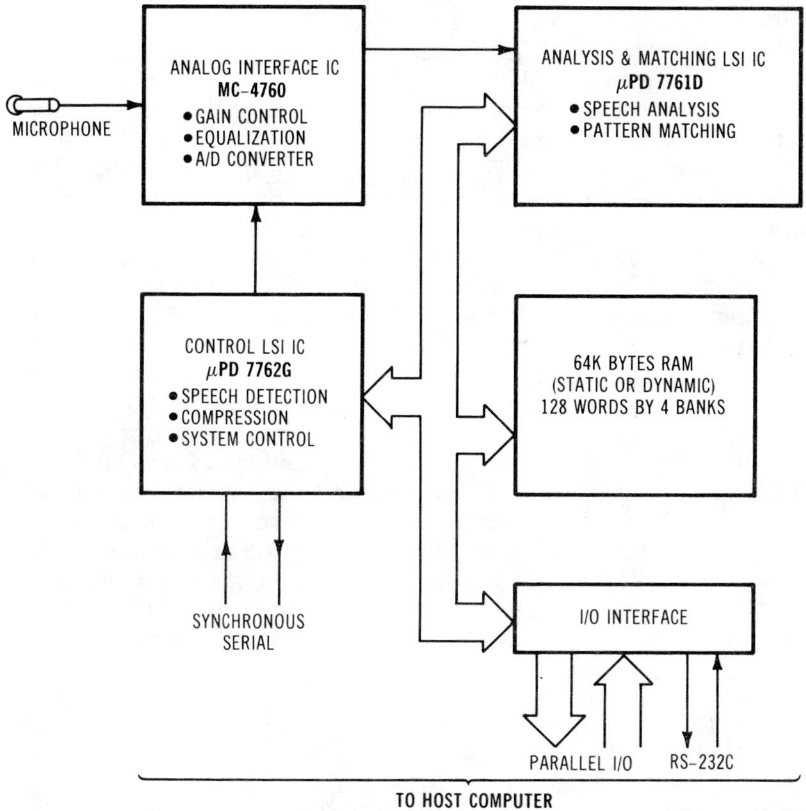

Figure 9-10.
A functional block diagram of the NEC three-chip Recognizer
(Courtesy NEC Corp.).

ous serial, and asynchronous serial RS-232C. The current cost of the chip set is rather inexpensive and is expected to continue decreasing as production efficiencies improve.

The products by NEC are quite varied from complete stand-alone recognizers to component level integrated circuits. Since they produce one of the few available connected speech recognizers, the people at NEC are obviously serious about speech recognition.

Scott Instruments

The voice-recognition products offered by Scott Instruments are designed primarily for the Apple® II family of computers. The products listed in Table 9-1 included the VET-2, the SHADOW/VET, and a software package known as the Voice-Based Learning System (VBLS). Although the people at Scott Instruments were very cooperative in supplying information on all of their products, they were reluctant, unfortunately, to provide publication rights to them. For this reason, one of the first personal computer voice recognizers to be listed has no accompanying photographs. On a more positive note, since the products are available for personal computers, they may be observed at many of your local computer stores and even operated for your own personal evaluation.

In describing the Voice Entry Terminal products, the hardware in the VET-2 and SHADOW/VET are very similar. Both are designed primarily for Apple® computers with the SHADOW/VET being the latest and most upgraded version. They consist of a hardware preprocessor with a software driving routine which resides within the host Apple computer. The preprocessor divides the incoming acoustic signal into two frequency bands, a low band from 300 to 1000 Hz and a high band from 1000 to 4000 Hz. The system counts the numbers of zero crossings during speech activation and then measures the envelope amplitudes over both regions. These four pieces of information are used for specifying the vocabulary word matrix in the subsequent speech-recognition process. Vocabulary words may be up to 1.5 seconds in duration with each word requiring approximately 115 bytes of template storage. Thus, the normal 40-word vocabulary will require somewhere around 4600 bytes of memory usage. The controlling software in the Apple memory needs about 6000 bytes so that a total memory space of around 11K bytes is needed for the VET-type recognizers.

The SHADOW/VET unit is designed to be compatible with computer languages such as Pascal, FORTRAN, BASIC, and many others. It is also designed to be used with Apple DOS 3.3 for system initialization. The computer requirements are an Apple II or Apple II + with 48K memory and at least one disk drive and peripheral slot available. System compatibility with the Apple IIe is not specified in the promotional literature; however, chances are it is compatible with the newest Apple computer also.

The final product listed under Scott Instruments is the Voice-Based Learning System (VBLS) software package. Scott states that this system is the first microcomputer-based instructional tool incorporating speech-recognition technology. It allows a student to talk to the computer, and control the pace of teacher-author instruction materials by voice command. The teaching subjects for each lesson are determined by the teacher and thus may include any subject taught in a classroom. The system is said to be flexible enough to support education of first graders through college seniors. Although the price listed for the VBLS system seems high, it also includes the Apple-compatible VET-2 unit *with* the learning software. In other words, this is a turnkey system designed for teaching students through voice control with Apple computers.

On the sidelines, Scott has announced a speaker-independent isolated word-recognition system for future introduction. The system, code-named "88," is a result of constant research on-going at the laboratories at Scott Instruments. Availability of the speaker independent system is expected in the near future.

SuperSoft-Techmar

As this book goes to press, the availability of a software/hardware speech-recognition interface package for the IBM Personal Computer has been announced. It is now available on the market. The system is designed to be used with the IBM personal computer as a voice-activated spreadsheet software package. The cost includes hardware and software that allow the user up to 97 commands in an isolated word-recognition mode. It basically gives you the capability to vocally command the software package "Scratch Pad." For further information on this product, contact the manufacturer listed in Appendix C.

Threshold Technology, Inc.

Threshold is offering a variety of speech-recognition products for commercial users and even personal computer hobbyists. They are probably best known for their newly acquired voice-recognition system: "The AURICLE." This unit has been on the market for quite some time as a peripheral for the personal computer market.

The first two products listed in Table 9-1 for Threshold Technology include stand-alone speech recognizers that interface to the host processor through RS-232-C or 20-mA current loop asynchronous serial ports. Baud rates may be selected from 50 to 19.2K baud. The less expensive of the two, the T-500/580, provides the user with a 16 character alphanumeric display for voice data entry verification. The second system, with essentially the same basic characteristics, provides a crt terminal and keyboard for system operation. Both units are extremely flexible and allow the storage of around 60 vocabulary words with the added availability of a feature called QUIKTALK®. This allows an entry speech rate of somewhere around 180 words per minute—very close to a connected speech rate.

The second type of unit offered by Threshold is the T-950 voice option plug-in board for the TeleVideo Model 950 terminal. The interface board is supplied as a Voice Option Board for installation inside of the TeleVideo 950 intelligent terminal. According to Threshold Technology, no wires need be added and no soldering is required for installation. All hardware needed for converting the T-950 is included within the interface package. Once installed, the voice system allows up to 80 words or phrases in the vocabulary with a three-pass training sequence. (Each word must be entered three times.)

The last and probably most well-known recognizer from Threshold Technology is the AURICLE. This recognizer is a relatively small unit as shown in Fig. 9-11. It is a self-contained automatic speech-recognition (ASR) system that accepts speech input from a microphone and outputs digital characters to a host computer that identifies the spoken words. The interface connection may be through RS-232-C asynchronous serial data, the IEEE-488 (GPIB) bus, or an 8-bit parallel TTL bus configuration.

The AURICLE is produced in three configurations. The one previously described uses RS-232 for communication with any computer. A second unit is offered that interfaces with the HP-85, HP-86, or HP-87 from Hewlett-Packard to provide speech recognition over the HPIB interface bus. This unit, unlike the other AURICLEs, contains the capability for up to 120 words within its vocabulary. Other than that, the only real difference between the units is the addition of the IEEE-488 interface bus option on the rear panel of the AURICLE-1. This is shown in the upper right corner of the unit in Fig. 9-12. The third configuration

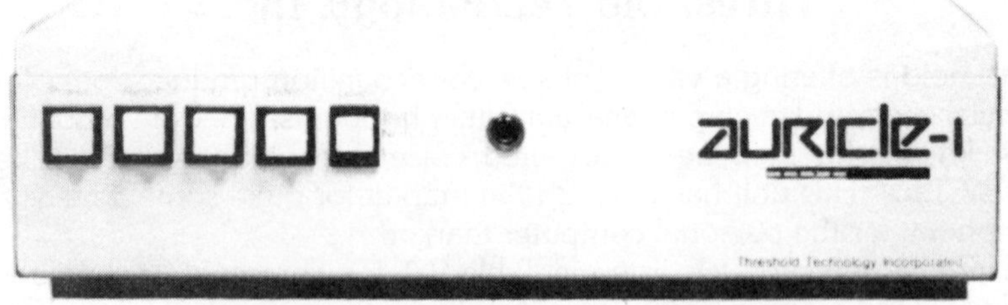

Figure 9-11.
The AURICLE-1 Speech Recognition Unit
(Courtesy Threshold Technology, Inc.).

Figure 9-12.
The rear panel of the AURICLE-1 Automatic Speech Recognizer
(Courtesy Threshold Technology, Inc.).

offered is a single-board recognition module, the AURI-1/RM. It is a single printed circuit board containing the AURICLE-1 speech system designed for production volume use.

The operation of the AURICLE-1 recognizer is based upon a hardware preprocessor which electronically separates incoming speech data into 15 frequency ranges. The ranges are digitized and then used to provide vocabulary enrollment and recognition. Fig. 9-13 shows the functional block diagram for the flow of information within the AURICLE series of speech recognizers. The specific microprocessor used on board the AURICLE is the Z-80 unit. The bandpass filter block referred to as the speech processor is a custom circuit manufactured for Threshold Technology. By utilizing switched-capacitor filters, the single-chip preprocessor performs the function of a large number of analog circuits required for voice filtering. The integration of the analog preprocessor into the AURICLE circuits is shown in Fig. 9-14 to illustrate the complexity within this single-chip function.

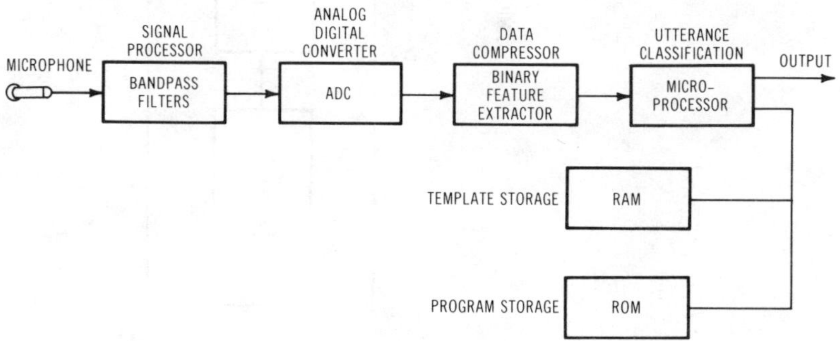

Figure 9-13.
The flow diagram of the AURICLE-1 Automatic Speech
Recognizer (Courtesy Threshold Technology, Inc.).

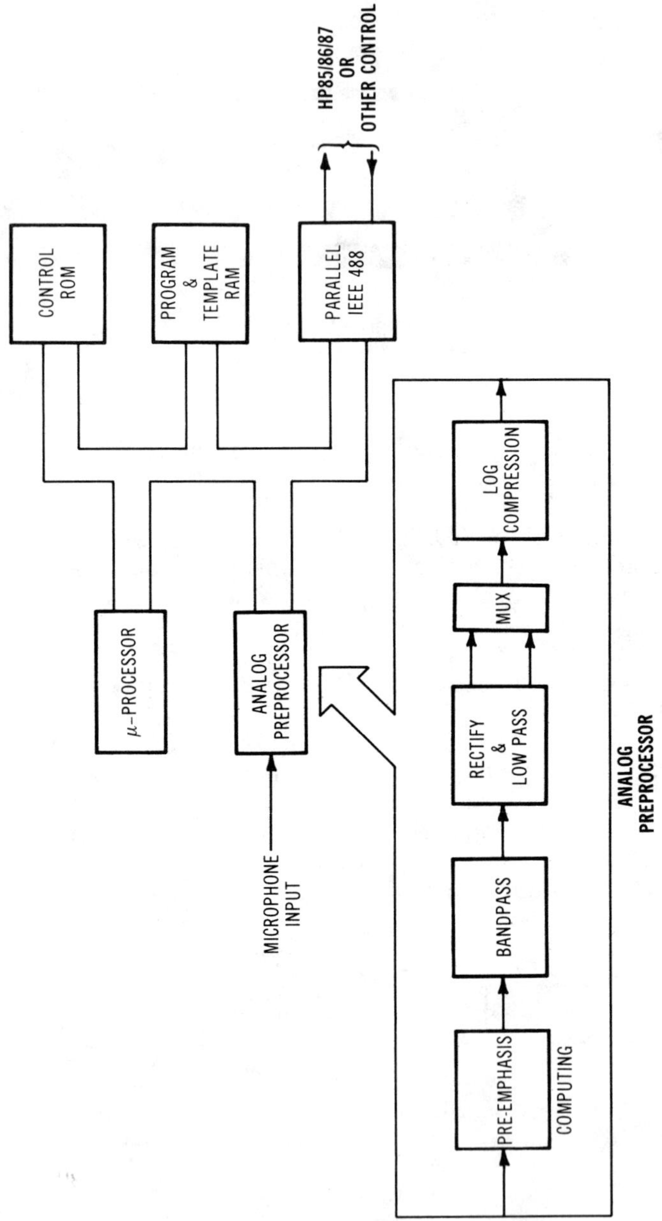

Figure 9-14.
The analog preprocessor in the AURICLE-1
(Courtesy Threshold Technology, Inc.).

The AURICLE series of recognizers allows nine major controlling commands that may be used to control the recognition process. These are entered through the RS-232C port from a host computer or crt/ keyboard terminal. Recognition accuracy is 99% or better with a response time of approximately 300 milliseconds with a full vocabulary. Although this is a rather expensive peripheral for home computers, it is certainly one worth investigating, considering its reputation.

Texas Instruments Incorporated

The entry of Texas Instruments into the speech-recognition market is very cautious. Although this is a company to really watch (based on the introduction of their TMS-320 digital signal processor), the flow of commercially available products using this device is still at a trickle.

Probably the first and most important speech-recognition unit offered by Texas Instruments is the interface board for the TI Personal Computer. It is based on the TMS-320 signal processor and plugs into a peripheral slot in the Texas Instruments computer. Rumor has it that if the last few inches of the printed-circuit board—which have been conveniently left completely vacant—are physically removed by cutting the pc board, it will also fit into the IBM Personal Computer. Of course, in time, this unit will certainly be available for the most prevalent computers such as the IBM PC and others.

The TI speech board is designed as a turnkey speech recognizer. Unfortunately, very little information is given about the recognition process itself. Eventually computer hobbyists will delve into the internal firmware of the TMS-320 board and have available to them an extremely high speed speech processing system. For the time being, however, the board is considered purely a voice input module/recognizer for the TI PC.

Verbex

It stands to reason that a company with backing as large as Exxon is going to have a pretty impressive product. And they do. The Verbex 3000 Voice Data Entry data terminal shown in Fig. 9-15 is a user-friendly voice input peripheral designed specifically for industrial environments. It can operate in a background noise level as high as 85 dB with a recognition accuracy of greater than 99%.

The 3000 system consists of two main parts, the small user work station and the larger speech processing unit. As in the previously described NEC DP-200, this speech recognizer also accepts *continuous speech* with a recognition vocabulary of up to 360 words. (120 words is the standard vocabulary.) The system will respond to the user's voice

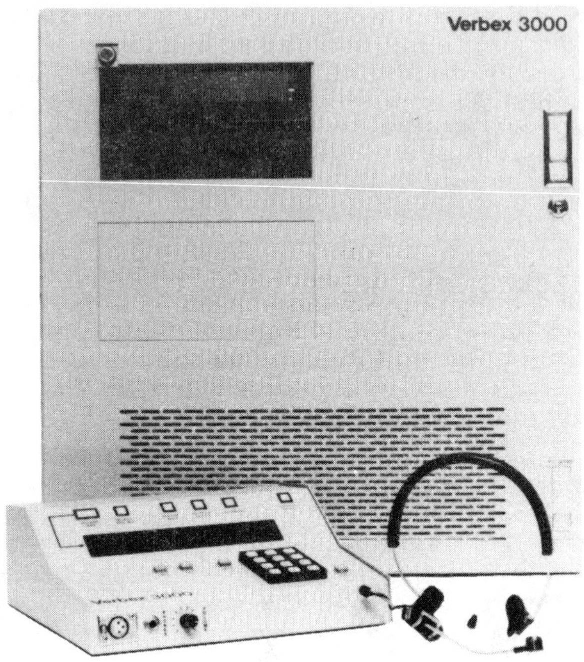

Figure 9-15.
The Verbex 3000 Continuous Speech Recognizer
(Courtesy Verbex).

input within 300 milliseconds with either visual or optional audio feedback to verify an input message.

Since the unit is specifically designed for the industrial environment, there is considerable customer support from Verbex in terms of software and hardware interfacing. Also since the host computer interface from the Verbex 3000 is through RS-232-C asynchronous data, the recognizer can be easily interfaced to most computers. One of the more unusual options offered by Verbex is a wireless headset which allows the operator to roam away from the recognizer free of connecting wires.

A fairly recent entry into the speech-recognition market from Verbex is the Model 3000 SPADS terminal. This addition to the original 3000 allows development of speech applications software in a resident mode. The SPADS system provides you with a speech-development system for evaluating speech recognition and creating the operating software for the system's ultimate use. If Verbex ever decides to enter the personal computer market with speech input peripherals, watch out for some pretty impressive products.

Voice Machine Communications, Inc.

VMC, through the introduction of their recent Voice Input Module (VIM), is providing the personal computer market (specifically the Apple II and Apple IIe) with a relatively low-cost voice-recognition peripheral. The complete VIM package designed for the Apple computer is shown in Fig. 9-16. It is available for the Apple II, II+, and IIe, and other Apple-compatible computers.

Supplied with the hardware is the software package allowing vocabulary training and recognition within the Apple computer. Optional accessories for the VIM are a wireless microphone, a head-mounted boom microphone, and a foot-pedal microphone switch.

Performance specifications for the Voice Input Module include a vocabulary of up to 80 discrete words or phrases, greater than 98% recognition accuracy and a response time of less than 150 milliseconds. Within the Voice Input Module hardware, there is a custom-designed spectrum analyzer integrated circuit which splits the voice band up into 16 frequency bands through switched capacitor filtering. The microprocessor used to control the hardware spectrum analyzer is the 68B03

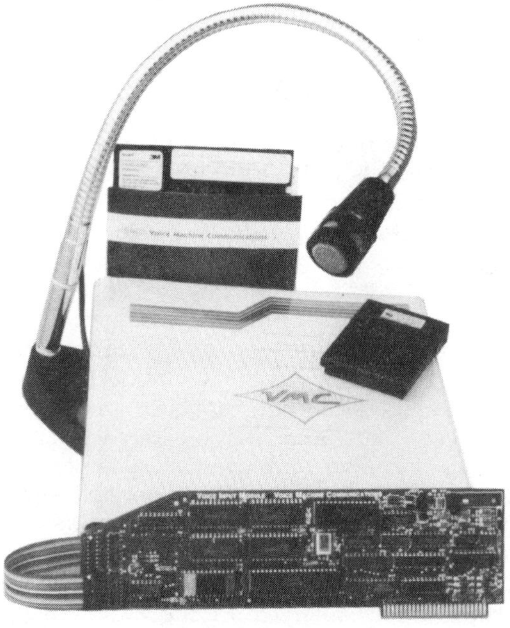

Figure 9-16.
The Voice Input Module (VIM) for the Apple® II, II+, IIe, and
compatible computers (Courtesy Voice Machine
Communications, Inc.).

chip from Motorola. Memory included within the system is an 8K byte bank of RAM and 4K bytes of EPROM firmware. Installation is performed by simply inserting the recognizer module into a spare peripheral slot in the Apple computer with a bus cable intercept from the keyboard to the Apple computer circuit board. This connection allows the VIM to directly replace the keyboard for operating such programs as VisiCorp's VisiCalc spreadsheet program by utilizing only voice commands. For the price, the system is quite impressive in the personal computer market. This relatively new corporate entry into the field of speech recognition has quite a future if their product is accepted in the speech-recognizer market.

VMC also offers (as a turnkey package for the medical profession) a system known as the Voice Operated Computer System for medical management (VOCS). The hardware consists of three Apple computers, a 32-megabyte Winchester disk drive, an Epson printer and crt monitor, and three microphones. The software package supplied is a menu driven program which allows a doctor's office to verbally examine and maintain patient records, and business transactions. Although the system cost is relatively high as shown in Table 9-1, the time savings offered to a medical office could be tremendous.

Votan

This company is another one fully involved in the speech-recognition market. Their total products which include speaker dependent and independent hardware *with* speaker identification included are listed in Table 9-1. Although a rather large offering of units is listed from the V-1000 through V-8000 recognizers, some of these may be withdrawn from the market as the more popular ones proliferate.

The V-5000 speech-recognition unit is designed as a stand-alone recognizer for development purposes or as a voice input/output peripheral for use with a host computer. The V-5000 shown in Fig. 9-17 integrates into one small system the capability for speaker-dependent recognition and speech generation. It also allows voice response, voice store and forward, vocoding and even speaker identification. The V-5000 is housed in an 11- x 18- x 3½-inch portable unit that contains the entire system electronics. Vocabulary capacity within the unit is 256 words in either the stand-alone or host connected configuration. The primary method of interface to the host computer is via RS-232-C asynchronous serial data, so interfacing is a relatively simple matter.

Another product within the Votan family is the V-6040 which features the first low-cost implementation of speaker independent recognition (SIR). It is said to be able to recognize any voice speaking a predefined vocabulary without prior training. The V-6040 shown in Fig. 9-18 also includes the capability of being used as a stand-alone or host-interface

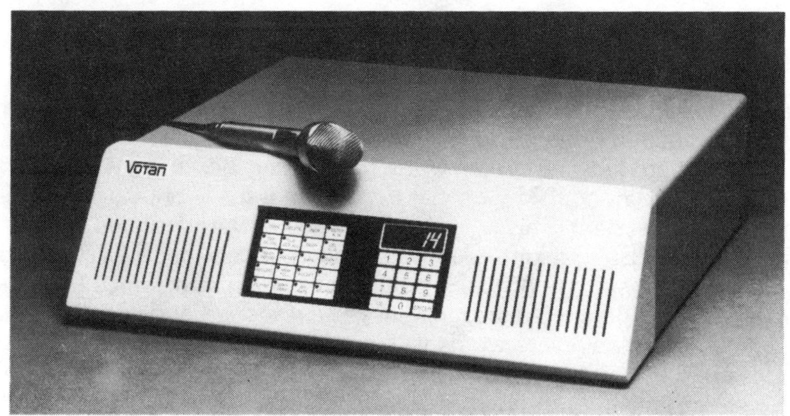

Figure 9-17.
The Votan V5000 Speech Recognizer
(Courtesy Votan).

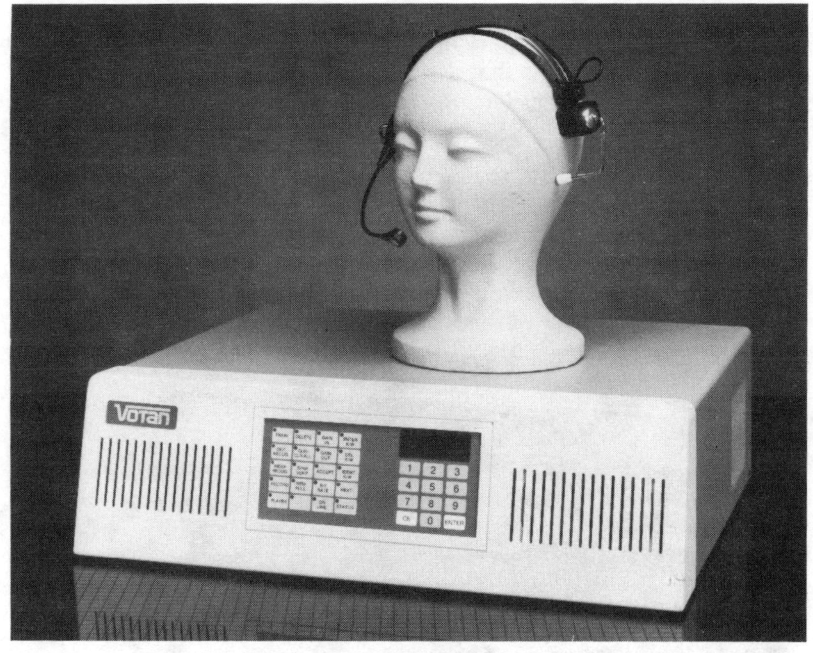

Figure 9-18.
The Votan V6040 Speaker Independent Speech Recognizer
(Courtesy Votan).

peripheral speech recognizer. The vocabulary in this unit initially includes the digits 0 through 9 and the words yes and no. Custom vocabularies for the V-6040 are also available and may be developed in any language. Since this unit is speaker independent, there is no operator training required prior to use of the system.

One last product from Votan worth mentioning, because it is designed to interface with the IBM Personal Computer, is the V-8000 series Integrated Voice system. This unit, shown in Fig. 9-19, is designed to interface with the IBM Personal Computer and operate with IBM's standard disk operating system. Available software for the system which features speaker dependent word recognition, voice response, and vocoding will allow you to manipulate words within a vocabulary file, add or delete from a file of voice messages, and even swap templates in and out of vocabulary memory through single commands. The vocabulary size in this system—like the other Votan products—is 256 words or phrases. Votan also offers many other speech associated products, including telephone line interfaces and single-board voice-controlling systems.

The operation within the Votan recognizer products is probably more complex than those recognizers normally found in home computing or personal computing systems. The recognizer operation shown in the flow diagram in Fig. 9-20 provides a graphic representation of the recognition process. The primary difference between this and many of the less expensive systems is that the digital spectral transform block computes 128 spectral coefficients over the speech band, equalling a bar-

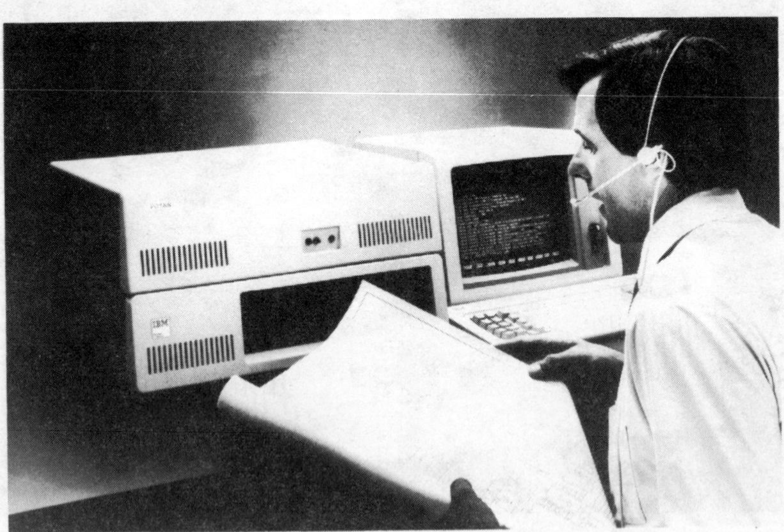

Figure 9-19.
The OBM PC-compatible Votan V8000-series
Integrated Voice System (Courtesy Votan).

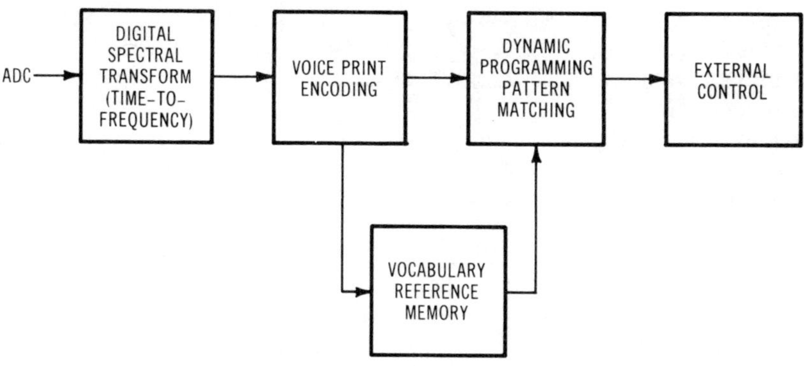

Figure 9-20.
The Votan voice-recognition process
(Courtesy Votan).

rage of 128 analog filters. Surprisingly, the Discrete Fourier Transform is not used because of the time consumption required. Instead, Votan uses a proprietary mathematical technique for spectral analysis and separation. In addition to the complex mathematical speech processing, there is also a dynamic programming algorithm to compensate for varying word lengths during recognition. The hardware within the Votan systems allows for voice compression and reconstruction in addition to recognition. A typical block diagram of a Votan recognizer is given in Fig. 9-21. Although it looks somewhat like a generic diagram for a speech recognizer, it follows very accurately the guidelines for speech recognition given in Chapters 4 and 5 of this book.

The speech recognition products from Votan are varied but extremely sophisticated. Although their cost puts them slightly above the personal computing hobbyist market, they have excellent application in the industrial and corporate environment.

Weitek Corporation

The last products to be reviewed are the Weitek speech-recognition chips. These are currently two products by Weitek for speech recognition. The WTV008 is a demonstration kit which illustrates the capabilities of the WTV108 single-chip recognizer. It is reported to be speaker independent with a vocabulary of up to 16 words. Recognition accuracy is greater than 90% with a real time response. Other information about the Weitek chip is rather sketchy but full information should be available through the manufacturer listed in Appendix C.

So there you have it, the lineup of most currently available commercial products for speech recognition. There has been no intent to slight

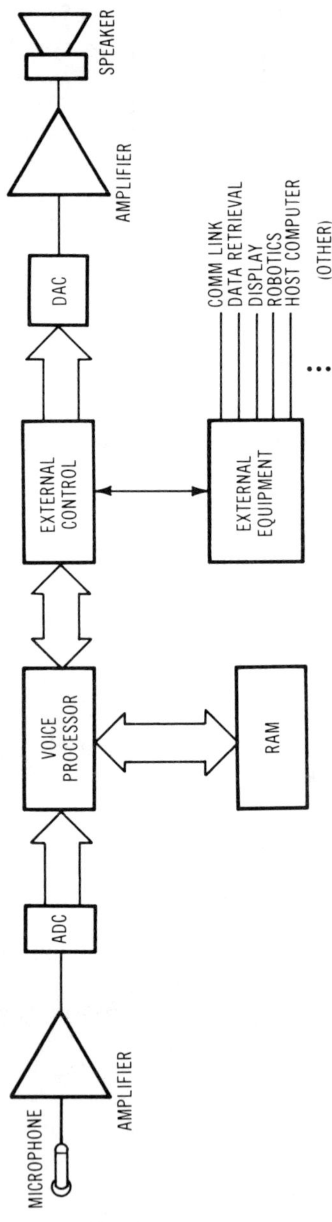

Figure 9-21.
Typical block diagram of the Votan Recognizer
(Courtesy Votan).

or accent any one manufacturer's products over the others. They are all excellent technological advances in speech recognition. Since the marketplace is changing so rapidly, if you have an interest in a particular line of products, then you should consult the manufacturer directly for the most recent information on product advances and introductions. If you would like to evaluate the operation of voice recognition without spending the typical $800 and up cost for the recognizers, *and* you enjoy diddling with hardware, then the next chapter should really capture your spare evenings for the next few weeks. In it you will find the instructions for assembling the hardware and software for your own speech-recognition system.

CHAPTER 10

Building a Working Voice Recognizer

This chapter is presented as a design guide for those of you who would like to attempt the construction of a voice-recognition system. Although it would be very desirable and convenient to present the information in this chapter like the step-by-step illustrations in a Heath Kit®, the complexity of the circuitry and concepts of a speech recognizer tend to prevent such details in a single chapter on voice-recognition construction.

In contrast, this chapter *will* present design concepts and circuits which, when copied and integrated together, will provide for your computer a working voice-recognition system development station. The hardware and software will allow you to develop and fully understand the voice-recognition process.

The target microprocessor described in the interface circuits is the 6502 microprocessor found in many 8-bit personal computers. However, the computer interface circuits within this chapter's diagrams may be modified for other existing processors such as the Z80, 8088, and 8080.

The construction descriptions given herein are intended for the experienced computer hardware hobbyist. Software designs presented which operate the speech-recognition hardware consist primarily of examples of BASIC programs and 6502 assembly-language–coded subroutines. What you will have if you decide to attempt some of the construction projects within this chapter is a series of relevant circuits which will allow you to trace and understand the recognition process. It is highly recommended that you have at your disposal an audio oscilloscope for circuit checkout following construction. Although the major portion of the circuitry presented was constructed and tested on a Wire-Wrap® prototyping board, some of the analog input circuitry was point-to-point wired utilizing soldering techniques for minimum noise susceptibility. Depending upon the recognizer complexity that you would like to incorporate within your system, the cost of the components needed to complete the described circuits will range from $50.00 to $300. With those precautions in mind, proceed carefully through the remainder of this chapter. As you construct and connect the circuits to your computer, there is always a possibility of component damage if the circuits are not carefully constructed and meticulously wired. Be especially careful when connecting the computer interface circuits to your personal computer, for there is nothing worse than having your computer system go up in a puff of smoke when you finally apply power to your experimental circuits. On an encouraging note, all of the circuitry given in this chapter has been constructed and tested to be operative and of sound design.

If you are not really interested in constructing your own voice recognition system, then you may learn some circuit techniques by simply following the circuit descriptions and design discussions which follow.

Hardware Construction

The best place to start the circuit design descriptions is at the beginning of the speech recognition system: the microphone input.

Speech Input Circuitry

Without belaboring the point of microphone selection given in Chapter 2, you should have a good microphone in mind before starting this project. A typical acceptable microphone will be a high quality noise-cancelling dynamic microphone with an impedance of somewhere between 200 and 50K ohms. The first electronics following the microphone are referred to as the speech input amplifier circuits. Fig. 10-1 illustrates an amplifier and prefilter circuit to boost the input voltage from your microphone to more usable levels for the remainder of the system. The first operational amplifier is configured as a differential amplifier with a gain of eight to eliminate hum and noise which may be picked up by the microphone cable. It is followed by a 2-pole, 240 Hz, high-pass filter with a low-frequency rolloff rate of 12 dB per octave. Thus, at 120 Hz, the response is 12 dB down, while at 60 Hz, the response is 24 dB below the gain within the passband of the filter. The addition of this circuit filter tends to reduce 60- and 120-Hz hum pickup

---

Wire-Wrap is a registered trademark of Gardner-Denver Co.

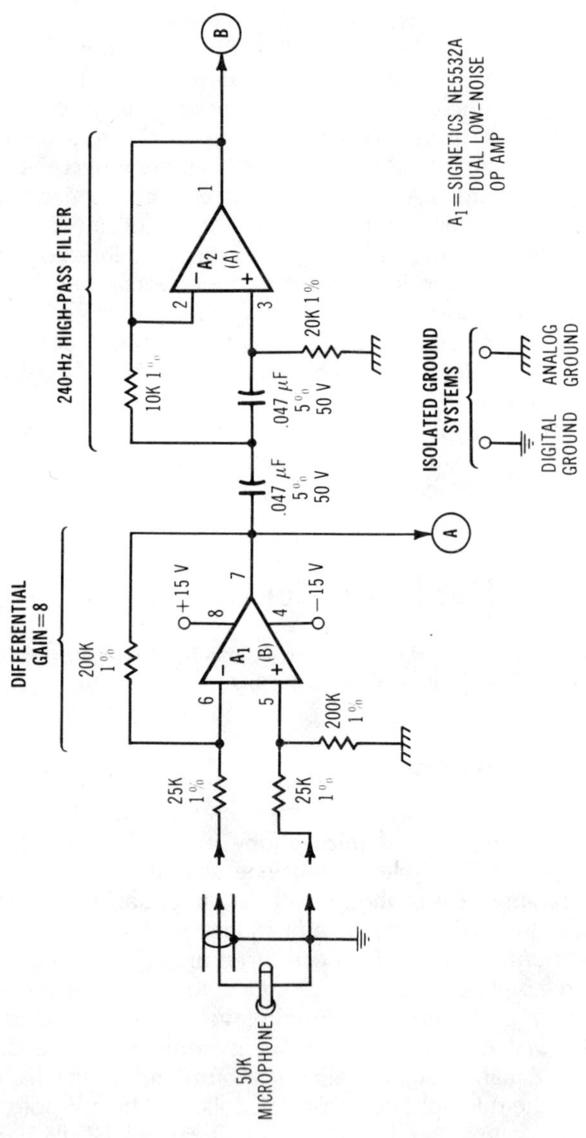

Figure 10-1.
Speech input amplifier circuits.

from power-line sources. Since the filter's response at 240 Hz is only 3 dB down, it has very little effect on the lowest formant frequencies of speech. The cut-off frequency was chosen to provide an optimal compromise between noise elimination and speech fidelity.

The only precautions to be taken with this circuit include point-to-point solder construction to prevent noise pickup by wire-wrap pins and open wiring. The two amplifier functions are contained in a single eight-pin mini-DIP package so it may be compactly wired away from digital circuits where noise pickup is more critical. Remember that the input to this amplifier circuit is on the order of a few millivolts while the remainder of the computer system has switching voltages typically around 5-volt levels. It does not take much stray noise pickup to introduce a whine or a whistle into the microphone amplifier chain. The amplifier/filter output terminals Ⓐ and Ⓑ are wired to the remainder of the circuitry; and if located more than a few inches away from the next stages, should be wired with shielded cable.

A few notes about circuit details. The dual amplifier used for this circuit is highly recommended because of its *low noise* characteristics. If you cannot obtain an NE5532A, then other amplifiers may be substituted; however, the noise performance will suffer and your system may be fighting circuit noise during speech recognition. A standard wiring procedure to be followed is physically separating the analog ground from the digital ground. This also prevents noise pickup from any switching circuitry in close proximity. Although the voltage level between the two grounds is basically zero, ac noise *will* exist between them. They are carried separately and connected only at a single point in a later schematic.

Speech Presampling 3-kHz Low-Pass Filter

As you remember from Chapter 4, the digitization of speech may create alias frequencies if the speech bandwidth exceeds one-half the sampling rate. This circuit is included to prevent that condition from occurring. Since most of the speech information is carried in a band of frequencies below around 3 kHz, we may selectively eliminate those higher frequencies, thus allowing a slower sampling rate.

The low-pass filter in Fig. 10-2 is a 3-pole Chebychev filter with a 0.5-dB passband ripple characteristic. It does an excellent job of filtering the higher frequencies above 3 kHz with a rolloff rate of 18 dB per octave. Thus, one octave up in frequency from 3 kHz gives us an 18-dB attenuation of signal level at 6 kHz. As we will later see, if we choose a sampling rate of 7–8 kHz, then we have sufficient attenuation of speech frequencies above one-half the sampling rate to prevent severe aliasing.

The low-pass filter is noncritical in its construction; however, the component values need to be quite close to those listed or the filter charac-

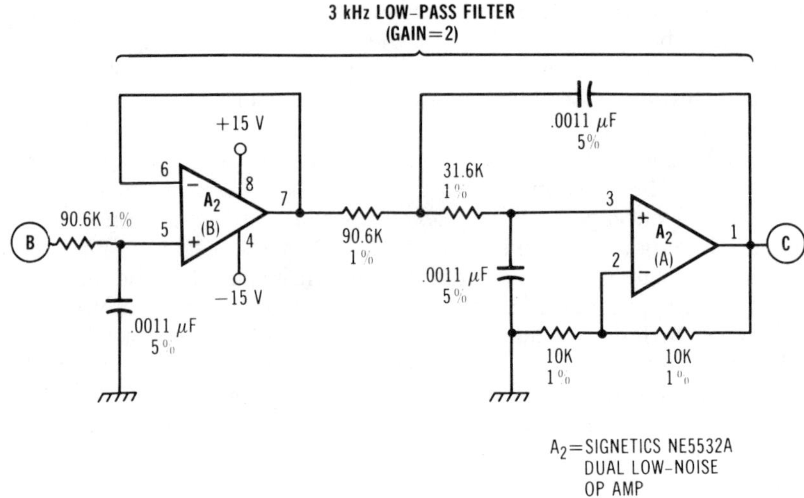

Figure 10-2.
The speech presampling 3-kHz low-pass filter.

teristics will suffer. Since the design equations for these components are all simultaneous equations, equal values listed need to be carefully matched together. The 1% resistors listed should be used in this circuit to prevent resistor long-term drift and also provide a lower resistor noise contribution over carbon composition resistors. The amplifier pair in this combination is identical to that in the speech input amplifier, an 8-pin mini-DIP Signetics NE5532A low-noise dual operational amplifier. While I recommend that this circuit be hand wired with extremely short connections, it may be wire-wrapped if you desire. Since the signal levels are still relatively low as they pass through this filter, it should be physically isolated from surrounding digital circuits. (Notice again that the ground referenced in this schematic is the analog ground.)

Speech Boost Amplifier and Bandpass Filter

So far in the circuitry presented, the speech signal has been amplified, high-pass filtered to reduce hum, and low-pass filtered for presampling to prevent aliasing. The input Ⓒ to Fig. 10-3 is a speech signal which has been preconditioned but is still at a relatively low amplitude. The first amplifier in Fig. 10-3 provides a gain of up to 25 which will yield a full 10-volt peak-to-peak swing of the preconditioned speech signal. This first amplifier also contains the volume control (gain control) for the entire speech system which should be preset so that at normal speaking amplitudes the output swing is approximately 10 volts peak-to-peak. The second stage in Fig. 10-3 is a bandpass filter/level shifting

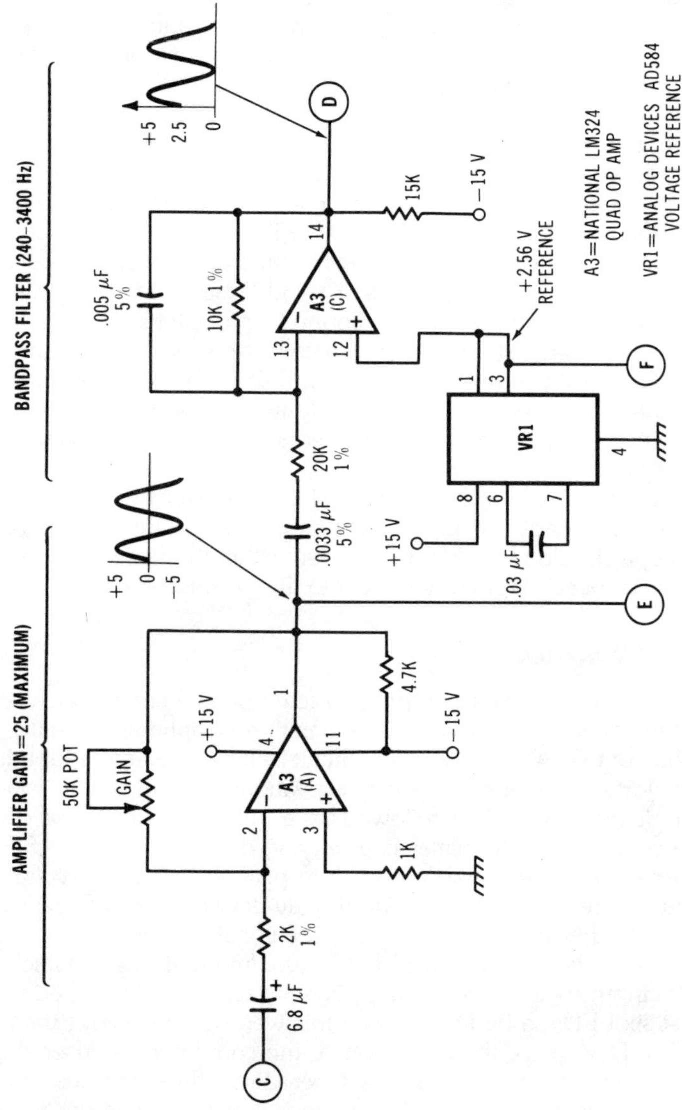

Figure 10-3.
Speech boost amplifier and bandpass filter.

amplifier which puts a final limit on the frequency response of the speech signal, and also dc level shifts the speech signal for proper digitization in the analog-to-digital converter which follows. Since this filter circuit has a gain of one-half in its passband and it must supply a 5-volt peak-to-peak ac signal to the A-to-D converter, its input level is adjusted for the previously mentioned 10 volts peak-to-peak for normal speech.

The voltage reference used in this circuit produces a very stable 2.56-volt reference voltage at the input to the final filter stage which is directly reflected at the output terminal Ⓓ as a dc offset level of 2.56 volts. The primary reason for doing this is so a 0 to 5 volt A-to-D converter may be used for digitization, thus avoiding the problems normally associated with bipolar converters. Terminals Ⓔ and Ⓕ are utilized in the next portions of the circuitry for speech controlling functions.

There are no critical components within the speech boost amplifier and bandpass filter. Amplifier A3 is an LM324 quad operational amplifier available from several sources. Only two of the four amplifier sections are used in this schematic. The remaining two will be used in the upcoming schematic.

The output Ⓓ is a speech signal which has been fully conditioned and amplified, ready for sampling. Output waveforms viewed on an oscilloscope should resemble those given within the circled balloons for a sinusoidal speech input (a whistle into the microphone).

Bells and Whistles

The circuitry in Fig. 10-4 comprises a few optional circuits which may be added for show in a speech-recognition peripheral. Actually, the upper half of the bells and whistles circuit is quite convenient for adjusting the voice level during speech activation. It consists of a speech rectifier circuit and dc filter followed by a buffer amplifier. The output voltage of the buffer amplifier is a varying dc level from 0 to 5 V dc corresponding to the equivalent peak-to-peak speech signal voltage at the input to the a/d converter. The display device is an LED bar graph array and driver assembly from National Semiconductor, the NSM39168. It is basically an LED VU (volume unit) meter which displays the input speech amplitude by lighting sequentially colored LEDs. The first six LEDs to be lit are green followed by two yellow, then two red LEDs. During speech activation of the computer, the user should attempt to keep his voice at a level where the VU meter is just starting to light the second red LED. This assures that the maximum range is being utilized on the a/d converter during digitization. The circuit resistor constants have been chosen so that as the last red LED is being lit, the analog-to-digital converter is just approaching maximum input saturation. The use of this display is not only convenient, but very effective in providing a visual indication that all speech circuitry is operating correctly.

The lower portion of the bells and whistles circuitry consists of two

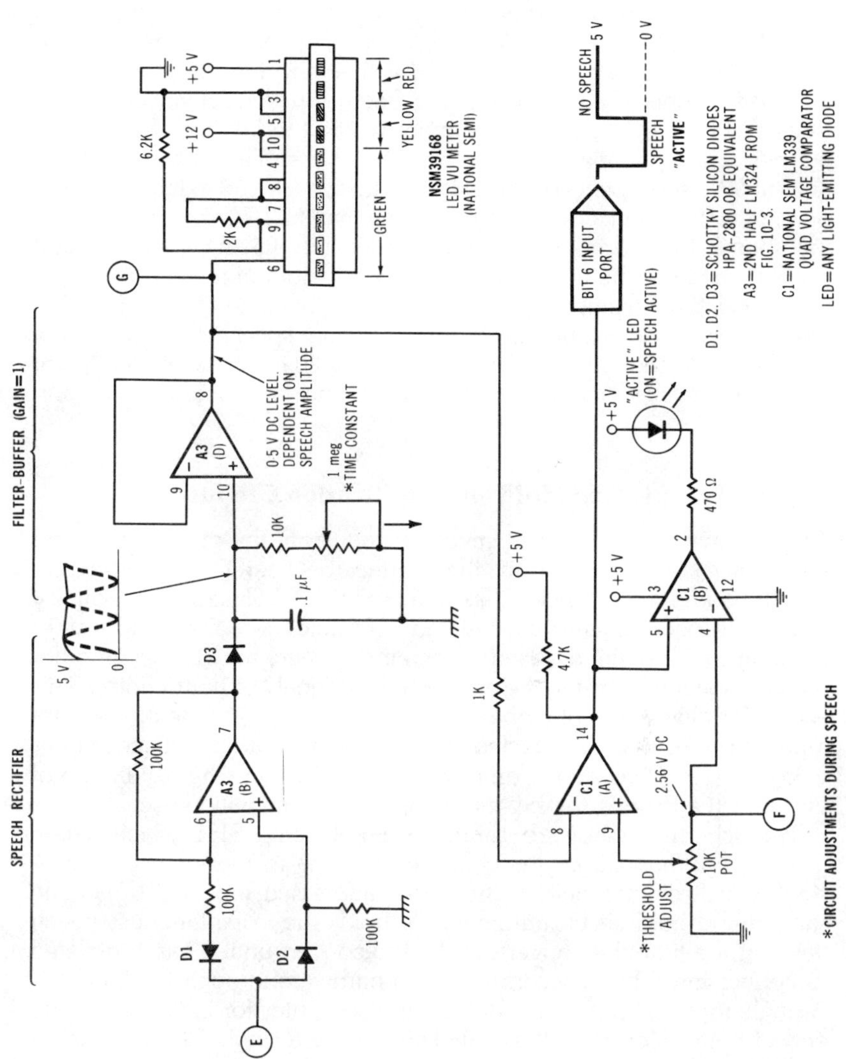

Figure 10-4.
Optional bells and whistles speech circuit.

comparators (half of C1) which provides a threshold input bit for computer testing to see if speech is over a preset threshold. The way that the circuit is adjusted is through the *threshold adjustment* potentiometer at the lower left of the figure. If you decide to use this circuit, which provides the computer with an indication of speech activity (and you with a visual LED showing threshold activation), then the threshold is adjusted like this. With the room quiet and no speech activity, adjust the threshold pot slightly above the point where the "Active" LED extinguishes. Then, try speaking into the microphone. The LED should illuminate for a short period of time during the speech and extinguish upon or shortly after silence. The length of time that the LED remains on after the speech has occurred may be adjusted through the time constant potentiometer in the upper part of Fig. 10-4. Both of these controls are marked with an asterisk (*) to ease identification.

If you opt not to include these circuits in your speech recognizer, then the system will still operate correctly and exactly the same as with them; however, as the circuitry name implies, you lack a few "bells and whistles."

Speech Sample-and-Hold and Digitization Circuits

To get down to the heart of speech recognition, the sample-and-hold and digitization circuitry forms the interface between the analog signals and the computer. The circuit shown in Fig. 10-5 illustrates a relatively low-cost speech digitizer which is quite flexible. As a matter of fact, in addition to the direct digitized speech input, there are also seven other analog inputs which may be connected to signals of your choice. This allows for digitization of game paddles, joy sticks, etc. One of the extra inputs may be even connected to the rectified and filtered speech envelope signal Ⓖ as shown on input 1. This will allow the digitization of the speech envelope for experimental speech-recognition use.

The schematic shows a sample-and-hold chip SH1 which, when given a command from the computer (writing to the address XXX0–XXX7), will digitize one of the seven addressed inputs (I0–I7). The sample-and-hold circuit automatically holds the instantaneous speech value at the time the converter is told to convert until it has completed its conversion. This is accomplished in hardware through flip-flop FF1. A single-input-bit port is needed on the computer for indication of the end of conversion (EOC) signal. This can be a single PIA input bit of any 8-bit input port. When the bit is low, the converter is busy converting. As it goes to a high (+5 volt) level, it signals the computer through the input bit that it has completed its conversion task. Maximum conversion time for this system is 100 microseconds so the capability exists for digitizing at a sample rate of up to 10 kHz. This will allow for more than adequate sampling of a speech signal for accurate and fast speech recognition. The only unspecified circuit component within this sche-

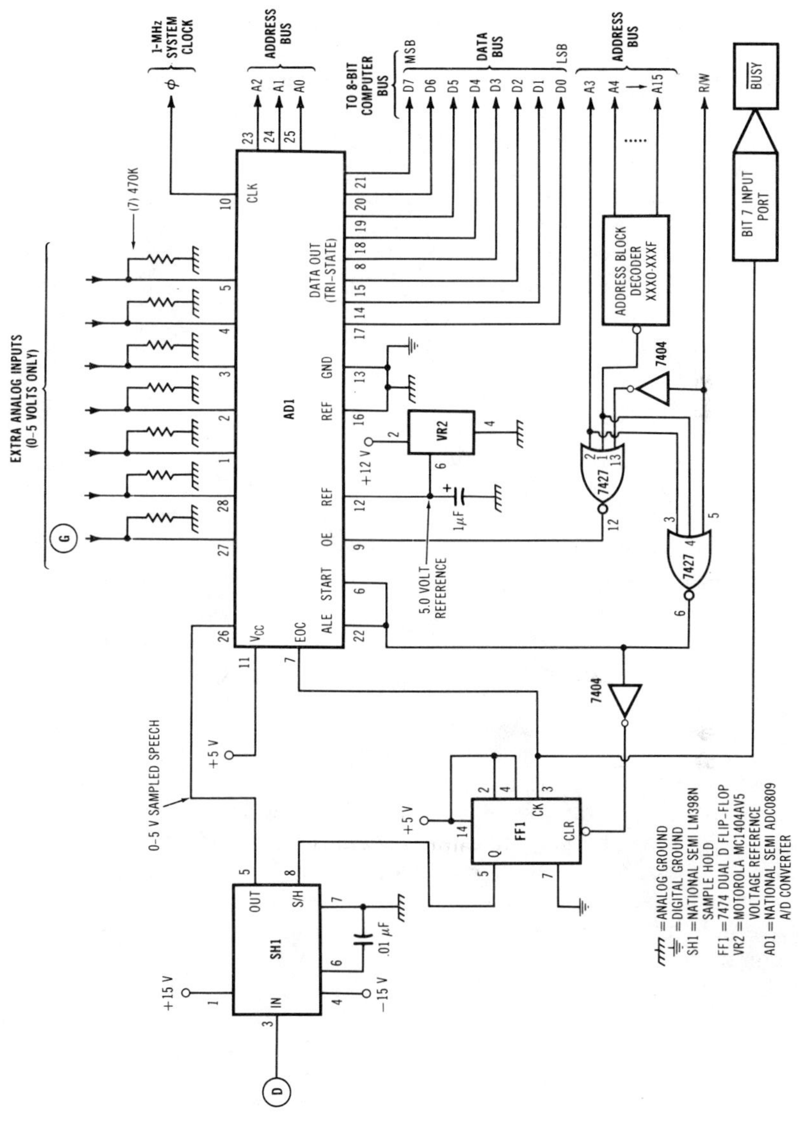

Figure 10-5.
Speech sample-and-hold and digitization circuits.

matic is the address block decoder box. This is the same decoding mechanism used to decode memories, input/output ports, etc. The address may be of your choosing; however, the decoding should be for only one specific combination of addresses A4 through A15 in an 8-bit computer. The remainder of the addresses A0 through A3 are properly decoded by the circuit itself. Thus, when a particular address combination of A4 through A15 is presented to the address decoder block, the output goes low and consequently enables the analog conversion circuitry.

To start the conversion of any specific addressed input (input 0 through input 7), the computer must simply *write* to an address XXX0 through XXX7, respectively. Once the system has been told to convert an input, the computer monitors the busy input line for the end of conversion signal. When the conversion end (EOC high) is indicated, the computer may *read* any port XXX0 through XXX7 address to determine the converted, addressed input value.

The operation of the analog conversion circuitry is extremely simple in software because of the hardware hold-command flip-flop. Normally the software would be required to sample and hold the speech signal and then command the a/d converter. At the completion of the conversion, the computer would then release the hold line to allow the sample-and-hold chip to return to the sample mode. The flip-flop FF1 alleviates all of these problems and provides a perfectly adequate means of sampling the input signal and holding it automatically.

TMS32010 Digital Signal Processor (Optional)

The circuits given up to this point are adequate for digitizing speech and storing the sampled speech information within the computer memory. Exactly how those speech samples are processed during the recognition program depends on the software complexity and level of accuracy and speed desired. The particular circuit given in this section is for the advanced hobbyist who wishes to experiment with the newest available circuit technology. Using the schematics which follow, you can add an extremely high speed speech processing circuit to your 8-bit microcomputer system.

In addition to being rather complex, the cost of the Texas Instruments TMS32010 alone is somewhere around $130. This cost can really boost the expense of the speech-recognition development system; however, when finished, you will have at your disposal a 32-bit (internal) microprocessor that operates at an instruction rate of five million instructions per second! If you remember the description in Chapter 5 of the TMS32010, it is 32-bits wide internally so when you add this extremely fast parallel processor to your 8-bit system, you have expanded your computing power to be the same as in a small mainframe computer.

(You will also have given your computer the capability of multiplying two 16-bit numbers with a 32-bit result in 200 nanoseconds!)

The additional circuitry required to interface the TMS32010 to an 8-bit computer requires around 14 extra chips excluding the TMS32010. The schematic for the major portion of the digital signal processor interface is given in Fig. 10-6. The entire circuit may be wire-wrapped since only digital signal levels are present. There is, however, one extremely important point to remember: the speed of the TMS32010 is so extreme that the wiring between the interface and the TMS32010 should be very short to reduce delays in wire lengths and signal coupling between lines. The four static memory chips used (TMM2016P-1) are 2K by 8-bit static RAM chips. The -1 option *must* be used here because the signal processor requires a maximum memory access time of 100 nanoseconds. If you desire to substitute other 2K by 8-bit memory chips, then they must have an access time of 100 nanoseconds or less!

There is one slight conceptual difficulty within the DSP interface circuitry which should be thoroughly understood. That concept is in the mapping of a 4K by 16-bit memory space for the DSP chip into an 8K by 8-bit memory array for the 8-bit microprocessor interface. This is the reason that the lowest address line A0 from the microcomputer connects to the data bus transceivers rather than the memory array itself. The transformation maps a single 16-bit instruction word for the TMS32010 into two sequential 8-bit memory addresses. This process may be more easily understood by observing the block diagram of the DSP interface in Fig. 10-7. Notice that the address decoder for the microcomputer address bus not only enables the correct locations in memory for each address signal, it also alternately switches between the high and low 8-bit portions of the 16-bit DSP memory data bus. This is one of the few ways that the 16-bit bus can be mapped into an easily accessible 8-bit data bus system. This will be further clarified in a few later paragraphs.

The remainder of the DSP interface is quite simplistic in nature with no tricks or special devices needed to make the system play. When this interface was constructed and connected to the author's personal computer, there was both exhilaration and astonishment when during the first attempt to force the TMS32010 to multiply two numbers together, the resultant answer was correct! In less time than the 8-bit processor had taken to tell the DSP chip to start, and then return to look for answer, the program had executed and left the TMS32010 twiddling its thumbs waiting for the 8-bit processor to return for the answer. This type of computational power is really hard to get used to, but if you realize that, for instance, in an Apple computer the 6502 microprocessor requires anywhere from 2 to 6 microseconds to complete one instruction, the TMS32010 will have executed from 10 to 30 instructions during that time.

If you plan to add this signal-processing peripheral to your computer,

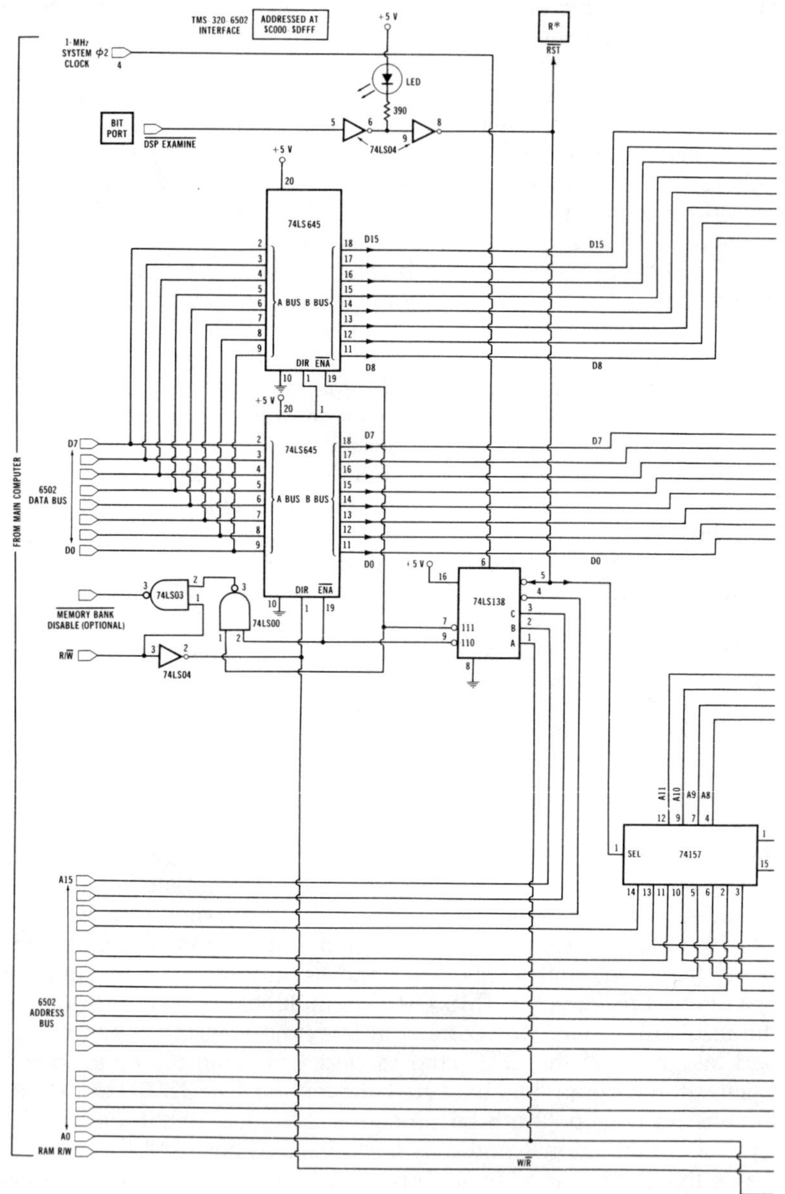

Figure 10-6. A TMS32010 digital

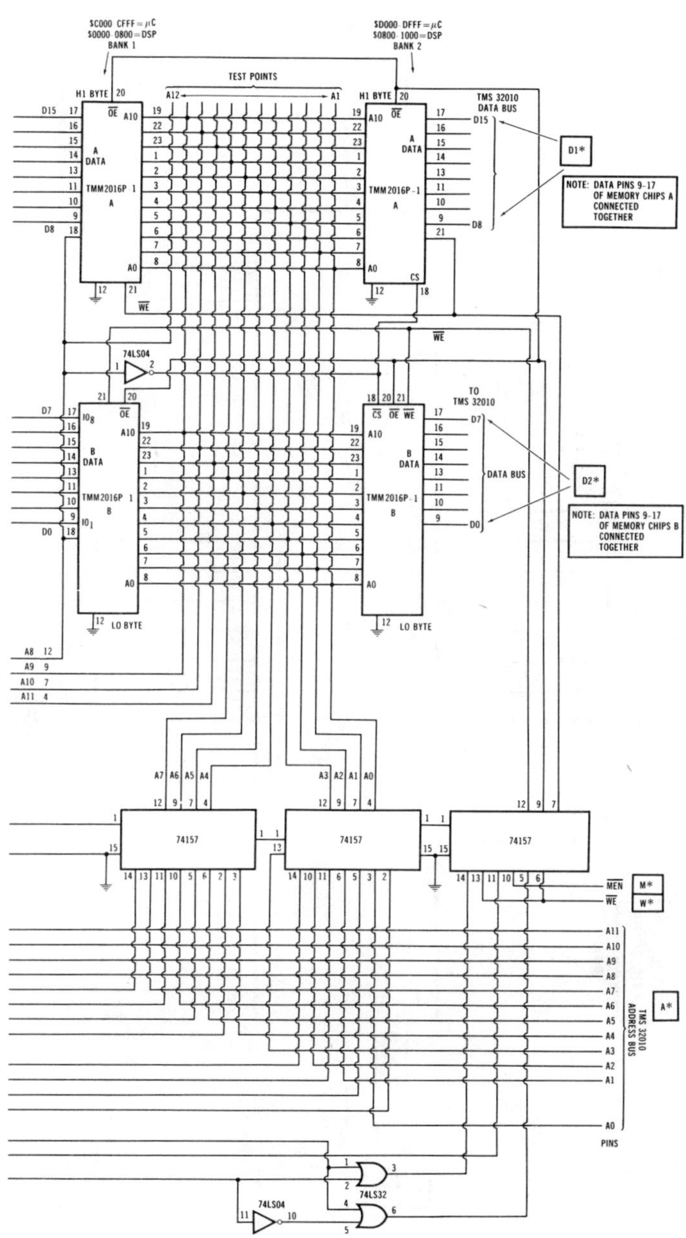

signal processor interface schematic.

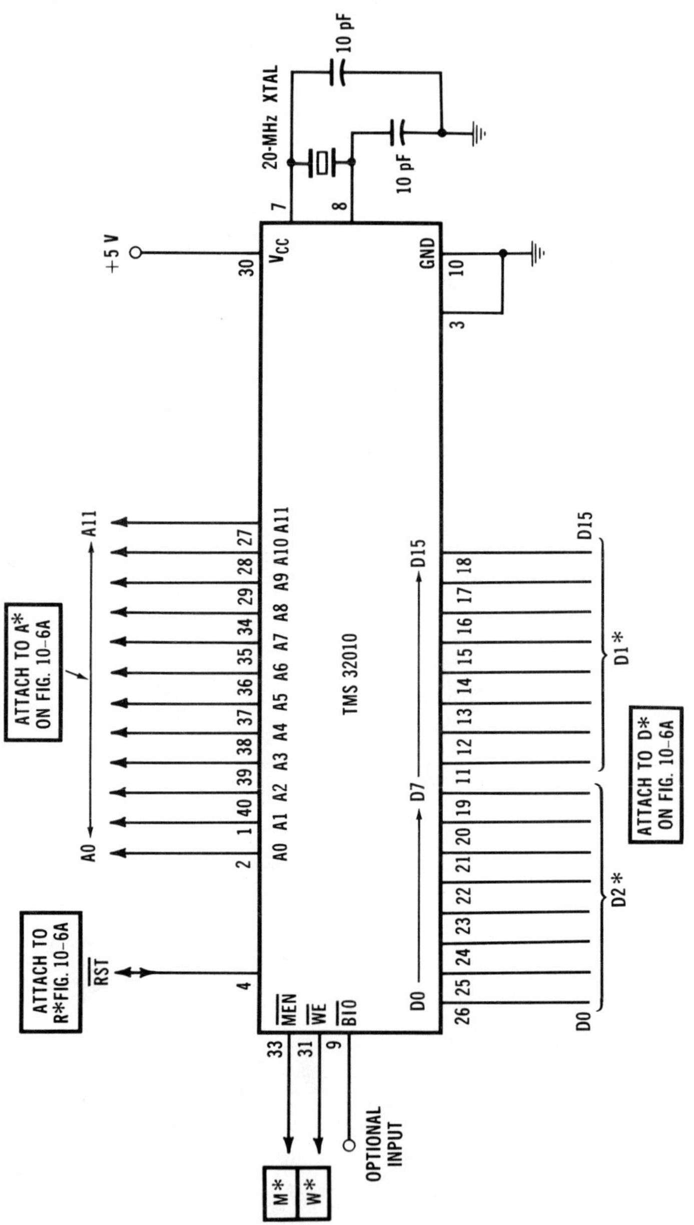

Figure 10-6—Continued
A TMS32010 digital signal processor interface schematic.

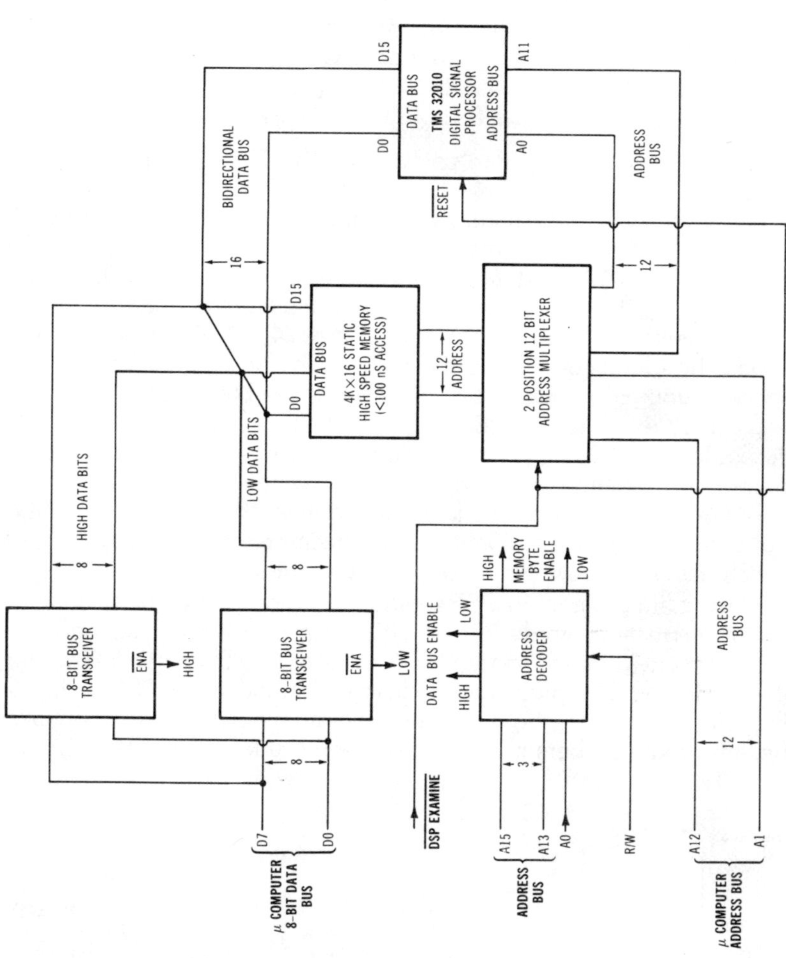

Figure 10-7.
The TMS32010 DSP interface block diagram.

then I strongly recommend that you contact Texas Instruments and obtain the complete data package for the TMS32010. The package is quite informative and the user's guide alone has almost 370 pages of information on using the powerful DSP chip. The address to write for more information is:

> Texas Instruments Incorporated
> Literature Response Center
> P. O. Box 401560
> Dallas, TX 75240

Simply request the literature package on the TMS32010 digital signal processor.

Now, returning to the memory organization and operation of the DSP interface. First of all, the memory mapping decoder used in Fig. 10-6 places the port-shared static memory from address C000 to DFFF (hexadecimal) for the 8-bit microprocessor. If this memory location block is inconvenient for your system, then the 74LS138 decoding circuit should be modified to place the memory block within an appropriate space in your computer system. The single line named DSP EXAMINE is used by the 8-bit microprocessor to halt the TMS32010 and gain access to the DSP memory. This line is normally connected to a single output port bit and may be toggled by software to control access to the DSP system. As soon as the line is taken high, the TMS32010 is taken out of the reset mode and immediately begins execution of the program which has been prewritten into the DSP memory.

Placing the program in DSP memory is accomplished by splitting the 16-bit instruction words for the DSP chip into 8-bit bytes and then placing them in the addressed DSP memory, low byte first, followed by the high byte. The procedure is illustrated in Fig. 10-8. Notice that on the left of this figure, the 8-bit data spaces have a group of six arbitrary hexadecimal numbers in the first six memory locations C000 through

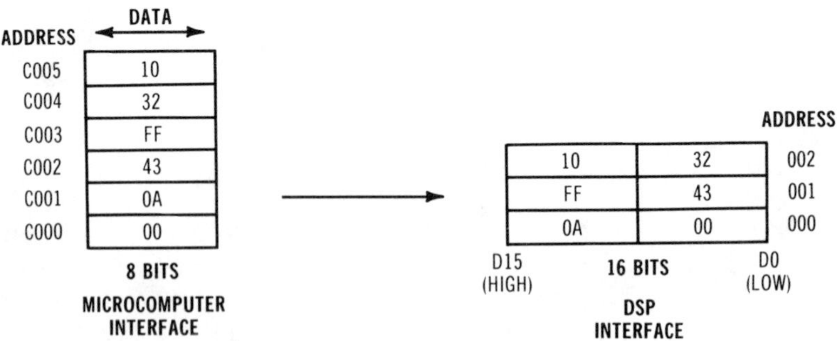

Figure 10-8.
The 8- to 16-bit data-bus transformation.

C005 (hexadecimal). When the memory bank is handed over to the TMS32010, the memory multiplexer no longer accesses the data as 8-bit bytes, but rather views the bytes two at a time to create a 16-bit wide instruction bus. The equivalent addresses for the DSP chip are also changed to a starting address of 0. If you track the movement of each data byte into the 16-bit space, then you can see how the instructions are acquired by the TMS32010 in reverse order. The whole process is somewhat rather arbitrary, according to the design of the memory multiplexer; however, if you duplicate this circuit exactly, then this is the way you must put data into memory for any digital signal processing program.

There are a few features left off of this minimal circuit which would certainly be convenient in a complete system. Some of the most important omissions are the input/output ports to enable the digital signal processor to talk with other devices. There is, however, a means by which the circuit shown can communicate with the controlling 8-bit processor. It is through the first eight 16-bit wide locations in the DSP memory. If, during a program, the TMS32010 outputs to any one of the eight "OUT" ports 0 through 7, that output data simply gets stuck into the first eight locations in memory (0 through 7) with the current circuit diagram. The 8-bit microprocessor may at any time acquire control of the DSP memory and examine the first *sixteen* 8-bit wide memory locations to acquire direct data transfer from the DSP chip. While the entire procedure is quite intricate, if you get into this system and begin to understand the workings of the TMS32010, then these comments will become more relevant *and* understandable.

So, overall, the digital signal processing interface given here is basically a starter circuit for any readers interested in getting into extremely highly sophisticated speech-recognition experimentation. If this subject—presented briefly here—were covered fully for everyone's understanding, then you would now be reading a book on use of the TMS32010 rather than speech-recognition principles (and it would probably be longer too).

Digital-to-Analog Signal Reconstruction

The final optional circuit, which is recommended in a speech-recognition development system, is a digital-to-analog converter. This device will allow you to replay or simply listen to any digitized speech information which may be stored in memory. This also allows you to investigate diverse signal processing techniques like digital filters, and even creating interesting sound effects as shown later in this chapter. The circuitry required is extremely minimal, requiring only a single chip and an 8-bit output port. The schematic in Fig. 10-9 shows an 8-bit digital-to-analog converter which may be used to reconstruct any sampled data stored in computer memory. While not absolutely necessary

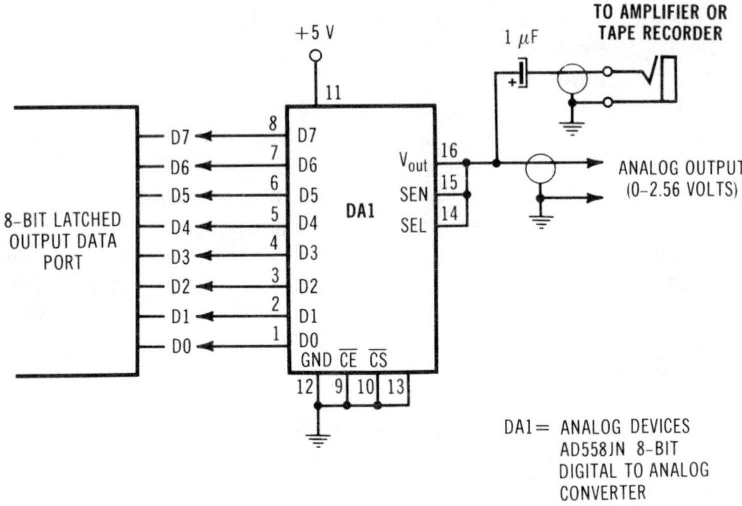

Figure 10-9.
An analog reconstruction d/a converter circuit.

for the voice-recognition process, this single-chip addition can really provide you with some confidence-raising feedback about what is being stored into your memory and used as sampled speech data.

Hardware Summary

Well, that's it. With the circuitry previously presented, you can construct a working voice-recognition development system for your own personal computer. If you decide not to attempt the advanced experimentation approach, thus omitting the digital signal processing interface, you will have added somewhere around 13 extra chips to your computer circuitry. Not bad for a speech recognizer.

Before attempting any development in speech-recognition software, it is mandatory that all of your speech input circuits work correctly *and* interface properly to your personal computer. The best way to do this is to assemble the system. Then connect the microphone and input an audio tone into the microphone while checking the signal points at the various terminals in the previously given schematics. Fig. 10-10 gives a complete run down of the labeled signal points so that you may, with an oscilloscope, check for correct voltage levels and therefore determine correct circuit operation. When testing for the signals in Fig. 10-10, ensure that the waveform frequency that you are observing is between the lower and upper cut-off frequencies of the speech circuitry (240 to 3000 Hz).

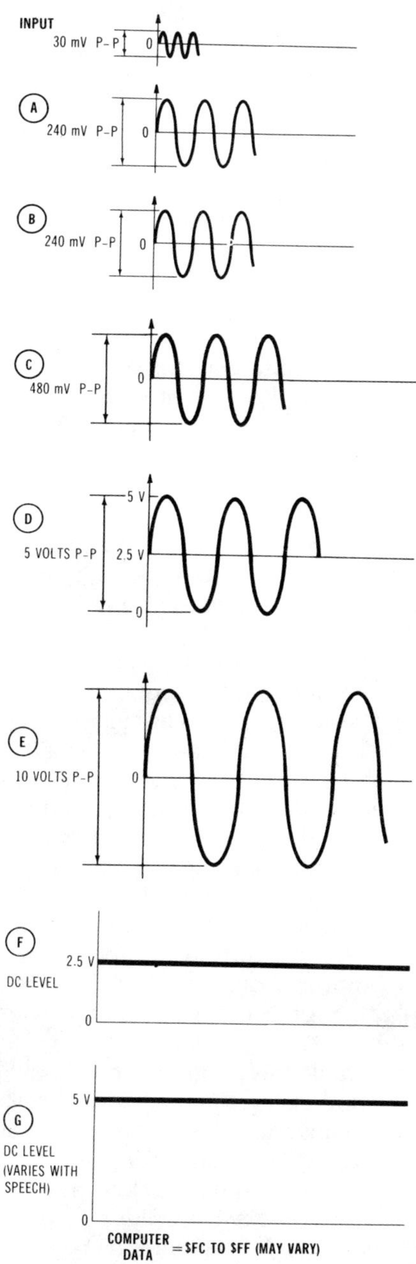

**Figure 10-10.
Signal waveforms through speech circuits.**

Once you have constructed, tested, and verified that the circuits are operational you are ready to begin software testing of the system.

Software Design

The software listed in this section primarily consists of several machine language subroutines designed for the 6502 microprocessor, in addition to an *automatic speech-recognition program* written in a standard Microsoft BASIC. Although all of the software relies on the utilization of hardware presented in the previous section for operation, if you presently have the ability to digitize speech, store it within memory, and then play it back through a digital-to-analog converter, the programs described will still work in your computer. While it may seem unbelievable that you can create a speech recognizer with only a digitized speech input, it *is* possible. The short BASIC program to accomplish this feat is given at the end of this section.

If you currently have a speech digitization capability within your computer, then you should simply compare the listings given (which follow) to ensure a compatibility with the ones you now use for digitizing and storing speech in memory.

The first listing is a 6502 assembly language program which may be used as a diagnostic for assuring that your speech digitizer and DAC circuits are operating correctly. The extremely short program listing is given in Listing 10-1. The only system-oriented changes to make in this program listing are the modification of a few address locations to match your own system's addressing of the analog-to-digital and digital-to-analog converter. There is also a test for a break key (BREAK) to enable you to easily exit this program once entered. If you have no such break key or interrupt key available, then simply push your reset button to exit. Since there is no timing loop within the machine language listing, the analog-to-digital converter runs at full speed—about 8 to 10 kHz. The flow of the program in Listing 10-1 is given in Fig. 10-11. This simplifies the visualization of exactly what is happening within this simple diagnostic subroutine.

As you enter and execute this program, you should be able to speak into your microphone and observe your speech directly from the output of the digital-to-analog converter. If you connect the audio output connector in Fig. 10-9 to a tape recorder or audio amplifier, then you should hear your speech very clearly with low distortion.

Assuming that program works correctly; and you verify that your speech *does* propagate through your computer system and exit as real digitized speech, then you are ready for an assembly-language program that acquires digital speech and stores it in memory. The main use of this program will be to service the recognition program in BASIC, pre-

Listing 10-1.
AD2DAC—A Speech Diagnostic Subroutine for the 6502.

```
01-0010   2000                         ;LISTING 10-1. SPEECH TO OUTPUT DAC TEST ROUTINE
01-0012   2000                         ;
01-0013   2000                         ;
01-0014   2000                         .OPT SYM,ERR
01-0015   2000              BREAK  =$FF50              ;BREAK KEY - BIT 7
01-0020   2000              SPCH   =$FF42              ;BIT 6! SPEECH "ACTIVE" BIT
01-0025   2000              DACDIR =$FF33              ;SET UP DAC PIA FOR OUTPUT
01-0030   2000              DAC    =$FF32              ;DAC OUTPUT PORT
01-0045   2000              SPECON =$FF71              ;WRITE TO CONVERT SPEECH
01-0050   2000              ADCRED =$FF70              ;READ HERE TO GET CONVERTED VALUE
01-0055   2000              ENDCON =$FF42              ;BIT 7 SIGNALS END OF CONVERSION
01-0060   2000                         *=$A000
01-0065   A000  A9 FF       AD2DAC LDA #$FF            ;DAC PORT TO OUTPUT
01-0070   A002  8D 33 FF           STA DACDIR          ;NOW SET IT
01-0075   A005  2C 42 FF    START  BIT SPCH            ;TEST FOR SPEECH ACTIVITY
01-0080   A008  70 FB              BVS START           ;IF NOT LOOP BACK TO START
01-0125   A00A  8D 71 FF    GOON   STA SPECON          ;CONVERT SPEECH
01-0145   A00D  2C 50 FF           BIT BREAK           ;TEST FOR ABORT KEY (BREAK)
01-0150   A010  30 01              BMI BUSY            ;NO KEEP GOING
01-0155   A012  00                 BRK                 ;ABORT INPUT IF BREAK KEY HIT
01-0161   A013  2C 42 FF    BUSY   BIT ENDCON          ;WAIT FOR CONVERSION
01-0163   A016  10 FB              BPL BUSY            ;WAIT FOR EOC HIGH
01-0165   A018  AD 70 FF           LDA ADCRED          ;GET CONVERTED VALUE
01-0170   A01B  8D 32 FF           STA DAC             ;OUTPUT IT TO DAC
01-0175   A01E  4C 0A A0           JMP GOON
01-0180   A021               .END


SYMBOL TABLE 0002


BREAK    FF50    SPCH    FF42    DACDIR  FF33    DAC     FF32
SPECON   FF71    ADCRED  FF70    ENDCON  FF42    AD2DAC  A000
START    A005    GOON    A00A    BUSY    A013

END OF ASSEMBLY = A020
```

sented later in this chapter. You may also use it to digitize speech directly; and then manually examine memory to confirm the storage of values within your computer.

The program for acquisition of speech data is given in Listing 10-2. It is very much like the previous program with the exception of the subroutine STORIT. Rather than output the analog-converted value to the d/a converter, in this program it is stored into a memory location pointed to by a buffer memory pointer WHEEL. The storage buffer exists from $1000 to $1FFF (hexadecimal). If these locations are inconvenient or incompatible with your computer's address decoding, then change the values in line 160 and 410 to match your needs. A flowchart for the listing is given in Fig. 10-12. This allows you to examine how the data is digitized and stored into memory. Also notice that the break key and speech "ACTIVE" flags are used to abort the program during execution. Of course, the program will completely fill the buffer and exit the subroutine by itself within approximately 0.5 second after speech begins, but if anything goes wrong, it is nice to have an escape route. In this program, as in the last one, if you do not have a "break" key available, or have not implemented the "ACTIVE" bit function in Fig. 10-4, these

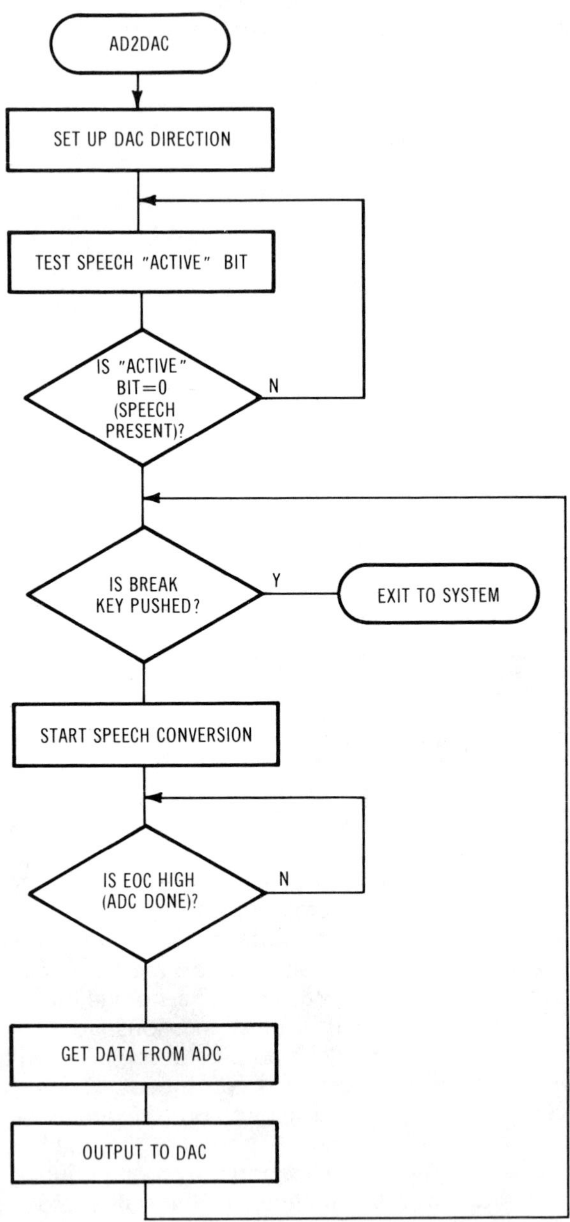

Figure 10-11.
A flowchart of Listing 10-1 for converter checkout.

Listing 10-2.
GETBUF—A Speech Acquisition Subroutine for the 6502.

```
01-0010   2000                        ;LISTING 10-2. SAMPLES SPEECH AND STORES IT
01-0020   2000                        ;(4096 SAMPLES) IN MEMORY
01-0030   2000                        ;
01-0040   2000                        ;
01-0050   2000                            .OPT ERR,SYM
01-0060   2000            BREAK   =$FF50      ;BREAK KEY BIT PORT(BIT 7)
01-0070   2000            SPCH    =$FF42      ;SPEECH "ACTIVE" BIT PORT(BIT 6)
01-0080   2000            WHEEL   =0          ;ARBITRARY BUFFER POINTER LOCATION
01-0090   2000            SPECON  =$FF70      ;WRITE TO CONVERT SPEECH
01-0100   2000            ADCRED  =$FF70      ;READ HERE TO GET CONVERTED VALUE
01-0110   2000            ENDCON  =$FF42      ;BIT 7 SIGNALS END OF CONVERSION
01-0120   2000                        *=$0400
01-0130   0400                        ;
01-0140   0400                        ;
01-0150   0400   D8       GETBUF  CLD
01-0160   0401   A9 10            LDA #$10    ;SET UP SPEECH BUFFER AT $1000=START
01-0170   0403   85 01            STA WHEEL+1 ;SPEECH BUFFER POINTERS-HIGH BYTE
01-0180   0405   A9 00            LDA #0
01-0190   0407   85 00            STA WHEEL   ;LOW BYTE
01-0200   0409   2C 50 FF NOACT   BIT BREAK   ;WATCH FOR BREAK KEY TO ABORT INPUT
01-0210   040C   30 01            BMI GOON    ;NO BREAK KEY
01-0220   040E   00               BRK         ;EXIT TO DOS
01-0230   040F   2C 42 FF GOON    BIT SPCH    ;TEST "ACTIVE" BIT FOR SPEECH
01-0240   0412   70 F5            BVS NOACT   ;NOPE KEEP LOOPING
01-0250   0414   8D 70 FF         STA SPECON  ;WRITE TO A/D FOR SPEECH CONVERT
01-0260   0417   2C 42 FF BUSY    BIT ENDCON  ;NOW WAIT FOR EOC LINE HIGH
01-0270   041A   10 FB            BPL BUSY    ;STILL LOW -- KEEP WAITING
01-0280   041C   AD 70 FF         LDA ADCRED  ;GET CONVERTED VALUE FOR SPEECH
01-0290   041F   20 25 04         JSR STORIT  ;NOW GO SAVE IT IN SPEECH BUFFER
01-0300   0422   90 E5            BCC NOACT   ;KEEP GOING IF BUFFER NOT FULL
01-0310   0424   60               RTS         ;RETURN TO CALLING PROGRAM
01-0320   0425
01-0330   0425                    ;SAVE SPEECH DATA IN BUFFER FROM $1000 TO $1FFF
01-0340   0425
01-0350   0425   A2 00    STORIT  LDX #0
01-0360   0427   81 00            STA (WHEEL,X) ;SAVE LAST SPEECH VALUE IN MEMORY
01-0370   0429   E6 00            INC WHEEL   ;INCREMENT POINTER
01-0380   042B   D0 0A            BNE NOTDUN
01-0390   042D   E6 01            INC WHEEL+1 ;CARRY FOR UPPER BYTE
01-0400   042F   A5 01            LDA WHEEL+1
01-0410   0431   C9 20            CMP #$20    ;TEST FOR BUFFER FULL=$2000
01-0420   0433   D0 02            BNE NOTDUN
01-0430   0435   38               SEC         ;BUFFER FULL- SET CARRY
01-0440   0436   60               RTS         ;RETURN TO GETBUF
01-0450   0437   18       NOTDUN  CLC         ;BUFFER NOT FULL -CLEAR CARRY
01-0460   0438   60               RTS         ;RETURN TO GETBUF
01-0470   0439                    .END


SYMBOL TABLE 0002

BREAK    FF50    SPCH     FF42    WHEEL    0000    SPECON   FF70
ADCRED   FF70    ENDCON   FF42    GETBUF   0400    NOACT    0409
GOON     040F    BUSY     0417    STORIT   0425    NOTDUN   0437


END OF ASSEMBLY = 0438
```

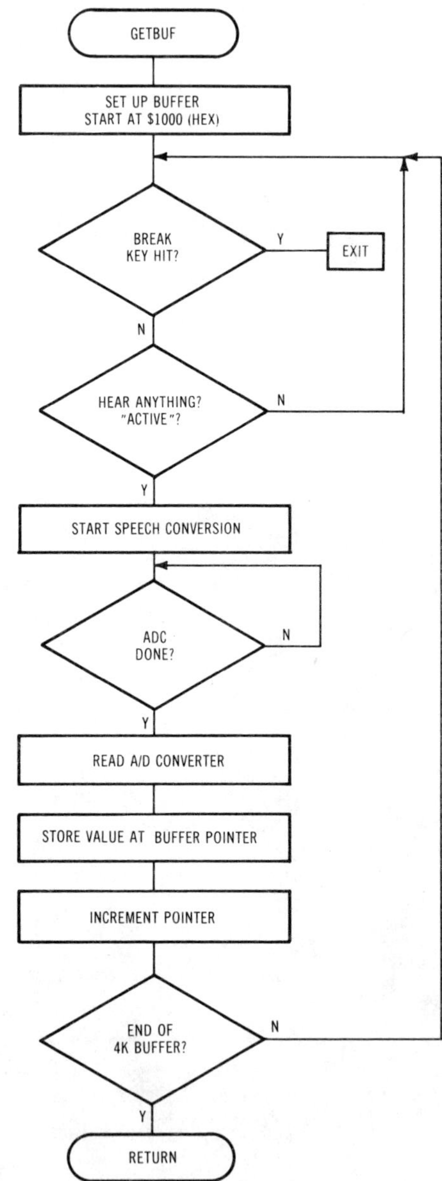

Figure 10-12.
Speech acquisition program flowchart of Listing 10-2.

Listing 10-3.
DELAY—An Echo Program for 6502 Systems With
a D/A Converter.

```
01-0004   2000              ;LISTING 10-3. A FUN ECHO PROGRAM FOR TESTING
01-0005   2000              ;YOUR SPEECH CIRCUITS AND DAC OUTPUT
01-0006   2000              ;
01-0007   2000              ;
01-0010   2000                      .OPT SYM,ERR
01-0015   2000              ;SET UP YOUR LOCATIONS HERE
01-0020   2000              BREAK  =$FF50            ;TOP BIT BREAK KEY (BIT 7)
01-0030   2000              SPCH   =$FF42            ;BIT 6! SPEECH "ACTIVE" BIT
01-0040   2000              DACDIR =$FF33            ;DAC DIRECTION REGISTER
01-0050   2000              DAC    =$FF32            ;DAC DATA REGISTER
01-0060   2000              WHEEL  =$8               ;ARBITRARY POINTER IN ZERO PAGE
01-0070   2000              SPECON =$FF71            ;WRITE TO CONVERT SPEECH
01-0080   2000              ADCRED =$FF70            ;READ HERE TO GET CONVERTED VALUE
01-0090   2000              ENDCON =$FF42            ;BIT 7 SIGNALS END OF CONVERSION
01-0094   2000              ;
01-0095   2000              ;
01-0098   2000              ;DELAY ROUTINE STARTS HERE *******
01-0099   2000              ;
01-0100   2000                      *=$A000
01-0110   A000   A9 FF      DELAY  LDA #$FF          ;SET UP FOR DAC OUT DIRECTION
01-0120   A002   8D 33 FF          STA DACDIR        ;NOW SET IT
01-0130   A005   A9 B0            LDA #$B0          ;BUFFER MEMORY STARTS AT $B000 (HEX)
01-0140   A007   85 09            STA WHEEL+1       ;SET UP HIGH POINTER
01-0150   A009   A9 00            LDA #0
01-0160   A00B   85 08            STA WHEEL         ;SET UP LOW POINTER
01-0170   A00D   2C 50 FF   NOACT  BIT BREAK         ;TEST FOR ABORT KEY (BREAK)
01-0180   A010   30 01            BMI GOON          ;OK TO KEEP GOING
01-0190   A012   00              BRK               ;SCREECH-STOP AND ABORT TO SYSTEM
01-0220   A013   8D 71 FF   GOON   STA SPECON        ;NOW CONVERT COMMAND
01-0230   A016   A1 08            LDA (WHEEL,X)     ;GET OLD VALUE IN BUFFER
01-0240   A018   4A              LSR A             ;DIVIDE BY 1/2
01-0244   A019   18              CLC               ;SET UP FOR ADD
01-0246   A01A   69 3F            ADC #$3F          ;NOW ADD 2.5 VOLTS FOR DAC OUTPUT
01-0250   A01C   81 08            STA (WHEEL,X)     ;PUT IT BACK
01-0260   A01E   2C 42 FF   BUSY   BIT ENDCON        ;TEST FOR EOC HIGH
01-0270   A021   10 FB            BPL BUSY          ;NOPE KEEP WAITING
01-0280   A023   AD 70 FF          LDA ADCRED        ;GET CONVERTED VALUE OF SPEECH
01-0290   A026   20 2F A0          JSR ECHROU        ;NOW DO AN ECHO SUM OF SAMPLES
01-0300   A029   8D 32 FF          STA DAC           ;OUTPUT IT TO DAC
01-0310   A02C   4C 0D A0          JMP NOACT         ;GO AGAIN
01-0320   A02F             ;
01-0330   A02F             ;
01-0340   A02F             ;THIS SUB-SUBROUTINE CREATES A BIG ECHO (1-2 SECONDS)
01-0350   A02F             ;
01-0360   A02F             ;
01-0370   A02F   A2 00     ECHROU LDX #0             ;SET UP X REGISTER
01-0372   A031   38              SEC               ;READY FOR SUBTRACT
01-0374   A032   E9 7F            SBC #$7F          ;SUBTRACT OUT DC LEVEL FROM NEW SAMPLE
01-0380   A034   18              CLC               ;GET READY TO ADD TO BUFFER
01-0390   A035   61 08            ADC (WHEEL,X)     ;ADD NEW VALUE TO 1/2 OLD VALUE
01-0400   A037   81 08            STA (WHEEL,X)     ;PUT IT BACK INTO ROTATING BUFFER
01-0410   A039   E6 08            INC WHEEL         ;SPIN WHEEL
01-0420   A03B   D0 0C            BNE NOCARY        ;WATCH FOR WRAP AROUND PAGES
01-0430   A03D   E6 09            INC WHEEL+1       ;SPIN BIG WHEEL
01-0440   A03F   A5 09            LDA WHEEL+1       ;TEST FOR END
01-0450   A041   C9 C0            CMP #$C0          ;AT $C000 (HEX)
01-0460   A043   D0 04            BNE NOCARY        ;NOPE NOT THERE YET
01-0470   A045   A9 B0            LDA #$B0          ;YEP START OVER AT FIRST BUFFER LOCATION
```

Listing 10-3—Continued
DELAY—An Echo Program for 6502 Systems With a D/A Converter.

```
01-0480  A047  85 09              STA WHEEL+1      ;RESET BIG WHEEL TO START
01-0490  A049  A1 08       NOCARY LDA (WHEEL,X)    ;GET LAST SAMPLE VALUE
01-0500  A04B  60                 RTS              ;RETURN TO "DELAY" CALLER PROGRAM
01-0510  A04C         .           .END             ;WHOA


SYMBOL TABLE 0003

BREAK    FF50     SPCH     FF42    DACDIR  FF33    DAC     FF32
WHEEL    0008     SPECON   FF71    ADCRED  FF70    ENDCON  FF42
DELAY    A000     NOACT    400D    GOON    A013    BUSY    A01E
ECHROU   A02F     NOCARY   A049


END OF ASSEMBLY = A04B
```

parts of the listing should be omitted or the program will loop indefinitely for nonexistent flags.

A final assembly code listing which is provided for your own enjoyment produces, with the use of a d/a converter, an echo generator. The operation of the program in Listing 10-3 is very similar to the previous program in that speech data is acquired and then stored in a memory buffer pointed to by WHEEL. The major difference in this program is that as each new speech data sample is acquired, it is added to the rotating speech buffer while the previously stored value is divided by one-half and summed with the current sample. What this does is create a half-amplitude echo each time the buffer circulates upon itself. Since the 4K buffer gives somewhere around a one-half to one second delay in speech, the echo returns at one-half amplitude each second or so. Since the value in the buffer, upon each rotation, is divided by one-half and readded to the incoming signal, on the second rotation, the original signal returns at one-quarter of its original value, etc. The effect is quite interesting and simulates a very long delay line through a very simple data acquisition program.

A requirement to operate the echo program is that you must have added the DAC circuit in Fig. 10-9 to your speech-acquisition system. This will allow you to output the mathematically echoed information to a recorder or audio amplifier for your listening enjoyment. If you decide to expand or shorten the WHEEL buffer, you may do so by changing lines 130 and 470 to the new start values and line 450 to the new ending value. Notice that this program has a different assembly origin and also a different buffer space in memory ($A000 and $B000 to $BFFF, respectively). It doesn't really do much but it can be a lot of fun to experiment with, and utilize the power of digitized speech processing within a computer.

The final listing within this section is the real core of speech recognition. It is a very simple program written in BASIC which will work in conjunction with the GETBUF program in Listing 10-2 to acquire and *recognize* speech. Although no claims are made as to the speed of the program—it takes about 30 seconds per word—it allows you to experiment with speech recognition at very low cost while intimately observing the internal operations of a recognizer.

The program listing in Listing 10-4 is written in BASIC. There are several lines in the program which may be foreign to your BASIC because the program was written with a very expanded version. Line 10 of Listing 10-4 is a statement which executes a disk command and loads the machine language program GETBUF from the disk into direct memory. If your system has a different method of loading machine data through BASIC, then be sure that GETBUF is loaded before the program is run. Lines 15 and 16 of this listing illustrate a characteristic of this particular BASIC which is very nice to own, but not necessarily prevalent in most BASIC languages: The &"XX" is a method of writing hexadecimal numbers directly into BASIC. In this case, the two POKE statements are poking the numbers 0 and 4 into memory locations $96 and $97 (hexadecimal), respectively. Since each BASIC is a little different from all others, you will probably have to modify these two lines. The major action occurring here is the placement of the starting memory address of the machine language program GETBUF into the USR pointer as designated in your BASIC manual. If you reassemble the speech acquisition program GETBUF in Listing 10-2, don't forget to change these starting vector locations in the USR pointers.

The program is set up to accept up to 40 vocabulary words. If you have the patience to enter this number of words, then the system may operate very slowly toward the end of the training process. However, it should only require somewhere around 30 seconds per word to recognize or train the system for short vocabularies.

When the recognition program asks if you "Want to train?" or not, it simply wants to know if you are training for a new word or trying to recognize an old word. You must obviously train the system with some words before it can begin recognition. After answering "yes" to the training question, it will ask you "What is the word?" you are about to speak. Simply type in the word followed by a carriage return. The program will then ask you to "Please speak now." At this time, the GETBUF program is executed for around one second to fill the speech memory buffer, and then program control is returned to BASIC.

Line 107 has a remark which informs you that by removing line 108, you have the ability to plot the digitized speech either on your crt or a line printer. Since this option prints all 4,096 data points, it can use a lot of paper and require considerable time for plotting. That is the reason it is bypassed in the original program. However, to observe the digital speech in memory, simply remove line 108 and you will still have the option of answering the question "Want to plot speech?"

The general concept of recognition that is used in this program is that of digital filtering of speech within memory. The process is described in

Listing 10-4.
A Simple BASIC Speech-Recognition Program.

```
2 REM  LISTING 10-4. A CRUDE SPEECH RECOGNIZER PROGRAM
3 REM  IN BASIC  - - BUT IT WORKS (SLOWLY)!
4 REM
5 INPUT "WANT TO LOAD %SAM?",N$
6 IF N$="N" THEN 20
7 REM LOAD MACHINE CODE "GETBUF"
8 REM THIS MAY BE DIFFERENT ON YOUR BASIC!
10 DC"LOD %SAM"
12 REM SET UP FOR USER ROUTINE
13 REM SET POINTERS ACCORDING TO YOUR BASIC INSTRUCTIONS
15 POKE &"96",0
16 POKE &"97",4
20 VC=1:DIM LC(40,8),BC(40,8),HC(40,8)
25 DIM W$(40),WS(40)
30 INPUT" WANT TO TRAIN?",TR$
40 IF TR$="NO" OR TR$="N" THEN T=0:GOTO 90:ELSE T=1
50 INPUT "WHAT IS THE WORD?",W$(VC)
80 REM NOW DO SPEECH INPUT (CALL GETBUF)
85 REM CALL USER ACCORDING TO YOUR BASIC
90 PRINT"PLEASE SPEAK NOW!"
100 U=USR(0)
102 REM BACK TO BASIC
105 IF T=0 THEN 170
107 REM TAKE OUT THE NEXT LINE (108) FOR PLOTTING
108 GOTO 170
110 INPUT "WANT TO PLOT SPEECH?",ANS$
120 IF ANS$="N" OR ANS$="NO" THEN 170
130 FOR I=&"1000"TO &"1FFF"
140 A=PEEK(I)
150 PRINTTAB(A/4);"*"
160 NEXT I
170 STR=&"1000":SP=&"1FFF"
172 IF T=0 THEN PRINT"RECOGNIZING";:ELSE PRINT"ENROLLING ´";W$(
VC);"`";
175 MX=0
180 FOR I=STR TO SP STEP 512
185 LC=0:BC=0:HC=0
190 FOR SLD=I TO I+27
200 S0=PEEK(SLD)
210 S1=PEEK(SLD+1)
220 S2=PEEK(SLD+2)
230 S3=PEEK(SLD+3)
240 S4=PEEK(SLD+4)
250 S5=PEEK(SLD+5)
260 S6=PEEK(SLD+6)
270 S7=PEEK(SLD+7)
290 A4=(S2+S3+S4+S5)/4:A2=S3
300 A8=(S0+S1+S2+S3+S4+S5+S6+S7)/8
310 LP=A8-128:BP=A8-A4:HP=A4-A2
315 IF LP>3AND LF=0 THEN LC=LC+1:LF=1
320 IF LP<-3AND LF=1 THEN LC=LC+1:LF=0
340 IF BP>3 AND BF=0 THEN BC=BC+1:BF=1
350 IF BP<-3AND BF=1 THEN BC=BC+1:BF=0
360 IF HP>3AND HF=0 THEN HC=HC+1:HF=1
370 IF HP<-3AND HF=1 THEN HC=HC+1:HF=0
390 NEXT SLD
400 PRINT".";
510 SX=(I-4096)/512
515 IF T=0 THEN VX=0 ELSE VX=VC
520 LC(VX,SX)=LC
```

Listing 10-4—Continued
A Simple BASIC Speech-Recognition Program.

```
530 BC(VX,SX)=BC:HC(VX,SX)=HC
540 NEXT I
600 PRINT
690 IFT=1 THEN VC=VC+1:PRINT:PRINT:GO TO 30
695 MN=100
697 PRINT
698 PRINT"VOCAB. WORD","LOW #","MID #","HIGH #","TOTAL"
699 PRINT"----------------------------------------------
--------"
700 FOR IX=1 TO VC-1
705 LD=0:BD=0:HD=0
710 FOR SX=0 TO 7
720 LD=LD+ABS(LC(0,SX)-LC(IX,SX))
730 BD=BD+ABS(BC(0,SX)-BC(IX,SX))
740 HD=HD+ABS(HC(0,SX)-HC(IX,SX))
750 NEXT SX
755 PRINTW$(IX),LD,BD,HD,LD+BD+HD
756 WS(IX)=LD+BD+HD
757 IF WS(IX)<MN THEN VP=IX:MN=WS(IX)
758 PRINT
760 NEXT IX
770 PRINT
800 PRINT"THE WORD IS ...";W$(VP)
900 PRINT:PRINT:PRINT
1000 GOTO 30
```

Chapter 5 as a finite impulse response (FIR) filter, which in reality is nothing more than a moving average filter computation performed on the sampled speech values in memory. The unusual part of the program is that two moving averages are computed: an eight-point sliding average and a four-point sliding average. These correspond to 8-tap and 4-tap FIR filters. The third computation involves the direct sampled data with no averaging. The result of the mathematical filtering produces a frequency selective response in the BASIC program having the transfer functions of the 8- and 4-tap FIR filters with coefficients equal to one. Assuming that the speech acquisition program samples data from your microphone at the sample rate of approximately 8 kHz, the frequency response of the 8-tap FIR filter is equal to that shown in Fig. 10-13. Notice that the response of this filter has theoretical complete attenuation at 1 kHz with stop band ripple approaching 25% of the passband amplitude. While this is not extremely good for digital filtering, it provides for a fast and efficient filter for a crude but workable speech recognizer written in BASIC. The same frequency response of a 4-tap FIR filter with an assumed sampling rate of 8 kHz is given in Fig. 10-14. These responses are both created mathematically by the BASIC program through computation on the sampled speech values.

Between lines 290 and 310, the BASIC program performs a low-pass, bandpass, and high-pass filter function. The low-pass function is simply the response of the eight-tap FIR filter. The bandpass response is obtained by subtracting the 8-tap filter values from the 4-tap values,

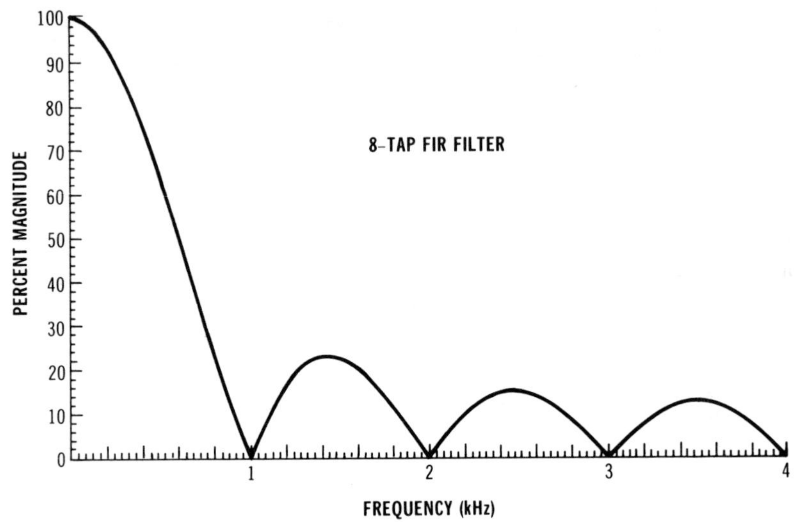

Figure 10-13.
The eight-tap FIR filter frequency response.

thus producing a bandpass filter response with a frequency peak at approximately 1 kHz. Finally, the high-pass function is performed by subtracting the 4-tap FIR filter response from the direct digitized-data values. This, in effect, inverts the 4-tap FIR filter response, providing a

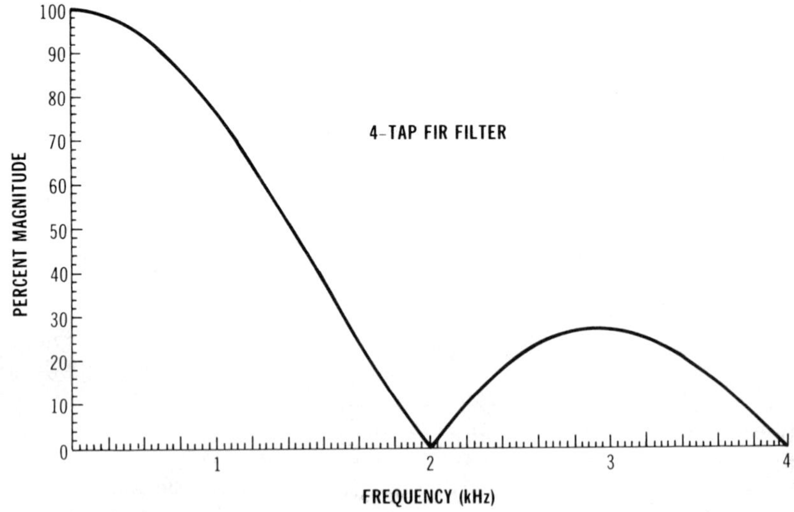

Figure 10-14.
The four-tap FIR filter frequency response.

2-kHz frequency peak response extending beyond the range of the presampling filter.

The computational filters are quite effective in selecting the various frequencies within the speech waveform. Each of these various filter responses is used as a feature of the incoming sampled speech for subsequent recognition.

The method of pattern recognition is similar to that shown in the flow diagram of Fig. 6-8 in Chapter 6. Rather than implement the three filter processes in hardware, at the sake of recognition speed (and/or low cost), the filters are implemented in software. The zero-crossing detectors and counters are simulated in lines 315 through 370. These counters for low pass, bandpass, and high pass are: LC, BC, and HC, respectively. To speed up program operation while sacrificing little recognition accuracy, the speech input waveform is segmented into 512 sampled frames. During each frame, the mathematical filtering is performed only 28 times before stepping to the next sampled frame. This produces, with a total of 4096 sampled points, only 8 sliding filter computational frames (4096/512 = 8). During the enrollment process, each frame is signified by the printing of a point. That's done primarily to let you know that the program is still working. For each frame of computation, the numbers in each of the three counters are stored (for that frame) with the associated vocabulary word. Thus, any vocabulary word in memory has associated with it 24 numbers, which correspond to 8 low-pass, 8 bandpass, and 8 high-pass counter values.

During the recognition process, the input word has the same mathematical transformation performed upon it, and then it is *compared* computational frame by computational frame with each previously enrolled vocabulary word. The comparison occurs in lines 700 through 760. The variables LD, BD, and HD correspond to the *differences* in values between each frame comparison, so the word with the *least difference* (or lowest score) is the match to the incoming word subject to recognition.

Following recognition, the program prints a scoreboard of difference values for each vocabulary word. This allows you not only to see all of the words within the vocabulary, but also to see the individual difference scores for each word. Finally, following the pattern matching process, line 800 produces the final answer based upon the lowest scoring word. If by chance there are two words which score the same low value, then the last one enrolled is selected for recognition. There are obviously many better ways of matching and comparing values; however, remember this is a speech-recognition development program. You are invited to go in and change values and print variables to see what is really happening during recognition and enrollment. That's one of the primary advantages of performing the recognition function in software.

If you would like to see what the program results look like (assuming you typed it in correctly), observe the program output in Fig. 10-15.

```
 RUN
WANT TO LOAD %SAM? Y
 WANT TO TRAIN? Y
WHAT IS THE WORD? YES
PLEASE SPEAK NOW!
ENROLLING 'YES'........


 WANT TO TRAIN? Y
WHAT IS THE WORD? NO
PLEASE SPEAK NOW!
ENROLLING 'NO'........


 WANT TO TRAIN? N
PLEASE SPEAK NOW!
RECOGNIZING........

VOCAB. WORD    LOW #        MID #        HIGH #       TOTAL
----------------------------------------------------------
YES             9            2            51           62

NO              7            4            4            15


THE WORD IS ...NO



 WANT TO TRAIN? N
PLEASE SPEAK NOW!
RECOGNIZING........

VOCAB. WORD    LOW #        MID #        HIGH #       TOTAL
----------------------------------------------------------
YES            10           16           39           65

NO             14           14           44           72


THE WORD IS ...YES



 WANT TO TRAIN? Y
WHAT IS THE WORD? COMPUTER
PLEASE SPEAK NOW!
ENROLLING 'COMPUTER'........


 WANT TO TRAIN?


WHAT IS THE WORD? STOP
PLEASE SPEAK NOW!
ENROLLING 'STOP'........


 WANT TO TRAIN? N
PLEASE SPEAK NOW!
RECOGNIZING........
```

Figure 10-15.
The speech-recognition program at work.

```
VOCAB. WORD    LOW #         MID #          HIGH #         TOTAL
-------------------------------------------------------------------
YES            11            22             50             83

NO             13            22             49             84

COMPUTER       6             13             27             46

STOP           10            23             49             82


THE WORD IS ...COMPUTER



 WANT TO TRAIN? N
PLEASE SPEAK NOW!
RECOGNIZING........

VOCAB. WORD    LOW #         MID #          HIGH #         TOTAL
-------------------------------------------------------------------
YES            10            17             64             91

NO             10            15             45             70

COMPUTER       11            12             67             90

STOP           7             8              15             30


THE WORD IS ...STOP


WANT TO TRAIN?
```

Figure 10-15—Continued
The speech-recognition program at work.

The first question is simply the loading of the machine code program
GETBUF in memory. Following the request for training, the word to be
enrolled is entered. In this case, it is "yes." The program will request
speech and immediately inform you that it is enrolling the new word.
This is where the time delay appears. Each of the dots following yes
requires around four seconds to appear so that the total enrollment time
is around 30 to 35 seconds. In the example in Fig. 10-15, there have
been two words enrolled before recognition is requested. Recognition
occurs by simply telling it that you do not wish to train. The system then
begins the recognition process. Following a 30-second delay or so, a
printout of the words in the vocabulary and their scores against the
recognition word in question appears. The first recognition table is obviously for the word "no." Remember that the lowest score wins, so
there is a very close match between the recognition word and the
prestored vocabulary frames for the word "no." The second word has
a much smaller difference but still is correctly identified as "yes." Since

it does not really matter how low the TOTAL is, the lowest one still wins. These numbers might be used in a more sophisticated system to judge the confidence factor in the recognition match. In other words, the lower the least value, the closer the match, and consequently the better the confidence in it.

The remainder of Fig. 10-15 shows that you may, at any time, train new words through enrollment and compare them against the previous vocabulary words. You may even enroll the same word twice which will obviously give you a better chance of matching that particular word during speech variations. It will still search through the vocabulary for the best match and pick the closest of the two identical vocabulary words.

If you have been very astute during the description of this program you may have noticed that most of the numerical values in the program are powers of two. There is no accident in the choice of these numbers. They were chosen so that the program can be easily converted to assembly-language code for tremendously increasing the program recognition speed. For instance, to perform an 8-point FIR filter function, a processor need only add eight values of sequential sampled points and then shift the sum right three places. A 4-point filter may be simulated in the same manner with four sequential additions followed by a dual shift right. The transformation from BASIC to machine code is relatively simple if you follow a line-by-line conversion. If you decide to rewrite this program in machine language for your particular processor, then you will probably find a recognition response time on the order of one to two seconds or less per word. This is a *much* more acceptable waiting time than that for the given BASIC program. But, still, the listed program can be used to evaluate and verify recognition principles with almost universal portability between computers. If you spend the time to try the recognition program, you should certainly be surprised at the results from such a simple listing.

Application Ideas for Your "Hearing" Computer

This section, like the previous ones in this chapter, assume that you have had the interest and energy to follow the construction and programming to this point. Although the applications for a voice recognition system with a 30-second response time may be rather limited, you can still enjoy the added feature of voice recognition in your computer. When you begin to tire of seeing your spoken word printed, then you are ready for some extra applications for your voice recognizer.

For instance, suppose that you have connected to your computer a text-to-speech synthesizer for computer speech output. If you include within the previous BASIC program a "PRINT" statement which outputs the recognized word to your synthesizer, then you can create a very long echo with synthesized speech.

On the more practical side, there are still a number of uses for which a speech recognizer (even with the long recognition time) can find application. For instance, once the computer has determined the word in the vocabulary, then the same program can be extended to perform actions upon that string variable. If there is an output port connected to the computer other than the recognizer, then the words can certainly be used to control relays for lights, printers, etc.

Those applications will be more practical if the program is rewritten in machine code for the increased speed and reduced recognition delay. However, remembering that this is primarily a speech-recognition development system, there are still a great many experiments to try with the system exactly as given here. One interesting application is the use of the speech recognizer as a language translator. This can be accomplished by a very simple procedure. Since the speech recognizer does not really care that sounds associate exactly with words, you may type in, for the vocabulary training word, a word in one language and then speak into the microphone the *same* word in another language. An example of this would be to type "house" for the vocabulary training word and then speak "casa" for the enrollment process. If you continue the sequence by entering English for the training and then enrolling the equivalent Spanish word, you will have created a Spanish-to-English translator. The operation is quite impressive since the computer appears to actually translate from one language to the next. Of course, you are doing the translation yourself during the training process, but it's not apparent during the recognition operation. Since the system has the capability of holding up to 40 vocabulary words, you may even enroll the foreign language and English version of the same word together into the system so that it will understand and recognize the English equivalent for *either* word.

Another experiment, which you might attempt, was tried with the author's system to test for speaker independence. There is some amount of speaker independence in this system. It may be illustrated by having one person enroll a large vocabulary followed by a second person attempting recognition with the same words. From this, you can see how close the speech dependence is between various speakers. You may even have one speaker enroll half of the vocabulary words, and another speaker enroll the other half. If either of those people use the system then they should be accurately recognized from their own enrollment words.

As you begin to use the speech-recognizer program, you will notice that the table of difference sums provides a means for you to learn which words most closely appear like other words. If you seem to be having trouble with the misidentification of a particular word, then simply enroll that word again to give the computer two choices to attempt to match.

There is only one precaution to remember when operating the software recognizer: if you exit the program and then type RUN, you will destroy *all* your previously trained vocabulary words. The simplest way to avoid this problem (if you do exit the software recognizer) is to reenter "GO TO 30." This will get you back into the program while keeping your vocabulary intact. Also remember that if you modify the program by changing a program line you will normally destroy your vocabulary. And, if you have spent the 20 minutes or so required to enroll 40 vocabulary words, this can be quite discouraging.

One last note on program operation. There is currently no way of deleting a previously trained vocabulary word if you happen to make a mistake. There are, however, two methods to defeat this disadvantage. The word can simply be reenrolled and the computer will usually choose the second enrollment over the first incorrect one; or you may exit the program into the BASIC operating system. Once there, decide which number in the vocabulary the word to be deleted carries. If the misenrolled word that is to be deleted is the fifth word in the vocabulary recognition table, then type *W\$(5)=" "*. Although that operation will not delete the vocabulary frame counts from memory, it will produce a null string, if the frame counts are recognized. Thus, no misrecognition will occur. Following the nulling of the vocabulary word string, type "GO TO 30" to reenter the program and continue running. If you happen to make a mistake and null the wrong vocabulary word, then you may gracefully cover your error by simply reexiting the recognizer program and correcting the error in the same manner that you made it.

All in all, the software speech recognizer is quite a bit of fun and a tremendous learning tool. Although it does not claim any kind of tremendous accuracy or recognition speed, it operates *completely* in software and *in the BASIC language* so that it is portable to almost any computer. After you have seen the operation of the voice recognizer, you will certainly understand where this technology is headed. As we begin to couple speech-recognition technology with increased computing power, we may formulate some projections about the future of speech recognition.

Future Directions of Voice Input Systems

"You're traveling through another dimension. A dimension, not only of sight and sound, but of mind. A journey into a wondrous land whose boundaries are that of imagination. Next stop, the Twilight Zone."

Rod Serling

Over the next ten years that quote may well become the theme for the development phases of the fifth generation computer (Fig. 11-1). During each stage of its development, the computer is acquiring more advanced intellectual powers and at some point in the future—not too far from now—our computers will begin to design and create their own offspring much as humans do today. A training process will then follow which might be likened to our educational system. As these computers begin to procreate, our task will be to retain control of the regeneration process through a series of checks and balances on the projected capabilities.

The first stages have already begun. Computers today are being used as human tools to design future computers more efficiently. In this generation process, the human is the key element to the eventual design. Man is still the creator and his machines are just tools. Over the next 10 to 20 years, the human element will play a decreasingly less important part in the creation process. This will happen because computers will be given more and more control over the design decisions. There will surely be many people made uncomfortable by this thought and an equal number that can envision a technological upheaval with won-

Figure 11-1.
Generation V (Courtesy Arnold Wieland, artist).

drous futuristic machines coming almost tomorrow. A rather bizarre analogy can be made between computer generations and the black monolith that pervaded the movie *2001: A Space Odyssey*. Each time the monolith was uncovered, mankind took a gigantic technological jump forward in a very short period of time. We are about to discover our next black monolithic slab in the early 1990s. Following that event, our technological development rate will begin to increase exponentially. It will occur in a manner much like today's research in computer memory chips which first gave us the 1K then the 4K and 16K memory chips. We are now observing the 64K and 256K chips being produced as easily as the original 1K chips, and for less cost! It's going to be a very exciting age. Only time will tell.

Intelligence Unlimited

Since the performance of speech recognition systems is so highly dependent upon their contained computer intelligence, any futuristic views of speech recognition technology must be based upon improvements in machine intelligence. Today's voice recognition devices understand isolated words and limited phrases from familiar speakers. As the processing power of computers becomes greater and greater, the restrictions on phraseology and speaker dependence will slowly disappear.

The single future event that will determine the speed at which machine intelligence improves is the creation of a computer that can program other computers. This is one area in which our technology is still in its infancy. While computers can help us create extremely sophisticated computer hardware, software that generates other software is still relatively unavailable. Although metacompilers, compilers, and assemblers might be put into this category, the general idea of self-sufficiency is missing. There must still be a human doing the origination of the creative thoughts in the software process. When we finally teach machines to program other machines, then such areas as pattern recognition, speech analysis, and other extremely complicated processes will be easily understood by the created intelligence.

As systems that can hear and think become more prevalent, we will begin to see other sensory inputs used with increasing frequency. For instance, the computer that sees and knows what it is seeing will become commonplace. It is also very likely that a computer link will be made directly to the human mind so that computers can intercept human thoughts and then perform actions based on thought commands.

A real problem exists in trying to forecast the future of machine intelligence. It is the lack of experience for future extrapolation. All previous experience in thinking has been human based. As we create machine intelligence, we are entering a new dimension. All the rules will be changed. Computers that can see will also read. The matter of teaching machines will be nothing more than supplying them with a library of reference material on the subjects in which we wish them to have knowledge. If we desire hearing and seeing computers to learn about world history and social sciences, then we may have to do no more than connect them to the local cable news network and tell them to learn everything through vision and sound.

One of the stranger goals in technology today is the fifth generation computer. From the sounds of all the predictions, this may be the last. But if not, consider the *sixth* generation computer. What will it be like? Can you even imagine a *tenth* generation computer? These may be machines that become independent of the human race. They may be put into corners to simply create and imagine, and even predict futuristic events with extremely high probabilities. The power of their thinking will be so tremendous that in the time it takes us to ask the computer a question, it will have processed more knowledge than most people acquire in a lifetime.

Those of you who have heard earlier predictions about futuristic computers which resemble solid masses of material without discrete interconnections have been given a clue to the future generations of computers. As computer scientists, philosophers, and medical doctors begin to collaborate in the field of artificial intelligence, there will be an awakening of a new subject: genetic engineering of computers. When these computers are created, they will be life forms. We will have a new

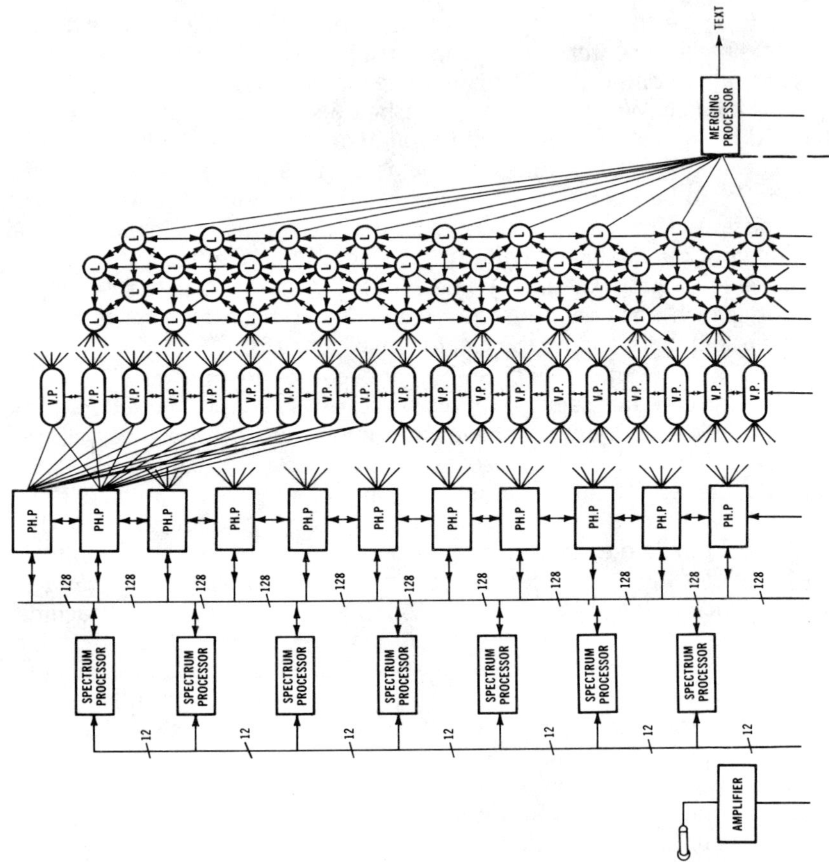

Figure 11-2.   A futuristic

species on earth. Pulling the plugs on these machines will be treated with legal terms such as "computer slaughter" with possible legal consequences for the humans involved. We might even have a computer rights amendment added to our constitution.

If all of this sounds like the future would be a fantasy world, it will be. Improvements in machine intelligence are self-regenerating. When the black monolith is finally touched by the human race, we will truly enter the twilight zone.

Tracking Technology

If we can relate predictable improvements in voice input technology to the previous changes in computer interface techniques, this will provide a somewhat cloudy window into the future. From the early days of the

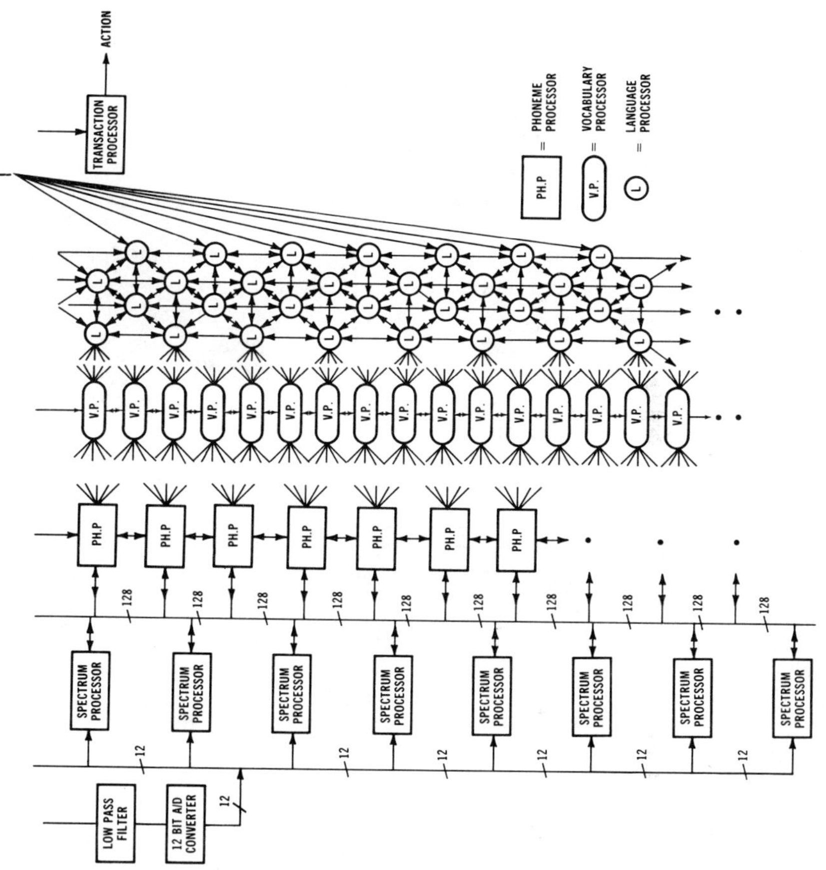

"Multifarious" speech processor.

Teletype® Model ASR-33 clunkers (which were preceded by even more archaic mechanical systems) to the modern, efficient crt terminals of today, we have passed through technology changes in ten years which should be equalled in the voice-recognition field.

The machines we talk to today are the equivalent of those Model 33 systems. With acceptance and experience, the manufacturers will continuously improve and expand the capabilities of our current speech recognizers. These expansions will occur primarily in the areas of vocabulary size, speaker limitations, and connected speech limitations. Future voice input terminals should be able to not only converse with a random individual (we do it daily), they should also be able to identify the speaker from his voice (as we also do). Although the *human* process of speech recognition is very complex, it shows us that what we are attempting to do in speech recognition *can be done*. If we were attempting to create a telepathic computer system, then we have no basis for our research. We have no model of telepathic operation. However, our speech-recognition model is highly defined and easily documented. The processes that occur are not completely understood but with each passing day more is being learned about how we hear.

The combination of our increased knowledge about hearing and our improved methods of digital signal processing is beginning to provide new working models of speech-recognition systems which outperform anything previously developed. Of most importance is the fact that we no longer need complete rooms full of computers to perform the speech processing computations. We now have available for our use single chip processing systems that can compute (in a limited environment) at rates exceeding those of mainframe computers from several years ago. Although colleges and universities are still performing a major portion of the basic research in speech recognition and processing methods, the commercial potential for speech recognition systems is creating quite a stir in the highly pragamatic corporations which originally thought speech recognition to be "too science fiction" oriented.

As the success of speech research gains public recognition, an increasing amount of informative material will become available for keeping track of the high speed technology. There will also appear public algorithms for speech-pattern recognition which are currently regarded as highly proprietary to particular organizations. As with any new field, the developments which are occurring at the present time are considered to be something like trade secrets with cloaks of secrecy far surpassing those used by governments.

Where Do We Go From Hear?

Our continuing struggle with the implantation of reasoning power into computers *will* eventually lead to some form of inferential reasoning by machines. That must occur in order to have the natural language speech recognizers that we so eagerly pursue. With some amount of luck and a great amount of scientific restraint, these systems will even have the courtesy to listen to us when we are speaking. It is also highly likely that at times their tasks will seem more important to their own reasoning than stopping to listen to a human speak. Our normal response to this type of mutinous action would probably be to stop the operating program, and go in and change a few memory locations to provide more obedience. But, a computer system that has been given intelligence close to human reasoning will not have a central identifiable operating program which can be changed at will. In the same manner that we lose many, many brain cells each day, the computer program may be modifiable only in large parts by removing chunks of intelligence. Also, a slip of the keyboard might be likened to a scalpel knife in a neurosurgeon's hands during brain surgery.

The only way that this analogy can even be imagined is if the intelligence within the speech-recognition system computer is composed of many, many independent processors, each having its own semantic function within the overall thinking process. Thus, the listening computers of the future will assuredly be multiprocessor systems with both shared and independent programming.

Fig. 11-2 illustrates a possible intelligent hearing computer architecture of the far future. The term "multifarious" means having great diversity; being of various kinds. The processing system shown has somewhere around 140 processors, each having specific functions. If the processors are assumed to be typical state-of-the-art processors available today (with capabilities of somewhere around 500,000 instructions per second), then this multifarious system as shown operates at a composite instruction rate of 70-million instructions per second! Of course, the hardware commitment to this system is quite extensive. The

Figure 11-3.
Cylindrical Thoughtwork **(Courtesy Arnold Wieland, artist).**

cost of 140 microprocessing systems with memory and the necessary ports would be quite costly. However, the system should perform the necessary computations in near real-time to provide both direct speech-to-text output and command interpretation and execution.

Notice that if we were to go into the system described above and disable a memory location or two, that very little damage would be done to the total system operation (with the exception of the merging and transaction processors). Thus, like the human mind, the system has much redundancy in its computing cells and, therefore, is not only extremely fast, but also highly reliable in terms of probablistic component failures. This type of processing system will obviously not appear overnight. When the entire circuitry can be implemented on a silicon chip—maybe four or five inches in diameter—then it will be economically producible and we will enter the age of the *wafer* computer system.

As ominous as the future world may seem with the advent of super intelligent computers (Fig. 11-3), you may rest assured that there will be regulatory agencies that will control the power of these systems and direct their application toward peacekeeping and goodwill. We are beginning to enter an age which will bring about staggering technology changes. If we accept them, we will be dazzled by their beauty. If we do not, then surely—somewhere out there—*something* will hear us.

APPENDIX 

Glossary

A

ACOUSTIC	Relating to sound or hearing.
A/D CONVERTER	An electronic circuit that changes analog voltage levels to numeric digital values corresponding to the voltage-level amplitude.
ADPCM	Adaptive Differential Pulse Code Modulation.
AFFRICATE	A consonant formed by the succession of two consonants such as j = D.ZH, resembles a fricative.
ALIASING	A condition or artifact occurring in signal sampling where a high frequency signal appears to be of lower frequency because of a low sample rate.
ALLOPHONE	Spoken variations of phonemes dependent on the phonemes and their placement within words.
AMPLITUDE	Magnitude, loudness, or volume of a signal.
ANALOG	Having capability of continuous variation without discrete discernible steps.
APHESIS	A speech defect characterized by the dropping of an unstressed initial vowel or syllable, i.e., example: zample; expect: spect.
APHONIA	Loss or absence of voice due to failure of vibration of the vocal cords.
ARTICULATE	To express orally.
ARTICULATION	A measure of speech intelligibility.

241

ARTIFACT — Something changed from its natural state by artificial means.

ARTIFICIAL — Produced by other than natural means such as artificial speech from synthesizers.

ARTIFICIAL INTELLIGENCE — Attributing the power of knowledge and reasoning to a computing machine.

ASPIRATION — To breathe out during speech.

ATTENUATE — To decrease the amplitude or energy of a signal.

AUDITORY NERVE — The group of neurons passing signals from the ears to the brain.

AURAL — Relating to hearing and sound.

AUTO CORRELATION — A method of signal processing created by delaying the original signal and then multiplying the delayed signal by the original.

B

BANDPASS — A filter allowing only a limited range of frequencies to pass.

BANDWIDTH — The important range of frequencies in a signal.

BASILAR MEMBRANE — Part of the inner ear which discerns frequencies.

BINARY — A number system with the base 2 with values of 0 or 1.

BIT — A single digit in the binary system.

BROCA'S AREA — A portion of the brain in the frontal lobe which relates to language perception and expression.

BYTE — A group of eight bits in sequential order.

C

CASCADE — Placed in series or sequence with each output feeding the next input.

CAVITY — A hollow area such as the throat or nasal cavity with associated resonances.

CEPSTRUM — The frequency spectrum of a frequency spectrum (an inside-out spelling of spectrum).

CHIRP — A wideband signal created by a rapid frequency sweep.

COCHLEA — The snail-like appearing part of the inner ear.

COGNATES — The related pairs of voiced and unvoiced fricative consonants.

CONCATENATE — To string together in sequence.

CONCHA — The part of the ear on which you hang your glasses, the outermost part.

CONNOTATION — The hidden meaning in a word or phrase.

CONSONANT — A speech sound in the category of a stop or plosive, fricative, nasal, liquid or glide, and semi-vowels; a non-vowel sound.

CONTINUANT — A static speech sound requiring no motion of the vocal tract other than the vocal cords and/or lungs.

CONTINUOUS SPEECH — Normal speech, without special pauses between words or unnatural emphasis.

CYCLE — A complete oscillation of a periodic happening or signal.

D

DAMPING — To cause a decrease in the amplitude of successive oscillations or cycles.

DECADE — The range of frequencies from one frequency to ten times that frequency.

DECIBEL (dB) — A quantitative unit of relative amplitude of two signals based on base 10 logarithms.

DELTA MODULATION — A type of digital encoding of an analog signal based on signal changes.

DFT — The Discrete Fourier Transform. It mathematically changes sampled data from the time to frequency domain.

DIALECT — A difference in speech patterns caused by social or geographical differences.

DIGITAL — Relating to specific states such as binary as opposed to analog.

DIPHTHONG — A speech sound formed between two spoken vowels.

DISTORTION — Imperfections in the replication of a signal.

DYSPHONIA — An impairment of the larynx which affects proper voice production.

E

ELECTRICAL ANALOG — An electronic simulation of a physical occurrence.

ENCODING — Converting a signal from one form to another.

ENVELOPE — A description of the variation in the peak values in a time varying signal; the shape of the amplitude variations.

F

FFT (Fast Fourier Transform)	A means of mathematically finding the spectral content of a signal.
FEEDBACK	A controlled reaction in a system based on its output to reduce error.
FIDELITY	The accuracy of signal reproduction; lack of distortion.
FIR FILTER	A digital filter with no feedback from the output to the input which has a finite impulse response.
FORMANT	A region of frequency prominence in the audio speech band; a speech resonant frequency.
FORMANT SYNTHESIS	A means of synthesizing speech based upon recreation of the formant frequency bands.
FRAME	A partial segment in the total time for a spoken phrase. Usually for speech 10 to 50 milliseconds.
FREQUENCY	The number of occurrences in a given period of time (usually one second).
FRICATIVE	A speech sound consonant having a broad frequency spectrum, usually characterized by a hissing sound.
FUNDAMENTAL FREQUENCY	The lowest frequency in a harmonically distorted signal.

G

GA (General American) DIALECT	A standard method of characterizing English speech in America.
GLIDE	A speech sound consonant (in the category of semi-vowels) consisting of Y and W.
GLOTTAL PULSE	The oscillation produced as air passes over the vibrating vocal cords.
GRAMMAR	Dealing with the formal features and use of a language.

H

HARDWARE	As opposed to software, the electronic components in a computer system and its peripherals.
HARMONICS	Distortions in a pure signal which produce integral multiples of the fundamental frequency.
HOMOMORPHIC FILTER	A filter which passes a desired signal while rejecting all undesired components.
HOMONYMS	Words spelled differently but pronounced identically, i.e., too, two.
HYPERBOLE	A linguistic exaggeration, i.e., I'm *dead* tired.

HYPERURBANISM — An erroneous speech sound change made in an exaggerated effort to speak correctly.

I

IIR FILTER — A digital filter with feedback from output to input which produces an infinite impulse response if the feedback coefficient is greater than 1.

IMPEDANCE — The apparent resistance of an electrical device to alternating current excitation.

INFLECTION — A means of "coloring" speech meanings with intentional pitch variations.

INSPIRATION — The pause in speech during which air is drawn into the lungs.

INTEGRATOR — An electronic circuit or system which performs a mathematical integration on a signal.

INTELLIGIBILITY — The clarity or understandability of speech.

INTENSITY — The loudness or amplitude of energy.

INTERPOLATE — To deduce internal quantities from the edge limits based on distance between limits.

INTONATION — Pitch changes in speech to express the importance of words or phrases.

ISOLATED WORD — A term in speech recognition meaning words spoken with emphatic pauses prior to and following the utterance.

L

LPC (Linear Predictive Coding) — A mathematical speech modeling method based upon digital filtering of voiced and unvoiced waveforms (parametric encoding).

LARYNX — The portion of the vocal tract in the throat containing the vocal cords.

LEXICON — A list of features of a language containing phonological, syntactic, and semantic features.

LIFTER — The name for a Cepstrum filter—specifically short-pass and long-pass lifters.

LINEAR — Moving along a line or continuous path as in an analog signal.

LINGUISTICS — The study of language.

LIQUID — A speech sound (also known as a semivowel) consisting of the consonants W and Y.

LISP
1. To speak with an impairment so that "s" sounds appear as "th" sounds. 2. A List Processing language developed for Artificial Intelligence applications.

LITOTES
To strengthen the meaning of speech by a deliberate understatement, i.e., *not too bright* for *stupid.*

LOUDNESS
A perceived hearing sense based on sound intensity *and* pitch.

LOW-PASS
An electrical circuit which attenuates high frequencies and passes low frequencies.

M

MATATHESIS
The exchange of the positions of sounds in speech whether intentional or accidental, i.e., *ax* for *ask, flim* for *film, pervent* for *prevent.*

MICROPHONE
A mechanism for converting sound waves to electrical signals.

MICRO-PROCESSOR
The heart of a computer; the central processing unit (CPU) where decisions occur in a single integrated circuit.

MODULATION
A means of signal encoding; to impress one signal upon another.

MONOTONY
Having a boring pitch inflection or intonation.

MORPH
A sequence of concatenated phonemes which creates a minimal unit of grammar or syntax.

MORPHEME
The smallest grammatical unit which cannot be further subdivided, similar to a syllable.

N

NASAL
1. Referring to the nose. 2. A group of speech sound consonants consisting of N, M, and NG.

NOISE
A signal containing no information other than randomness; a wideband signal.

NORMALIZE
To scale a signal or quantity to a reference value maximum.

NYQUIST THEORY
It states that to preserve fidelity, a signal must be sampled at least at twice its highest frequency component.

O

OCTAVE
The range of frequencies from one frequency to twice that frequency.

ONOMATOPOEIA
Use of a word to describe a sound, i.e., *boom* for an explosion, *tick-tock* for a clock sound.

OVERTONES	Integral frequency distortion of a signal; harmonics.

P

PALATAL	Pertaining to articulation with the tip of the tongue touching the roof of the mouth.
PARSE	To separate a phrase or computer program into the most elementary structural parts.
PHONEME	The basic sound unit of speech.
PHONETICS	The study of speech sounds and their production and perception.
PHYSIOLOGY	The science of living organisms, their parts, and functions.
PITCH	The predominant frequency sounded by an acoustic source.
PLOSIVE	A speech sound consonant also known as a stop consonant.
PORT	A connection from a computer to its peripherals.
PROSODIC	Relating to the stress patterns of an utterance, normally longer than one word.
PSEUDORANDOM	Having the appearance of randomness over a limited period of time.

Q

QUANTIZATION	Converting from analog to digital or quantitative information.
QUEFRENCY	The horizontal axis in a Cepstrum.

R

RAM	Random Access Memory. Temporary read/write memory which holds data as long as power is on.
RANDOM	Equal probability of any occurrence.
RECONSTRUCTED SPEECH	Speech electronically regenerated from stored human speech.
RECTIFIER	An electronic element usually called a diode which allows current to flow only in one direction; used to convert alternating current (AC) to direct current (DC).
RECURSIVE FILTER	A filter with multiple feedback in a lattice configuration.
REFLECTION COEFFICIENT	A predictor value used for digital filtering in LPC speech synthesis.

RESONANCE   Having activity at a specific frequency while rejecting others.

RESONATOR   A mechanism which emphasizes certain frequencies over others.

ROM   Read Only Memory. A permanent computer memory normally used to store data or programs. The stored information remains with power off.

S

SEMANTICS   The study of word meanings as they are used.

SEMIVOWEL   A group of consonant phonemes consisting of the sounds W and Y.

SINE WAVE   An oscillating analog waveform described by the equation: $\sin 2\pi ft$ where f is the frequency and t is time. $(\pi(PI) = 3.14159\ldots)$

SLOPE   An artifact of delta modulation which causes signal dis-
OVERLOAD   tortion; it occurs when the delta modulator cannot keep up with signal changes.

SPEAKER   A speech recognition term indicating that a system re-
DEPENDENT   sponds properly only to the trainer.

SPEAKER   Computer verification of speaker identity through voice
IDENTIFICATION   patterns and frequencies.

SPEAKER   A speech recognizer with no preference of user or
INDEPENDENT   trainer. Will accept any tone of voice or inflection.

SPECTROGRAM   A plot of visible speech sometimes called a voice print; made on a machine called a spectrograph showing the frequencies of speech.

SPECTRUM   The complete description of all frequencies within a signal.

SPEECH   Computer indentification of spoken words.
RECOGNITION

SPEECH   The means for generating artificial human speech.
SYNTHESIZER

STOP   Also known as a plosive; speech sounds consisting of
CONSONANT   b, d, g, p, t, and k.

STRESS   Applying added volume and emphasis to a particular syllable or phoneme.

SYLLABLE   A segment of speech or writing longer than a phoneme but shorter than a word (except for single syllable words).

SYNTAX   The pattern or structure of word order in a phrase or sentence.

T

THRESHOLD | A fixed quantity or amplitude value used to select signals above or below that value.

TONGUE | The major speech muscle. The center of articulation.

U

UNVOICED | Speech generated without the use of vibrating vocal cords.

UTTERANCE | A spoken phrase or passage.

V

VOCABULARY | The list of words or multiword phrases that a voice recognizer can understand.

VOCAL CORDS | The larynx which generates the glottal pulse excitation for voiced speech.

VOCODER | A shortened term for voice coder; any means for electronically coding speech.

VOICE CONTROL | Computer or machine control through speech activation.

VOICE RESPONSE | A process produced by a synthetic speech generator. Voice output by computer.

VOICE STORE AND FORWARD | A real time encoding, compression, and storage of speech for later retrieval . . . a verbal mail system.

VOICED SPEECH | Any speech generated with the glottal pulse excitation (vibrating vocal cords).

VOWEL | A speech sound other than a consonant. A voiced sound of which there are 12 in GA speech.

W

WAVEFORM | A general shape of an analog signal (as seen on an oscilloscope).

WHISPER | Human speech generated with totally unvoiced sounds.

WHITE NOISE | A completely random signal waveform that contains all frequencies; acoustically, it sounds like a hiss.

APPENDIX B

Suggested Readings and References

Physiology of Speech

R. Curry, *The Mechanism of the Human Voice,* David McKay Co., Inc., New York, 1940.

P. B. Denes and E. N. Pinson, *The Speech Chain,* Waverly Press, Inc., Baltimore, MD, 1963.

H. Fletcher, *Speech and Hearing in Communication,* Van Nostrand Co., Inc., Princeton, NJ, 1953.

G. W. Gray and C. M. Wise, *The Bases of Speech,* Harper & Brothers, New York, 1946.

H. M. Kaplan, *Anatomy and Physiology of Speech,* McGraw-Hill, New York, 1960.

W. R. Zemlin, *Speech and Hearing Science: Anatomy and Physiology,* Prentice-Hall, Inc., Englewood Cliffs, NJ, 1968.

Linguistics

N. Chomsky and M. Halle, *The Sound Pattern of English,* Harper and Row, Publishers, New York, 1968.

G. Fairbanks, *Voice and Articulation Drillbook,* Harper and Row, Publishers, New York, 1960.

Z. S. Harris, *Methods of Structural Linguistics,* University of Chicago Press, Chicago, 1951.

R. Heffner, *General Phonetics*, University of Wisconsin Press, Madison, 1950.

A. A. Hill, *Introduction to Linguistic Structures*, Harcourt, Brace and World, New York, 1958.

D. Jones, *The Phoneme: Its Nature and Use*, Heffer, Cambridge, U.K., 1950.

J. Lyons, *Introduction to Theoretical Linguistics*, Cambridge University Press, Cambridge, U.K., 1968.

P. A. M. Seuren, *Semantic Syntax*, Oxford University Press, London, U.K., 1974.

R. W. Shuy, *Discovering American Dialects*, National Council of Teachers of English, Urbana, IL, 1967.

Speech, Recognition, and Signal Processing

N. Ahmed and T. Natarajan, *Discrete-Time Signals and Systems*, Reston Publishing Company, Inc., Reston, VA, 1983.

J. P. Cater, *Electronically Speaking: Computer Speech Generation*, Howard W. Sams & Co., Inc., Indianapolis, IN, 1983.

J. L. Flanagan, *Speech Analysis, Synthesis and Perception*, 2nd Edition, Springer-Verlag, New York, 1972.

J. D. Markel and A. H. Gray, *Linear Prediction of Speech*, Springer-Verlag, New York, 1976.

A. V. Oppenheim and R. W. Schafer, *Digital Signal Processing*, Prentice-Hall, Inc., Englewood Cliffs, NJ, 1975.

A. Peled and B. Liu, *Digital Signal Processing, Theory, Design and Implementation*, John Wiley and Sons, New York, 1976.

R. K. Potter, G. A. Kopp, and H. G. Kopp, *Visible Speech*, Dover Publications, New York, 1966.

L. R. Rabiner and B. Gold, *Theory and Application of Digital Signal Processing*, Prentice-Hall, Inc., Englewood Cliffs, NJ, 1975.

L. R. Rabiner and R. W. Schafer, *Digital Processing of Speech Signals*, Prentice-Hall, Inc., Englewood Cliffs, NJ, 1978.

M. Rigsby, *Verbal Control with Microcomputers*, Tab Books, Blue Ridge Summit, PA, 1982.

R. Steele, *Delta Modulation Systems*, Halsted Press, London, 1975.

E. R. Teja, *Teaching Your Computer to Talk*, Tab Books, Inc., Blue Ridge Summit, PA, 1981.

Artificial Intelligence in Computers

A. Barr and E. A. Feigenbaum, *The Handbook of Artificial Intelligence*, William Kaufmann, Inc., Los Altos, CA, Vols. I and II.

P. R. Cohen and E. A. Feigenbaum, *The Handbook of Artificial Intelligence,* William Kaufmann, Inc., Los Altos, CA, Volume III, 1982.

D. R. Hofstadter, *Gödel, Escher, Bach: An Eternal Golden Braid,* Vintage Books, New York, 1980.

P. C. Jackson, *Introduction to Artificial Intelligence,* Petrocelli/Charter Publishers, Inc., New York, 1974.

J. Krutch, *Experiments in Artificial Intelligence for Small Computers,* Howard W. Sams & Co., Inc., Indianapolis, IN, 1981.

P. McCorduck, *Machines Who Think,* W. H. Freeman and Company, San Francisco, CA, 1979.

L. Siklóssy, *Let's Talk LISP,* Prentice-Hall, Inc., Englewood Cliffs, NJ, 1976.

Periodicals and Tabloids

First Computer Chronicle
502-B Oakland Avenue
Austin, TX 78703

Machine Intuition Magazine
P.O. Box 1432
Carrales, New Mexico 87048

Speech Technology Magazine
525 East 82nd Street
New York, NY 10028

VoiceNews
Stoneridge Technical Services
P.O. Box 1891
Rockville, MD 20850

APPENDIX C

Manufacturers of Speech-Associated Products

The listed companies offer speech recognizer products and/or software and components for their construction.

Analog Devices Incorporated
One Technology Way
P.O. Box 280
Norwood, MA 02062
(617) 329-4700

Dragon Systems, Incorporated
173 Highland Street
West Newton, MA 02165
(617) 527-0372

Intel Corporation
3065 Bowers Avenue
Santa Clara, CA 95051
(408) 987-8080 (Of course!)

Interstate Electronics Corporation
1001 East Ball Road
P.O. Box 3117
Anaheim, CA 92803
(714) 635-7210

National Semiconductor Corporation
2900 Semiconductor Drive
Santa Clara, CA 95051
(408) 737-5000

NEC Corporation
Microcomputer Division
One Natick Executive Park
Natick, MA 01760
(617) 655-8833

NEC Corporation
Systems Division
532 Broad Hollow
Melville, NY 11747
(516) 752-9700

Scott Instruments
1111 Willow Springs Drive
Denton, TX 76201
(817) 387-9514

Signetics Corporation
P.O. Box 9052
811 Arques Avenue
Sunnyvale, CA 94086
(408) 739-7700

SuperSoft-Techmar
1713 South Neil Street
Champaign, IL 61820
(217) 359-2112

Threshold Technology, Incorporated
1829 Underwood Boulevard
Delran, NJ 08075
(609) 461-9200

Texas Instruments, Incorporated
P.O. Box 401560
Dallas, TX 75240
(214) 680-5096

Verbex
(A Division of EXXON Enterprises)
Two Oak Park
Bedford, MA 01730
(617) 275-5160

Voice Machine Communications, Incorporated
1000 South Grand Avenue
Santa Ana, CA 92705
(714) 639-6150

Votan
4487 Technology Drive
Fremont, CA 94538
(415) 490-7600

Weitek Corporation
VLSI Systems & Technology
3255 Scott Boulevard, Bldg. 2B
Santa Clara, CA 95054
(408) 727-6625

Index